Parallel Learning of Reading and Writing in Early Childhood

Parallel Learning of Reading and Writing in Early Childhood explores why it's important to provide a balanced language learning environment for young children and offers approaches for children to practice and explore language. Writing—a different but parallel process—can open the door to reading, and an effective writing approach in the home and early childhood classrooms leads to the development of phonemic awareness, understanding of phonetic principles, vocabulary, fluency, and comprehension. Effective early childhood teachers are those that extend the knowledge children have amassed at home and use the knowledge of how children learn naturally in the world to inform their practice.

This book offers the purpose, context, and outcomes of including writing right from the start in young children's literacy learning. Through analysis of writing samples, research, and principles of best practices, Shea outlines the essential ingredients for early language learning and provides a developmentally appropriate approach to language learning. Throughout the chapters, Shea integrates discussion of assessment, classroom environment, instructional/teacher scaffolding, and differentiating instruction across developmental levels along with the supporting theory.

Special Features:

- Vignettes and descriptions of Pre-K, K, and Grade 1 classrooms that incorporate writing across the day
- Artifacts of children's writing that demonstrate an evolution of knowledge related to both message and word construction
- Concept labeling words and topic specific terms defined throughout the book to support the reader's understanding of professional terminology
- Discussion of seminal and current research as well as best practices
- Companion website with lesson ideas and abundant writing samples from a wide range of demographic, cultural, and language contexts for readers to view, analyze, and discuss

This text offers pre- and in-service early childhood education teachers the content and resources to develop a deeper understanding of language learning, to prompt an examination of current practice, and to stimulate curricular re-designs that foster meaningful, joyful, and motivated learning.

Mary Shea is a Professor and Director of Graduate Literacy Programs at Canisius College.

Parallel Learning of Reading and Writing in Early Childhood

MARY SHEA

 Routledge
Taylor & Francis Group

NEW YORK AND LONDON

KH

Please visit the companion website for this book at:
www.routledge.com/textbooks/shea

First published 2011
by Routledge
270 Madison Avenue, New York, NY 10016

Simultaneously published in the UK
by Routledge
2 Park Square, Milton Park, Abingdon, Oxon OX14 4RN

Routledge is an imprint of the Taylor & Francis Group, an informa business

© 2011 Taylor & Francis

The right of Mary Shea to be identified as author of this work has been asserted by her in accordance with sections 77 and 78 of the Copyright, Designs and Patents Act 1988.

Typeset in Sabon and Neue Helvetica by Book Now Ltd, London
Printed and bound in the United States of America on acid-free paper by Edwards Brothers, Inc.

Library of Congress Cataloging in Publication Data
Shea, Mary.
Parallel learning of reading and writing in early childhood / Mary Shea.
     p. cm.
Language arts (Early childhood) 2. Reading (Early childhood) 3. Early childhood education. I. Title.
LB1139.5.L35S54 2011
372.6—dc22   2010045395

ISBN13: 978–0–415–88298–9 (hbk)
ISBN13: 978–0–415–88299–6 (pbk)
ISBN13: 978–0–203–84118–1 (ebk)

SUSTAINABLE FORESTRY INITIATIVE
Certified Fiber Sourcing
www.sfiprogram.org

2/28/12

Dedication

This book is dedicated to my granddaughters, Skylar and Emma.

Contents

Preface

This Book

From the moment of birth, children are totally immersed in the language functions of their family and community. Just as they do with any other experience or object in their environment, young children fashion their own experimentations with language, attempting to understand it and use it in ways they've observed. They don't separate language into categories; they work on all aspects of it through self-directed explorations that serve their purposes. While engaging with language holistically, young children become increasingly aware of its components and conventions.

This book is about children developing an understanding of how print works. It is also about how adults in the child's world scaffold that knowledge building in incidental and intentional ways. Parents and teachers mindfully mediate learning in a developmentally appropriate manner that respects the child's uniqueness. It's about children's natural inclination to include literacy explorations in their individual and group play—where they direct the content and pace of learning. Most importantly, young writers and readers discover how the language processes contribute to the quality of their lives.

This text offers pre-service teachers an introduction to concepts on emergent literacy and related research. Numerous examples bring ideas to life; text supports enhance comprehension. In graduate courses with in-service teachers, the text becomes a springboard for deeper examination of pedagogical principles outlined and studies cited. Literacy coaches can use the content and resources as grist for extending faculty discussions on appropriate curriculum, activities, and assessment in primary classrooms.

Themes

In my own teaching, I've observed children write, conferred with them about their writing, collected samples, and assessed the data for message quality and print conventions. Aware of my deep and abiding interest in how literacy knowledge emerges, teachers, graduate students, parents, and friends have shared their stories and numerous samples of young children's writing with me. These are presented as demonstrations of children's propensity for logical thinking when figuring out the intricacies of the printed code.

I've completed research investigating preschool (four- and five-year-olds) children's concepts about literacy as demonstrated in a series of tasks. Recently, I visited schools in different parts of the country and collected monthly samples of students' writing. These research sites included pre-kindergarten (pre-K), kindergarten, and grade 1 classrooms, representing different socioeconomic status (SES) and demographic populations. In site descriptions, pseudonyms are used for teachers' names. Data came from tasks presented, center writing, free writing, journal entries, and writing in response to reading. Translations for children's writing in the bilingual classroom were completed with assistance from Dr. M. Fernanda Astiz, Associate Professor in the Adolescent Department at Canisius College. Examples are woven into discussions across the chapters of this book. Numerous other samples are offered at the companion website at www.routledge.com/textbooks/shea. These offer grist for rich discussions among pre-service and in-service teachers.

Language learning begins well before schooling. Children build conceptual foundations for literacy as they observe and participate in everyday events, behaviors, and activities. Adults, siblings, and peers in the child's world introduce him to literacy as part of daily routines. Mindful of this phenomenon, families and schools work in partnership to construct a sound foundation and firm structure for early language learning.

Effective teachers in primary classrooms appreciate areas of uniqueness and commonality in children's language learning experiences before schooling. They prepare an environment that welcomes diversity and reflects the appropriate implementation of best practice as validated by sound educational research. Language learning grows in such environments, along with each child's sense of self and appreciation for community. Children's work samples described in this book—as artifacts—attest to the effectiveness of instruction in these classrooms and the achievements children have attained.

Organization

The Introduction to this book establishes a premise that is carried throughout the text. Language functions are interconnected; growth in one area supports growth in other processes. The evolution of the language reciprocity concept is traced for readers. Understanding this synchronicity has implications for how we interact with children before schooling and design curriculum in primary classrooms.

Part One of this book presents a *logical argument* (Bruner, 1986) for the resolve that writing deserves a prominent role in young children's literacy development at home—and at school. The premise is supported throughout the text by the cumulative effect of conclusions from multiple researchers. Knowing what works at home—how children learn naturally in the world—informs practice in effective classrooms. The Introduction outlines the theory of reciprocity in language processes. Chapters 2–4 outline essential ingredients for early language learning. Although it occurs in different ways across cultures and communities, construction of a literacy foundation begins before children enter formal schooling. Effective primary classrooms provide environments that extend the knowledge children have amassed. Curricular design honors the way in which children learn; activities are developmentally appropriate and intrinsically motivating. Primary teachers build on children's strengths and guide each learner to an appropriate next step in the journey toward becoming literate.

Part Two (Chapters 5–10) of this text relates to language learning in school settings. Chapter 5 talks about getting started by setting the stage with the environment and pedagogy needed for effective language learning in primary grades. Chapters 6–8 describe pre-kindergarten, kindergarten, and grade 1 classrooms that incorporate writing across the day; each chapter includes artifacts of children's writing in these settings. Each classroom examined is unique in its approach to incorporating language, but writing is always prominent in their balanced approach for designing literacy curriculum. Additional information on particular concepts and instructional strategies for each grade is also included within these chapters.

artifact
object made by a human being, learner's work sample

Different experiences, background, interests, motivations, talents, cultural heritage, and other factors have shaped children's uniqueness— their *nonstandardess*. Effective primary curriculum recognizes the fact that "one size [curriculum] fits few" in schools (Ohanian, 1999, title). Children progress from emergent to fluent levels of language skills at different rates. Teachers continually assess children's responsiveness as they implement the practices described in Part Two. By differentiating teaching strategies, content, group size, and activities, teachers target instruction for learners at each stage. Chapter 9 discusses how to differentiate instruction, activities, and expectations to meet the needs of readers and writers who are ready to move beyond the emergent level. Chapter 10 is a conclusion that reviews some of the key ideas of the book.

Key Features

Children's writing samples, pictures, charts, and tables are offered throughout the text to clarify concepts described; they offer a translation to practice. Within chapters, stage levels for pieces of writing have been determined as a model for analyzing children's writing in any early child-hood classroom. Descriptions of the message quality and conventions used in each piece of writing are outlined as a model for examining the expansive collection of samples on the companion website accessible at www.routledge.com/textbooks/shea. Collaborative analysis of these additional samples helps teachers to construct theory that guides class-room practice; that reflective instruction generates more inquiry. And, the research cycle continues.

Throughout the book, concept-labeling words and topic-specific terms are defined in the margin. This supports the reader's understanding of professional terminology and overall comprehension of ideas presented.

Chapters begin with a notation of the "big ideas" in the chapter and conclude with prompts for extended discussions. Pre-service teachers can make connections to the classrooms in which they are completing service learning, participation hours, or student teaching. In-service teachers can make connections with their own students as they examine concepts and principles addressed in the text and represented in the artifacts and resources. Vignettes from the classroom are windows for readers to observe teachers and children learning together in communities.

The content and resources provided within this text and at the website are intended to develop deeper understanding of language learning, prompt an examination of current practice, and stimulate curricular re-designs that foster meaningful, joyful learning in primary grades and lifelong interest and motivation to engage in literate activities.

Acknowledgements

As a parent I had an opportunity to watch my children slowly grow and blossom into adults. The dynamics of our relationship changed as they did. Now we talk about the world, literature, and life—as friends. I taught them simple things; now, they teach me how to use my cell phone and digital camera.

I once heard that a child is someone who passes through your life and disappears into an adult. That's not true. The child each of my sons once was is forever imprinted on my heart. I can see that child without looking at a picture. Who I am—what I do today has been greatly influenced by my experiences as a parent—and as a grandparent.

This book is dedicated to my granddaughters, Skylar and Emma who deepened my continued interest in children's development in literacy. Watching their explorations into literacy is a gift. It's magical to see their renditions of Tracy Kane's fairy houses, use of expressions taken from literature, and their authorship. Skylar and Emma have been marinated in literacy right from the start. Their lives have been filled with books, learning experiences, grand conversations, and opportunities to ask about and experiment with print. When I talk about my grandchildren's "ah-hah"s, my friends usually open up with their stories.

There are numerous examples and stories in this text from the students, children, and grandchildren of friends. Delightful, revealing contributions came from Cathleen March, Nancy Roberts, Mary Wilson, Marcia Cleary, and Robin Shea. I appreciate the willingness of parents to allow their child's work to be used in this way. Hopefully, these examples will inspire a greater willingness to bring writing into the lives of young children.

Special thanks to Ardith Cole who helped me shape the concept for gathering writing samples from schools as a central part of this text. Ardith also hosted me whenever I met with teachers at a particular school site. Those visits were fun and productive. By our friendship, I have been enriched; through our conversations, my thinking has been expanded.

My sister, Peggy Hay, and her husband John also hosted me numerous times when I traveled to meet with teachers in New England. Another school site was near my grandchildren's home. That meant a number of extra visits and stays with them. Skylar and Emma are always fun-filled hostesses who made every visit an event.

The teachers who regularly saved work from students were all amazing people and professionals. The administrators at these sites were ones who respected teachers' professionalism; they gave them the autonomy needed to teach developmentally. Each site inspired me to tell the story of children who were learning literacy and loving it; children who were simultaneously learning complex language processes. They were writing into reading; their daily writing built an essential foundation of conceptual knowledge for understanding the reading process

I am grateful to the teachers who collected children's writing for this text and the administrators at each site who granted permission for the project. This includes Mary Wilson, Dawn Braden, Diane Frame, and Steve Finch; Nilda Carmona-Rivera, Margarita Torres, Stacy Altieri, and Sharon Jackson; Mary Ellen Towne, Julianne Lewis, and Karen Brackett; Ellie Liston; Lisa Wood; and Linda Schott and Ryan Schoenfeld.

My colleague in another department at the college gave generously of her time and knowledge to translate writing samples from Spanish. I remain very grateful to Dr. M. Fernanda Astiz for her help. Her insights influenced my analysis.

Friends and family have encouraged me throughout this long endeavor; that support has been a mainstay in my life. It keeps me afloat when I'm drowning in data and writing—when I need a break to refresh my thinking. Their invitation for a brief get-away is a welcome distraction; their insight clears my mind. Afterwards, I'm ready to get on with it.

Heather Jarrow, my editor at Routledge/Taylor & Francis, has shared her expertise for the publication of this work. I wish to also acknowledge all the other production, layout, typesetting, permission, and artistic editors at Routledge/Taylor & Francis; they are giants in their field. Special thanks go to Georgette Enriquez and Richard Cook and his team at Book Now. These specialists take the bones of a text and dress it up for the ball; they make it fabulous! Thanks to all for your passion, patience—and divine design.

part one
A Strong Foundation for Learning Language

one
Introduction

Big Ideas in the Introduction

- Essential components for reading competency
- Parallel learning of language processes
- Literacy learning at home and at school
- Creating effective literacy learning classrooms

phonemic awareness
understanding that words are made of separate, sequential sounds

phonetic knowledge
knowledge of the match between sounds and letters in a language

fluency
combined effect of reading pace, accuracy, and elements related to expression

vocabulary
understanding words used in oral and written communication and the ability to use words appropriately for expression

Essential Ingredients for Reading Competency

Phonemic awareness, phonetic knowledge, fluency, vocabulary, and comprehension have gained status as *the* essential components for reading competency (Cunningham, 2002; Moore & Lyon, 2005; NICHHD, 2000; Scanlon, Anderson & Sweeney, 2010). Schools quickly prioritized them and implemented programs of instruction focused on each. Skill in each of these components is important in becoming literate; that's not in dispute. What is in dispute is how to achieve balanced instruction. An obsession with teaching these skills in isolation (outside of their normal use) obscures the pivotal role of early writing and other language processes in young children's development. It also works against the concept of learning reciprocity.

comprehension
understanding meaning communicated in oral or written messages

balanced instruction
instruction that provides continuous teaching across all components deemed necessary for literacy

integrated instruction
instruction that provides demonstration and supported practice in using all of the literacy-learning components interactively

Synchronous Learning of Language Processes

Numerous researchers confirm the importance of learning reading and writing skills concurrently and interactively (Cecil, 2007; Martin, Lovat, & Purnell, 2007; Makin, Diaz, & McLachlan, 2007; Vukelich, Christie, & Enz, 2002). "There is a synchrony in learning to read, write, and spell. Development in one area generally coincides with advances in the other two areas" (Cecil, 2007, p. 106). A body of research supports a

reciprocity
a mutual exchange or interaction of knowledge in different domains

correlation
relationship where a change in one element is related to change in another

paradigm
set of ideas that establish a pattern or model

semiotic relationship
both reading and writing involve the functions of signs and symbols in a language

parallel processes
growing in the same direction simultaneously and distinctly

transactional processes
processes that interact with each other

correlation theory, indicating that development in one language process influences growth in the others (Bagley, 1937; Bissex, 1980; Clay, 1980, 2001a; Evans, 1979; Stotsky, 1975, 1983; Whitmore, Martens, Goodman & Owocki, 2005). Kenneth Goodman (1982) suggests, "skills displayed by the proficient reader derive from the meaningful use of written language" (p. 265). This view differs radically from paradigms that consider reading and writing to be reverse processes or mirror images with their own set of sub-skills (Ruddell, 1969; Sticht, Beck, Hauck, Kleinman, & James, 1974; Yoos, 1979).

Sub-skill or code emphasis approaches (Chall, 1967) emphasize learning discrete components of reading competency (i.e. phonemic awareness, phonics, fluency, and sight vocabulary) in isolation followed by practice with de-contextualized text (content that is neither story nor continuous text). Instruction starts with the smallest pieces of language (sounds and letters); eventually, lessons incorporate larger units (sentences, paragraphs, and stories) of text built with controlled vocabulary, rhyming words, and/or repetitive refrains. Children learn to perform skills in an automatic, rote manner, but some do not easily integrate this knowledge when navigating the complexities of real literature or writing personal messages (Temple, Ogle, Crawford, & Freppon, 2008; Vacca, Vacca, Gove, Burkey, Lenhart, & McKeon, 2009).

Yetta Goodman (1984) described the reading–writing relationship as *semiotic* (p. 102); children first begin to comprehend the interrelationship of reading and writing as representations of meaning when they actively participate in family literacy events (Whitmore et al., 2005). Squire (1983) described reading and writing as related in the similarity of demands placed on thinking. Similarly, Kucer (1985) explained the relationship as *parallel processes* after examining research findings in education, psychology, and linguistics; he concluded that reading and writing are "more appropriately conceived as running in parallel and utilizing many of the same basic mechanisms . . . drawing from a common pool of cognitive and linguistic operations [i.e. composing, comprehending]" (p. 319). Adding another dimension, Dahl and Farnam (1990) describe a body of research "showing reading and writing as transactional processes—each concurrently changing the other and becoming changed in the process" (p. 85).

The extent to which these concepts of semiotic, parallel, or transactional processing in reading and writing have become important in the field of early literacy development is evidenced by the numerous studies (Dyson, 1982; Harste, Woodward, & Burke, 1984; Pappas, Keifer, & Levstik, 1999; Taylor, 1983; Teale, 1982) that have explored young children's literacy development and reaffirm that "preschoolers employ similar strategies when generating meaning through and from print" (Kucer, 1985, p. 319). These researchers conclude a positive interactional effect (transaction) as these processes, involving an understanding of the signs and symbols (semiotics) of printed language, develop in parallel, employing and developing similar cognitive functions. Based on that finding, integrated instruction and practice in early childhood curriculum creates a balance that allows each process to develop and complement growth in the other (Roe, Smith, & Burns, 2005).

Despite the research supporting parallel learning, it appears that mandates and other priorities have made balanced inclusion of all language functions in early childhood classrooms the exception rather than the norm. In recent years, programs for teaching literacy have flooded the market. Each is based on the publisher's construct of essential components, rather than on substantiated research. Publishers characterize their model as *research-based* when any aspect of it can be traced to research; it's touted as based on research. This is completely different from whole practices that are *research-tested* and found to have significant positive effects. The caveat is to understand the difference between research-based and research-tested (Scanlon et al., 2010).

Along with packaged programs, commercial assessments for measuring students' literacy progress are a notable line item in school budgets. As publishers define curriculum and materials, one begins to wonder if the ready-made products greedily consuming classroom time and budgets are worth the sacrifice. Is there a better way to ensure children are acquiring literacy skills and applying them meaningfully?

The debate over approaches for teaching literacy and sequencing of instruction will likely go on—and on. The stakes are high; companies invested in publishing all the *teacher trappings* for a specific approach need to ensure their view is winning (Garan, 2004). Even though we've known for a long time that it's the teacher, not a program, that makes the difference (Bond & Dykstra, 1967; Cole, 2003a), some well-intended educators succumb to the silver bullet product pitch. However, not all classroom teachers are as easily swayed by glitzy ads. Years of experience have honed their persistence as reflective teacher-researchers; teachers are steadfast in analyzing what works and what doesn't. Prolonged up-front and personal observations in the classroom create the fabric of these authentic views and provide the data to verify them.

Literate Before Schooling

In seminal research—research that has endured the test of time—Delores Durkin (1966), a researcher and Professor of Education Emeritus at the University of Illinois, Urbana-Champaign, concluded that children who are exposed to *interactive* models (where they have opportunities to question and participate) of literacy, invited to playfully engage in literate activities, supported in the literacy tasks they choose, and allowed to experiment in their own way, come to school reading or learn to read with ease. This wasn't anything magical; these interactive models allowed children effective incidental language instruction—even when those around them didn't intend to teach—and abundant time to practice with lots of support. Her study of precocious readers "led to the eventual demise of reading readiness programs, highlighting the role of parents in literacy learning, and set the stage for later emergent views" (IRA, 1998, p. 28).

seminal research
study that notably influenced future thinking or events

interactive models
instructional models that incorporate student interaction in the learning process

FIGURE 1.1
Books as Comfortable Companions

FIGURE 1.2
Experimenting Like a Writer

Other research consistently supports these conclusions (Bissex, 1980; Clay, 2001b; Holdaway, 1979; Laminack, 1991; Torrey, 1969; Taylor, 1983; Taylor & Dorsey-Gaines, 1988; Rasinski & Padak, 2009). In other words, some children already know how to use component skills in reading when they arrive at school; others are in the process of acquiring specific skills while writing and reading back what they wrote. Those with even a modicum of proficiency in early reading and writing skills are more likely to attend to formal (school) literacy instruction because they know how the information will serve their needs; they're building on what they've already learned at home. The information has a use that's authentic and genuinely relevant to them. Maybe, just maybe, if instruction in early childhood classrooms looked more like the environments described in this body of research, we'd have successful, motivated learners right from the start.

Literacy at Home

Literacy instruction at home is usually implicit although it can be explicit at times. Often, adults don't even realize they're teaching the child about language skills. They offer *soft* teaching; they encourage, respond, coach, and answer questions in all the right ways. Children watch, reflect, and ask as their curiosity is sparked by the behaviors of significant others in their environment. They replicate observed reading and writing behaviors for their own purposes. Although done playfully, this is serious business. Play is a child's work; it "typically provides a meaningful context for children to construct new knowledge" (Owocki, 1999, p. 3)—one where the child is in charge and safely takes risks. Owocki (1999) suggests that "play is like a gold mine in its potential for facilitating literacy" (p. 3).

Early writing builds conceptual knowledge about how printed language works (Sinclair, 1989). It's much easier to assimilate (absorb) and accommodate (find a place for) learning related to the smaller pieces of language (e.g. words, letters) when the learner understands the broader purpose for the activity. In other words, appreciation of the functions of

soft teaching
incidental, casual teaching

conceptual knowledge
understanding of complex idea formed by combining thoughts on all of the characteristics related to it

assimilate
absorb, take in knowledge

accommodate
make room for new knowledge in personal schemata

FIGURE 1.3
Reading with Mom

schema
previously acquired (background) knowledge on a topic; schemata (pl.)— total background knowledge

macro literacy skills
skills in comprehension and composition; skills in working with larger units of meaning in a text

micro literacy skills
skills in words with letters, words, sentences, paragraphs; skills in working with smaller elements in a text

approximations
attempts that gradually approach the target performance

scaffold
provide temporary structure to support learners

developmentally appropriate practice
in harmony with the natural growing process

implicit
implied rather than stated

explicit
clearly explained and demonstrated

literate behaviors (the macro) precedes interest in its forms (the micro) (Owocki, 1999). Without the first, the second is more difficult to acquire. A rich literacy schema is constructed over time from demonstrations and immersion in all of the language functions.

This schema grows when children are given responsibility for learning, when their approximations are accepted and respected, and when they have ample time to safely *muck around*—be engaged cognitively, socially, and emotionally—with what they're learning (Camborne, 1988). These young writers, Durkin's *paper and pencil kids*, come to the classroom with an expanded repertoire of literacy skills—including ones they're expected to acquire in school—already in place.

Literacy at School

Researchers propose that we develop a curriculum that is characterized by literacy-rich experiences in pre-kindergarten (pre-K) and kindergarten—before children are expected to read and write conventionally (Allington & Cunningham, 1996; McGill-Franzen, 2006). Such activities model home-based scaffolded exploration with print (Cambourne, 1988; Taylor, 1983; Bissex, 1980)—the type Durkin's (1966) paper and pencil kids experienced. In fact, developmentally appropriate practice (DAP) must include print experiences since children seek these in their self-directed play (Bredekamp & Rosegrant, 1992). While traditional free-play environments enhance children's social skills, "what the child who is least ready for systematic reading instruction needs most is ample experience with oral and printed language, and early opportunities to begin to write" (Anderson, Hiebert, Scott, & Wilkinson, 1984, p. 29). Sadly, many classrooms follow drastically different methodologies.

Instruction in school can also be both implicit and explicit, although it has traditionally been more explicit and too often reduced to a "hierarchy of interrelated [and atomistic] isolated skills" (Taylor, 1983, p. 90) that doesn't include writing. Such segmentation differs significantly from the integrated nature of literate behaviors that young children observe in their world (Taylor, 1983).

Developmentally appropriate literacy instruction in early childhood classrooms is similar to the authentic literacy interactions children encounter at home. Analyzing such interactions has long been a focus of research (Bissex, 1980; Clay, 1987a, 1987b; Taylor, 1983). Rather than tell the child how to do something, Holdaway (1979) noticed that the parent

> sets up an emulative model of the skill in operation and induces activity in the child which approximates toward use of the skill . . . The activity is then "shaped" or refined . . . From this point of view, so-called "natural" learning is in fact supported by higher quality *teaching intervention* (p. 22).

Knowing what developmentally appropriate literacy instruction should be is the first step; next, we ask, "How do we get there?"

Toward a Reading-writing Classroom

So, what's needed to make this happen? First, a sensitive adult (teacher and/or parent)—one who responds to what each child is trying to do—no more, no less. That's essential! Such responding is the one difficult way to make learning to read easy (Smith, 1983). It's difficult to respond with just enough, but not too much information. But, finding that balance makes learning easy. Next, writing materials are required—preferably ones that are attractive, colorful, comfortable, fun to use, and that spark creativity (Mayer, 2007). That doesn't necessarily mean expensive equipment, but writing tools must be readily available. Freeman (2003) suggests creating a writer's kit as a convenient way to make them accessible (Figure 1.4). An easy-to-equip "writer's tool cart" is described in Chapter 5. Ideas for stimulating and supporting young children's journey into literacy are also outlined.

Research findings conclude that young children's experimentation with writing plays a pivotal role in learning to read (Farnan, Lapp, & Flood, 1992; Richgels, 1995; Cecil, 2007). Perlmutter, Folger, and Holt (2009) suggest that, "4-year-olds do not learn to read first and write later—children's beginning efforts at writing support initial forays into the reading process" (p. 15). But, many schools follow a reading-first approach, holding off writing until children have acquired a sizable sight vocabulary (Wells, 1986). Effective early childhood classrooms accommodate both language processes—right from the start; they provide

sight words, sight vocabulary
words known on sight, read automatically without an analysis of cues

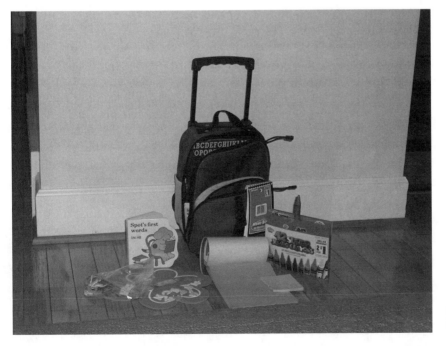

FIGURE 1.4
Writer's Toolbox

ideograph
picture (or design) symbolizing an idea

ideographic
ideas or objects are represented by graphic images rather than words or speech

encode
represent ideas and emotions in a sign system

decode
break the print code; figure out the words and understand the message

meaningful opportunities for children to write and read. "Rather than developing *after* reading, we now know that writing accompanies young children's growing interest in naming letters and reading print" (Cecil, 2007, p. 162). Children write into reading and, along the way, they acquire specific literacy skills. Other researchers concur that writing can precede learning to read or develop simultaneously (Montessori, 1966; Teale & Yokota, 2000). These outcomes in writing occur in environments (in school or at home) that offer quality ingredients in appropriate amounts of modeling, explanation, support, stimulation, feedback, choice, nudging, materials, and encouragement. These environments sensitively challenge, but never push; they expect and respect children's differences.

Durkin's (1966) paper and pencil kids flourished in such contexts, growing from ideographic message drawings to scribbling to random letters to semi-phonetic and phonetic representations and, finally, to more conventional forms. In the process of encoding their messages, children learn to decode their own words and the words of others. Stepping into reading is easier for them because they have already engaged with the functions and forms of print in personally meaningful ways.

Classrooms That Work

Early writing doesn't supplant reading instruction; it lays a foundation for understanding how print works. "Writers write for readers and readers read writing. The reading-writing connection lies at the heart of our work in classrooms" (Martin et al., 2007, p. 39). Children's writing samples in this text and on the companion website demonstrate the power of that connection.

At the national level, there's renewed interest in the vision of universal, high-quality pre-K and early childhood experiences. We need to seriously consider priorities for curriculum and materials if we are to fulfill the promise of bringing all children to literacy. In the midst of the hype about paraphernalia needed to teach and assess specific skills, it's good to know that children can learn all they need for success by becoming paper and pencil kids. And, we have all we need to assess their progress when we mindfully observe their literate performances and the products they create (Portalupi & Fletcher, 2005). The first step according to Freeman (2003) is "to absolutely expect your students to write. . . . treat them as writers, call them writers, make them believe they are writers. Have faith; *Build it and they will come* [italics as source]" (p. 3).

Researchers have consistently concluded that children learn literacy skills—even before coming to school (Durkin, 1966; Ferreiro & Teberosky, 1989; Whitmore et al., 2005)—most effectively while marinating in wonderful literature, engaging in grand conversations, and creating their own picture and print messages. These experiences become the cornerstone of conceptual knowledge about language and print. Do some children lag behind in developing these skills? Some might; others appear to be lagging based on contrived time norms for acquisition.

Norms (standard for average performance) for development in any area (i.e. height, weight, language acquisition, social development) are arbitrary measures established statistically using a sampling of the population; a second sampling would produce a different norm. Those who take longer (i.e. late bloomers) to reach a standard level of performance are not necessarily deficient when they fall below the current norm. Suspected lags may also be due to limited experience and opportunities. Or, perhaps, children just haven't learned to demonstrate their knowing in the manner that schools use to assess literacy knowledge (Whitmore et al., 2005).

Regardless of the causes of perceived or real learning lags, ensuring that the conditions enjoyed by children who learn literacy skills easily are provided for all makes the most sense. It's simple, effective, and enjoyable—and it's the least costly way! In the chapters that follow, we'll explore just how to do this.

Extending the Discussion

- Talk to parents of a pre-school-age child. Ask them to describe his/her explorations or experimentations with print. How did they support the child's interest and play with print?
- Observe teaching and learning in a primary classroom or examine the practice in your own classroom on a particular day. Describe the language learning opportunities that occurred. What language processes were included? What essential components for reading competency were most notable?
- Review curriculum plans for pre-K classrooms. Take note of literacy activities that are integrated. What are they? How often are they included? Are they well-developed? Share your thinking with others.

two
Function Before Form

Building Concepts About Print

Big Ideas in Chapter 2

- Research on emergent literacy—Durkin's study
- Study of preschoolers' concepts of reading and writing
- Conditions for literacy exploration and experimentation
- Building concepts about print
- Successful literacy curriculum
- Solid foundation in literacy

Research in Emergent Literacy

A body of research from close to 50 years of studies reveals how literacy develops, the factors that motivate children's explorations with language, and the concepts children have constructed about language and print. Many researchers conclude that preschool experiences play a significant role in children's literacy development (Durkin, 1966; Heath, 1983; Holdaway, 1979; Martens, 1998; McNaughton, Parr, & Smith, 1996; Morrow, 1983; Neuman, 1997; Paratore, 2003; Schickedanz, 1990; Schulze, 2006; Smith & Elley, 1997a; Soderman & Farrell, 2007; Taylor, 1983; Taylor & Dorsey-Gaines, 1988; Teale, 1982, 1984; Weinberger, 1998). As previously mentioned in Chapter 1, Durkin's (1966) seminal research on children who came to school reading, or learned to read with ease, set the stage for research in emergent literacy (IRA, 1998).

Durkin's Study and Findings

socioeconomic status
a group's position in society based on combined social and economic factors

Durkin's (1966) study identified several common factors in early readers. Notably, IQ or socioeconomic statuses (SESs) (i.e. professional, working class) were not among them.

Early readers

- were highly *motivated* to engage in literate activities. This motivation wasn't innate; it germinated during positive, supported, and engaging literacy experiences;
- were broadly exposed to print and print forms, including an array of real world genres from books to newspapers, magazines, and environmental print;
- had engaged in meaningful interactions with others focused on print;
- had witnessed numerous demonstrations of purpose-driven literate activities;
- had their queries about print and how it works answered with enough, but not too much, information;
- had opportunities to create print messages; they were writers.

environmental print
print found in the world
(e.g. signs, posters, charts, maps, on products)

Writing was a gateway into reading for these children. In the process of encoding their own messages, they learned how print works. Durkin's (1966) findings outlined the stages of young children's evolution as writers. Other research supports her findings, concluding that concepts about print develop in stages as a result of children's supported exploration in writing and reading (Cecil, 2007; Clay, 1993; McGill-Franzen, 2006; Schulze, 2006; Sulzby, 1990; Vukelich, Christie, & Enz, 2002). Stages offer a lens through which to understand children's writing rather than rigid benchmarks for measuring achievement. Children's work often reflects elements of multiple stage levels.

benchmark
expected level of performance at a given point in time

stage
a step in a process or development

Durkin's Stages of Early Writing Development

Durkin's (1966) research concluded that young writers progressed through developmental stages that could be broadly described. Children moved through them at their own pace and in their own way.

Stage 1—Drawing and Scribbling

Children draw and scribble. Sometimes they do one or the other; sometimes they use both forms to create messages. Iredell (1898) stated, "scribbling is to writing what [as] babbling is to talking" (p. 235). Platt (1977) reiterated the analogy, explaining that controlled scribbling initiates the representational use of print for ideas.

The next two stages are very closely related. They can be considered separately or combined as a beginning and later phase of the same stage when tracking children's progress (see Chapter 5, Figure 5.4).

Stage 2—Letter-like Forms

Children begin to create letter-like forms. These include all kinds of distinct shapes, lines, and angles. The child has learned that message making with print is different from drawing and scribbling; it has distinct

FIGURE 2.1
Madison Draws and
Writes

and repeated marks with lines and curves that form letters and words
(Kempton, 2007; Meek, 1991).

Stage 3—Copying Objects and Letters

Children copy print found in the environment; they use letters they've
learned to form when constructing messages.

Stage 4—Asking Questions About Spelling

Children continue to use logic and experiences to compose messages, but
they're beginning to recognize constancy in print representations. When

FIGURE 2.2
Emily Draws and
Writes Hearts

FIGURE 2.3
Skylar Copies from
Book

dissonance
lack of agreement, state of unrest, incompleteness

conventional print forms
correct in spelling, grammar and usage

that understanding causes dissonance, they seek help for particular forms. Durkin (1966) suggested that in *ask the expert* stage, children might query, How do you make ... (meaning spell)? Children's efforts to write at this stage reflect growing appreciation for conventional print forms, but their message making remains genuinely self-directed. Meek (1991) states "in the case of writing, composing [constructing personal messages] counts for more than copying" (p. 96).

Stage 5—Reading One's Writing

Children read their own messages and gradually the messages written by other authors. Their reading informs their writing; continued writing stimulates growth in reading.

Durkin's (1966) findings have been thoroughly examined over time. After reviewing several studies replicating her seminal work, Anderson, Hiebert, Scott, and Wilkinson (1984) confirmed Durkin's findings. Their

FIGURE 2.4
Emma Writes About Clifford and Mouse

conclusions were reported in *Becoming a Nation of Readers*. More recently, Dickenson and Tabors (2001) identified multiple correlations between early literacy opportunities at home and children's success in kindergarten.

Yet, too often, these findings from research are not the driving force in early childhood classrooms. The full body of research referenced throughout this text—which includes both quantitative and qualitative studies on young children's emergence into literacy—provides evidence of a significant positive effect for young children's engagement in authentic literacy activities. The study described next demonstrates young children's early concept building—constructions made from the fabric of experiences and observations in their family life and community.

quantitative
empirical research characterized by numerical data and statistical analyses

qualitative
research characterized by analyses of non-numerical data (i.e. descriptions, interviews, case studies) in search of patterns

A Study of Preschool Children's Concepts About Print

In a research project focused on pre-kindergartners' concepts about print, four- and five-year-olds engaged in a series of literacy related tasks (Shea, 1992). Children observed and participated in tasks involving reading and writing behaviors.

The Study

The sample included pre-K classes at schools representing diverse populations. The study was designed to reveal pre-school children's working hypotheses about written language, to identify universal patterns across their theories, and to examine the results obtained against findings from other research. Children's responses on a series of tasks demonstrate the concepts they hold about reading and writing. Data from the study reveal that all children construct an intricate web of theories about print as they go about the business of life in the company and care of adults who respect, accept, and support their approximations as novices. For example, they learn that:

diverse populations
various cultural communities

working hypotheses
theories (ideas) being tested

- writing is different from drawing;
- writing stands for ideas and messages—writing can be read;
- print is mapped onto the page from left to right with a return sweep;
- written words are constructed with letters;
- there's a limited set of letters to use for writing;
- words have a variety of letters—a string of the same letter isn't a word;
- words have different sequences of letters (generative principle).

Data from this study also reinforce findings from the body of research on emergent literacy. Literacy learning, like other learning, is a social event. Children respond to "an explosive force from within ... to express themselves" (Goodman, Smith, Meredith, & Goodman, 1987, p. 34). They "do not wait for formal instruction before they read and write" (Whitmore et al., 2005, p. 299). Children jump right in, explore, and use

approximations
attempts at doing a task that come closer and closer to the expected level of performance

print. Demonstrations and invitations to participate in daily literacy occasions (e.g. writing grocery lists, reading coupons) provide opportunities for explaining how and why tasks are done. Frequently interjected, "I know you can do this" statements from adults build children's confidence and persistence with literate activities (Shea, 1992).

Two separate tasks in the study clearly demonstrate children's concept-building in reading and writing. The nature of communication throughout the researcher–subject interactions in the study led to unexpected findings, which validate the power of high expectations and positive affirmation for increasing children's confidence and motivation to engage in literate activities.

Reading Task

contextual surroundings
everything around the element (i.e. objects, words) analyzed

This task reveals what children know about reading. Children were asked to identify and *read* photographs with environmental print; each enlarged photograph had additional contextual surroundings.

FIGURE 2.5
No Parking

FIGURE 2.6
Bridge Closed

They were asked, "Is there something to read in this picture?" and "Can you point to where it is?" Then, they were asked what it said. If a child responded, "I don't know; I can't read yet" it was suggested that he pretend to be Mommy or Daddy. What would that person say if asked to read it? Without fail, gentle coaching for pretend reading allowed the few hesitant ones to respond with what they imagined the adult would say. Sometimes, it took a pregnant pause of silence followed by a smile of encouragement before a slow start with "Hmmmm ..." produced a response similar to ones that follow. Patience and complimentary nudges from the adult were always rewarded with an answer, even though some responses were more logical than others as predictions.

When asked how they (or Mommy or Daddy when they were reading) knew what it said, children's answers reflected the use of *historical context* (Shea, 1992) in some cases. They connected objects in the picture with familiar ones and events. An example of historical context is: "It says *Don't Park Here* because I saw that sign at my Grandma's house." Children also used *immediate context* to assign meaning to print or situations in the photograph.

An example of immediate context: "It says *Broken Road Be Careful Where You Go You May Fall In* because the road is broken right there [in the picture]."

Although not conventionally correct, these children systematically used contextual clues to read embedded print messages. They demonstrated awareness of print around them and an assumption that meaning is associated with the situation in which print is found.

historical context
background knowledge (schema), similar to immediate context (situation)

immediate context
everything that's right there in the situation (i.e. in a visual, other words on a page) and available as a clue

contextual clues
clues embedded in the words or sentences; clues in visuals (i.e. charts, pictures)

Writing Task

Children reveal their knowledge about the functions and forms of writing in this task. When asked to write, a few children played it safe; they'd fill the paper with huge letters, spelling their name or writing it repeatedly.

These children would typically say, "I don't know how to write; I'll learn that when I go to school." Sadly, they had fully internalized an idea,

Example 15

FIGURE 2.7
Filling the Page

probably transmitted in their environment by well-meaning adults; writing must be correct and the mechanics would be introduced formally in school. Concern about correctness becomes a gatekeeper to early exploration with print—experimentation that builds interest, motivation, concepts, and confidence as a language user. Any loss of opportunity to play with language is regrettable.

Similarly, Heath (1983) found that Roadville (a white working-class textile mill community in the Piedmont Carolinas) mothers typically allowed children to use pencils and crayons under supervision; they didn't encourage scribbling. Roadville children were encouraged to follow a system when coloring or labeling—with the same expectations of correctness and neatness they'd meet when filling in workbooks in school.

Contrary to rigid "up tight, gotta be right" behaviors, other children—the literacy explorers in the study—responded differently. Identified across cultural and SES groups, these adventurers had been allowed to experiment with reading and writing in their own way; they showed no trepidation.

Literacy explorers dove into the materials available (including colorful smelly markers), creating drawings and print messages. The literacy explorers composed; their writing was a communication. Ray and Glover (2008) discuss children's composing as a process of creating—representing *their* feelings, thoughts, or ideas. Composing can be done in different sign systems (i.e. written language, art, music, dance); it's a matter of choice—and talents. People compose when they encode (represent thinking and feeling) in art, music, dance, or in print. Young children compose in all of these sign systems too. Supporting composition developmentally—across sign systems—expands several horizons.

sign system
symbol system used to record thinking or feeling in a communicative form for others

When children have access to an array of attractive supplies, they explore and experiment playfully with each (Coles & Goodman, 1980; Klenk, 2001). If children said they didn't know what they had written when asked to read it, a suggestion to describe what they were thinking about while writing was offered. The adult responded to the child's description with, "Well, I'd guess it says what you just told me." Children usually agreed with this logic.

The concept conveyed was that writing represents ideas; what you think can be spoken, what you say can be written down with marks and what you write can be read. The children's writing also represented a wide variety of forms from scribble to initial letters and some correctly spelled personally important words (such as Mom, Dad, names, love).

Sometimes, there was ambivalence about the difference between drawing and writing, but this was expected. Young children typically move freely from one expressive process to the other (Mayer, 2007). The children would frequently say, "I'm writing a house. I'm writing the flowers" when they were actually drawing a house with flowers.

But, drawing was often the path into marking. Eventually, the child added marks and expressed what his *writing* said. Messages were often a compilation of ideographic (picture writing) and graphic (scribble, marks, letter-like forms, and letters) symbols (Temple, Nathan, Temple, & Burris, 1993). Graves (1994) defines writing as a process of composing that connects covert ideas with the marks, letters, and/or words used to make them readable.

Some children worked with intentionality, knowing from the beginning what they wanted to say; they harnessed the power of the print, making it work for them. Others began making marks and decided what the writing said as they wrote or when they were *reading* it. But, whenever children used marks to communicate, it was acknowledged as writing (Calkins, 1994; Graves, 1994; Harste, Burke, & Woodward, 1983; Schulze, 2006). Children's efforts were encouraged; their compositions received praise. Remarks of encouragement and affirmation were spontaneous—unplanned and unscripted; the outcomes attributed to them were unexpected.

Unexpected Findings: The Power of Expectation and Positive Affirmation

A strong expectation for success was communicated to children when introducing each task in the preschool study. It began with, "I know you're going to like this activity. I can tell that you're clever." The intention was simply to establish rapport and support risk-taking by making it clear that the request was based on a belief that they would like to read or write and *could do it*.

kid writing
writing at various early stages before conventional or standard form

For example, in the writing task, children were invited to create a personal message using their own version of *kid writing*. They could be in charge of how the writing would go, but they would need to read it back when they finished. The request was, "Since I'm used to grown-up writing, I might get stuck on some of the words in kid writing. I'll need your help to read it." Cambourne (1988) states that expectation is the most critical condition for learning; the other conditions (discussed in Chapter 3) are moot without first communicating a vision of the child as a natural born learner. The young writers and readers who *gave it a go* had learned (directly or indirectly) that they are capable; they were willing to explore and expand their thinking. Parents and family members had nurtured their interest and efforts, inviting them to join the literacy club (Smith, 1988). Once children are empowered with a *can do* attitude, amazing things happened.

Several parents of children at one of the sites attended a session where the study was described. Before the meeting, a parent whose daughter had been involved in the study had a story to share. She explained that her daughter had not shown the same interest in literacy activities that an older brother had demonstrated when he was the same age. This had caused the parent some concern until a recent episode occurred. It seems that she and the child were driving in the car when an 18-wheeler passed them. The child calmly proclaimed, "Mommy, I know what it says on that truck." Assuming that this was impossible since there were no pictures accompanying the print, but wishing to encourage interest in reading, the mother asked the child what it said. The child responded confidently, "It says 'mushrooms', Mommy." Indeed, the word "mushrooms" was boldly printed on the truck along with other smaller print. The mother said she almost drove off the road in her astonishment. Upon collecting her composure, she asked, "How did you know?" The child nonchalantly replied, "Because Mrs. Shea said I'm a clever girl" (Shea, 1997).

We can't know with certainty how this child learned the word "mushrooms", but her attribution for knowing the word is important. Simple words expressing genuine expectations of capability are powerful and have far-reaching effects. Confidence to inquire and experiment lays the foundation for learning. When a child believes she can make sense of print, she is motivated to notice it. Perhaps this child queried options on a pizza menu to be sure mushrooms were either included or excluded as an ingredient. With that examination, she may have learned the word. Although not verified, one can reasonably suggest that self-confidence sparked the attention that led to word recognition.

It's during the process of attending to and mucking around with print that essential conceptual understandings are constructed. Sinclair (1989 in Ferreiro & Teberosky) points out that

> skills are quite secondary when it comes to understanding the nature and function of writing [and] ... learning to read and write cannot be reduced to a set of perceptual-motor skills, or to willingness or motivation, but must grow from a deeper layer of conceptual development (p. v).

perceptual motor
interaction between various senses and motor activity

In supportive environments, young children build deep layers of understanding about literacy. Knowing what works in these settings can inform curricular mapping for literacy instruction in early childhood classrooms, transforming practice and reducing the achievement gap (Taylor, 1993). The key is to provide ample time, lots of choice, and an environment that supports learning exploration. These ingredients nurture language seeds within the child.

curriculum mapping
designing lessons, units of study, and sequence of learning across grades

Children Experiment With the Functions and Forms of Print

Young children in any culture and community are surrounded with print and significant others using it in all kinds of ways; they are naturally curious about everything they observe. This leads them to explore the *functions* (uses) that they notice print serving. Young children label, list, make notes, and write stories with a focus on using print. Attention to its *forms* (e.g. letters and other conventions) is secondary, growing from experimentation as young writers attempt to refine their constructions (Owocki, 1999).

Newkirk (1989) suggests that list writing is the first sign of exposition when it is used to document what is known. Such play with the functions

exposition
informational writing

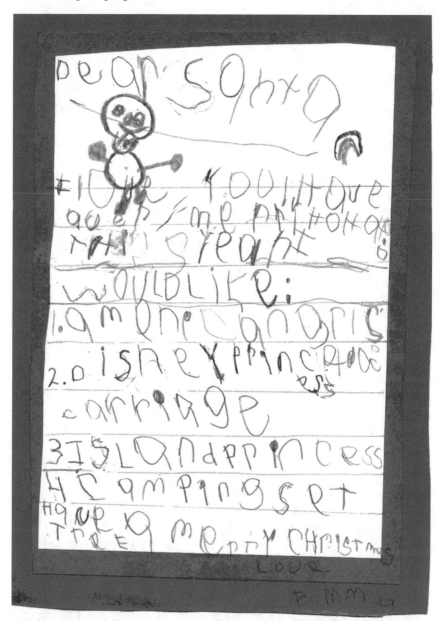

FIGURE 2.8
Emma's Santa Letter

of print draws children's attention to conventions, including how print is placed on the page, letter-sound relationships, spelling, and other conventions (Owocki, 1999; Whitmore et al., 2005).

This playful writing is the child's work; it's focused, consuming, and joyful. "Nobody needs to teach a child to play, but good teachers move play into new areas of learning … and relinquish control" (Kempton, 2007, p. 63). In their literacy play, children mimic how significant others in their world act, self-directing literacy learning. Vygotsky (1978) noted that in "play a child always behaves beyond his average age, above his daily behavior" (p. 102). Children's play as learning and learning through play is socially, emotionally, and cognitively fulfilling.

Young children typically scribble aesthetically when first presented with a marking tool. When they realize that others perceive a communicative intent in their playful marking, children begin to report messages for displays of marks (Goodman, 1989). They also become more aware of environmental and other print around them; they ask questions about it. Soon previously discussed stages (Durkin, 1966) can be identified in the child's progressive forays into composing.

These children are theory builders, following the logic of their observations, experimentation, and feedback from others (Gentry, 2005). "Children do not follow a learning path that goes from 'true position' to another, more advanced 'true position' ... [They] hold false theories as a necessary part of the process of learning to think" (Papert, 1980, pp. 132–133). This method is not deficient; it's one that allows children to flex cognitive muscles as they process experiential input on their way to conventional knowledge. But, too often, "our educational system rejects the 'false theories' of children, thereby rejecting the way children really learn" (p. 132). Young children learn most effectively when the environment complements natural learning paths—when they lead, but have the security of a sensitive guide at their side.

aesthetic
having a sense of the beautiful, involving emotion

pragmatic
practical point of view

true position
accepted as the correct understanding

false theories
considered an incorrect understanding

conventional knowledge
currently socially accepted as correct information

From Experimenting to Concept Building

Sometimes, there are false starts in children's concept building; their ideas about print can be a bit off target—even amusing—but the logic behind them is often quite sophisticated (Ferreiro & Teberosky, 1989; Goodman, 1996; Harste et al., 1984; McGee & Richgels, 1996; Owocki, 1999; Taylor, 1983). For example, Kristina's spelling reflects an ability to thoughtfully separate and represent sounds even though the results are not in standard form.

When blinded by a sense of *gotta be right* (conventional), it's easy to miss the significance of young children's early writing and dismiss it as inconsequential play. Mayer (2007) concludes that emergent writing (writing that intends to communicate) begins when children are around three to five years old. The preschool and primary grade years lay the foundation for refined aspects of writing expected in later years. The young child who has had opportunities for joyful concept building about print has a huge head start in knowledge, attitude, and interest; he's predisposed for success with formal literacy instruction.

Bissex (1980) clearly shows an accelerated learning curve in the documentation of her son Paul's writing development—knowledge that benefits early reading. "Learning to write at the same time as one learns to read adds much to the knowledge one needs to become a fluent reader" (Smith & Elley, 1997a, p. 44). Clay (1991) points out that the writing-child must break down ideas into their smallest parts (sounds and letters) and then synthesize these into words and sentences; gradually, the child writer begins to match symbols with sounds. When complete, the child reads the construction to confirm his meaning was represented. Clay (2001b) suggested that the classroom that "emphasizes early creative

FIGURE 2.9
Kristina's Thank-you

writing and succeeds will [also] produce … good readers" (p. 338). The pattern of this growth becomes evident when observing children's writing over time and across purposes that are playful, authentic, gently supported, and highly self-directed.

Engaging on Their Own Terms

Children intently observe the actions of significant others in their environment; they act scientifically. They're trying to make sense of the world they live in and become part of it. Children mimic and try on the behaviors they notice. We see this in their fantasy play with dolls or trucks; likewise, we see it with their drawing, marking, and writing. Children want to write when the conditions are right (Turbill, 1983). "Wanting to write motivates children to learn how print works. Learning to write often precedes learning to read" (McGill-Franzen, 2006, p. 197).

In their writing as play, children organize their responses and the way they behave according to the pretend situations they've constructed; they're in control. But, beyond the immediate activity, abstract thinking and metacognition are evolving (Dyson, 2003; Owocki, 1999; Whitmore et al., 2005). Most children—in a risk-free, supportive environment— take to writing like ducklings to water. Just drop them in, encourage and model, and away they go—competent and proud!

metacognition
ability to reflect on one's thinking, determine what is known, plan how to find out

From Journaling to Journalism

Rachel spent two years in preschool because she just missed the cut-off date for beginning kindergarten in the local school district. The preschool she attended has writing time every day—with both the three-year-old and four-year-old class. Paper used for writing has the alphabet—with upper and lower case letters—written across the top of the page. There's a space for drawing and the area for writing is delineated with bars and lines. Rachel writes on the line rather than using it to determine a height for lower case letters. In Figure 2.10 Rachel explains what she has represented in the picture. "Mom AnD DAD AnD I Ane KechinG BuDerflis" (Mom and Dad and I are catching butterflies). Rachel draws less in Figure 2.11, but documents something she's just learned in different lessons; the form is exposition. She proudly states what she knows about the heart. Newkirk (1989) argues that "as long as children have access to a variety of non-narrative forms, they will adopt them" (p. 24).

Novice Novelist

After numerous explorations into composing using kid writing, Mathew decided he wanted to write a book. On his own, Matthew (five years old) authors and illustrates a Pooh adventure (this can be found on the companion website). Pooh and his friends go to a local ice cream shop after getting together to play. Matthew follows story format, beginning "One day, Pooh was walking to his house." He introduces the setting

FIGURE 2.10
Catching Butterflies

(time and place) and main character, continues with events ("then ... "), and concludes with a simple resolution ("So they went to Anderson's to get ice cream."). His spelling reveals an ability to hear and record sounds with letters and use a repertoire of automatic writing words (known spellings). Both skills grow with this kind of meaningful practice.

In their uses of literacy, these children controlled the situations; they made decisions, experimented, and assessed the outcomes. Their early literacy experiences were risk-free, enjoyable, and personally meaningful, causing them to consistently engage and learn. It was just play in their minds—play with enormous potential for learning literacy.

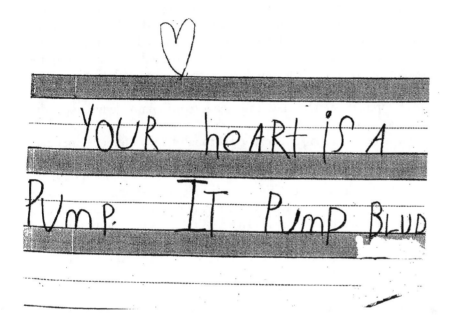

FIGURE 2.11
Heart

Play With a Consequence

The children described are building a conceptual framework of literacy knowledge—the big picture or *macro* knowledge. Cole (2004) explains that the macro is "the substance from which global understandings are constructed" (p. 20). Rachel and Matthew understand how print fits into their world and needs; they show interest in using it for personal reasons. When these children are exposed to formal instruction and the micro skills—whatever the program or methodology—they're able to tune into the teacher's frequency. They assimilate and accommodate the *micro content* of text. The *micro content* of text includes situational graphophonic (letter/sound), syntactic, and semantic cues and the integration of these (Cole, 2004). Formal literacy instruction makes sense to them because they know how they'll use the information. They're the lucky ones; they'll easily meet and exceed expectations established by schools. They already use print to encode ideas; they use reading to decode written messages.

cues
clues

graphophonic
relating to the grapho—letter and phonic—sound relationship in the language

syntactic
relating to grammar

semantic
relating to meaning

Literacy Curriculum That Works: Start Where They Are

Children's use of random letters indicates a budding awareness of the alphabet principle; letters are used to encode words. Young writers' phonetic spellings demonstrate the isolation and ordering of separate sounds (phonemic awareness) and matching of each to the letter or letters for spelling words. Children's word choice indicates the breadth of background knowledge and vocabulary they have amassed. Young writers soon acquire an automatic writing vocabulary; with frequent use, they remember how to spell words previously requested. When the child can independently write a word, he can most often read it. Thus, the young writer acquires a bank of sight words (sight vocabulary) that can be used in reading and as a basis for analyzing other words with similar sounds and patterns. As mentioned, formal literacy instruction makes sense to these children; they attach new knowledge to prior knowledge, expanding existing schema.

What these children have learned through family literacy experiences can be accelerated in children who come to school without a rich literacy schema. When children write—right from the start—in school, the process becomes a vehicle for establishing and strengthening macro literacy concepts; it also provides authentic practice of micro skills that are too often taught separately. There will always be a natural range of developmental levels in early childhood classrooms, but our curriculum and methodologies can lessen the gaps created by experiential differences. Transferring learning in isolation to personally meaningful applications also generates motivation to participate because children view the work as relevant. Persistent and prolonged engagement in meaningful literacy practice also increases children's performance on formal assessment measures.

Johnson (1999) reported that end-of-the-year reading tests given to her kindergarten students, who wrote throughout the year, documented their extensive phonetic knowledge. She hypothesizes that the "writing experience [in her classroom] gave the letters and sounds deeper meaning" (p. vii). Clark's (1987) research concluded that being encouraged to write and use temporary spelling (sound spelling) led to greater achievement gains for all children, including those who came to school with literacy experiences that do "not fit mainstream expectations in school, but achieve functionality and intellectual purpose in families' daily lives" (Whitmore et al., 2005, p. 303).

The writing samples in this text come from homes and classrooms that support children's writing right from the start; they document the range of literacy knowledge and specific skills (e.g. phonics) children acquired. Their writing provided a readiness curriculum for reading.

Setting up such conditions—ones that foster literacy exploration and build *can do* attitudes—establishes a conceptual framework for filling in specific literacy knowledge. "Children who are encouraged to write early and inventively perform better in reading, especially in word recognition,

---

automatic writing vocabulary
words children can write without stopping to think about phonemic (sound) elements and phonics (letter/sound match)

readiness
state of preparedness for learning a task

sound spelling
word spelling that represents sounds in the sequence they're heard using mostly appropriate letters

readiness curriculum
series of sequenced instructions that intends to develop readiness for reading

than children who do not have this practice" (Temple et al., 1993, p. 11). Ray (2004) suggests that the way to start is "no matter what, let them write every day" (p. ix). Concept construction begins at home when children have a purpose (e.g. making a note, writing a book, creating a list) for assimilating and filing literacy insights. It continues seamlessly in classrooms that reflect the same conditions. These classrooms significantly reduce achievement differences, allowing all children to thrive.

Ensuring a Solid Foundation for Literacy Learning

McGill-Franzen (2006) points out that

> if we are to improve literacy in our nation, we all have to embrace the belief that teaching reading [and writing] to 5-year olds can be a school [or family] experience that's every bit as playful, imaginative, inquiry-driven, and developmentally appropriate as anything John Dewey or Jean Piaget might have dreamed up. (p. 16)

Collaboratively, teachers can apply research findings to design such a curriculum and environment at their school.

This book describes classroom communities that make children's journey into literacy joyful—places that stimulate excitement for learning no matter how old you are! Schulze (2006) emphasizes that such classrooms are especially critical for the many children who have not had the empowering, concept-building preschool literacy experiences their peers have enjoyed. Knowing that the quality of children's literacy experiences from birth through age five has a profound effect on their success in school (Dickenson & Tabors, 2001; Strickland & Barnett, 2003), early childhood teachers fill any gaps that exist as soon as possible.

Meaningful early childhood curriculum includes instruction in specific literacy skills that's imbedded in authentic reading, writing, and discussion. Quality literature is central to learning activities. Children respond to story or information through conversation and writing. Writing is incorporated across the curriculum; children write to learn and show what they know. Specific skills are tools for the real job of literacy—not standalone goals.

Assessment of literacy development is focused on how children apply skills functionally; their writing verifies acquisition of separate skills and much, much more. The young writer's ability to accurately use the labyrinth of writing forms (structures and conventions) grows developmentally when adults provide patience, effective instruction, scaffolded practice, sensitive feedback, appreciation of effort, and audience for his message. The same ingredients led to Shaun White's competence in snowboarding and David Beckham's agility with a soccer ball.

When children write right from the start they understand right from the start that knowledge in isolation is not enough; one must be able to use skills—just as literate people use them in the world. "It is not surprising, therefore, that a major research finding in emergent literacy is that writing—if much experimentation is encouraged—can play a pivotal role in children's learning to read" (Cecil, 2007, p. 162). And grand conversations about life, literature, and the world around them get young writers started. Talk generates subject matter children know about, care about, and can write about; it sustains their composing.

The next chapter discusses the importance of frontloading children's background knowledge about the world, language structures, and meaning vocabulary through adult-guided immersion in quality literature and meaningful real or vicarious learning experiences. But, these adult-guided opportunities must include talking *with* (not just *to*) the child, respecting him as a partner. Such grand conversations produce learning. What's the connection to writing you might wonder? It's simple. One cannot write without something to say or without knowing how to map ideas onto the page. And, one cannot express thoughts interestingly, coherently, and persuasively without expanded word knowledge. Chapter 3 discusses the importance of talk in building knowledge, writing skills, and the motivation to use both.

Extending the Discussion

- Describe any early literacy experiences you recall from your own life. What do you remember about learning to read? Learning to write?
- Collect additional samples of young children's at-home writing. Discuss what these reveal about the children's acquired literacy concepts.
- Reflect on the *function before form* premise for learning. Think about a new skill you recently learned (e.g. how to play golf, cook, quilt, ski, build a deck). What were the understandings you had about functions for that skill that inspired you to persist in learning the details of form?

three
Talk

An Essential Tool for Writing

Big Ideas in Chapter 3

- Building a bridge to written communication
- Building language reservoirs
- Write like the authors of favorite books
- Talk: practice for written expression
- Time and place for writing

A Bridge to Written Communication

Talking, visually representing (drawing), and writing are sign systems—modes for communicating ideas and messages. Children explore and develop skills in each expressive language form as they think and interact with others in their world. They typically start with talking and drawing—formats that serve as a foundation for written expression.

Learning Language

Verbal interactions, at home and in literacy-rich classrooms, illuminate children's lives, helping them notice, describe, and make sense of new experiences; they set the stage for writing. Ong (1982) purposed that "orality ... is destined to produce writing" (p. 15). Children immersed in story and supported as storytellers enjoy sharing their tale with an audience. Such literate experiences become incentives for learning how ideas can be written down, just like the narratives in books, and retold over and over.

orality
the state of being in an oral mode

There's a recognized line of research that describes the development of children's knowledge related to the importance, purposes, and forms of speech in their community (Ehri, 1975; Ferreiro & Teberosky, 1989;

Halliday, 1975; Heath, 1983; Karpova, 1966; Wells, 1986; Whitmore et al., 2005). Findings consistently point out that "talk is the root of literacy" (Kempton, 2007, p. 47).

From the moment of birth, a child produces sounds. As soon as he connects vocal productions to responses from others, a symphony or cacophony erupts depending on the child's mood, wants, or needs. At this early stage of development, a most simplistic form of vocalization is used to communicate—gurgling, gooing, fussing, or wailing. In a matter of months, the newborn begins to babble the consonant and vowel sounds needed to produce his home language (Morrow, 2004; Pappas et al., 1999; Wells, 1986). Bloomfield (1933) identified this language acquisition process as the "greatest intellectual feat any one of us is ever required to perform" (p. 29). Positive interactions from those around him encourage the baby to continue generating these sounds; he's delighted with the affectionate reactions. The baby repeats the behavior to maintain the attention; in the process, he continues to refine utterances as adults mediate the child's language productions by repeating, rephrasing, extending, and elaborating them (Burns, Snow, & Griffin, 1999; Hart & Risley, 1999; Morrow, 2004; Vygotsky, 1978; Wells, 1986).

This back and forth interplay (between baby and adult) serves to reinforce the child's learning of his home language. "Talking with young children is thus very much like playing ball with them—The adult [is] doing a great deal of supportive work to enable the ball [or conversation] to be kept in play" (Wells, 1986, p. 50). Such language activities set the stage for transitioning expression to a written mode.

"When they [children] write, it is only natural they want their voices to echo from the page" (Graves, 1983, p. 161). Engaging children in conversation as equal partners provides linguistic practice where they can refine the structure, form, sophistication, and length of expressions used. Children's talk establishes roots that anchor language learning (Hart & Risley, 1999; Kempton, 2007; Wells, 1986).

The quality of children's utterances increases when we provide interesting experiences to talk about and engage them in grand conversations (Kempton, 2007). The depth of their learning also increases. "Talking and [language] learning go hand in hand" (Wells, 1986, p. 67). Models, supportive practice, and positive response ensure development and continued refinement of skills across the range of everyday language functions (Graves, 1983; Hansen, 1987; Heath, 1989; Newkirk, 1989; Wells, 1986).

Case Studies of Language Development

Halliday's (1975) documentation of his son's oral language development revealed young Nigel's use of language for universal purposes. Even when early speech attempts are telegraphic, they reflect *intentionality* that aligns with functions utilized by fluent speakers. Language helps children to make sense of their observations, building understanding of themselves, others, and the world around them. Their language has content. But, the child's expressions also reveal perceptions of his relationship

---

vocalization
voiced sounds used to communicate

babble
to voice sounds intended as words; indistinct, imperfect articulations

language acquisition
process of learning and using a language in all formats

mediate
to bring differences into alignment (i.e. the utterances and intended communication) to restore harmony between ideas, performances or parties

linguistic
pertaining to language

telegraphic speech
a few words are used to represent a longer message

intentionality
a purpose, a design, an expected result

with the listener. Halliday calls this the *ideational* and *interpersonal* dimensions of language (1994). In the process of language development, children "learn how to mean" (Halliday, 1975, p. 7). They express ideas, wants, and needs. Children assimilate responses from listeners; they become social members of a community.

Nigel's speech could be:

- regulatory (Do what I tell you.) "Push." (meaning: "Push the swing for me.")
- instrumental (I want …) "Juice, Mommy."
- interactional (You and I …) "Want to play with me?"
- personal (I … "I run fast.")
- heuristic (Why … ?) "Why it boom?" (meaning: "What makes thunder?")
- imaginative (Let's pretend …) "Let's play dress-up."
- informative (I have something to tell) "I show you how."

In fact, once children start speaking, they employ the full spectrum of language functions they've observed. And, they never seem to stop. They're the most delightful (but sometimes exhausting) pint-sized chatterboxes. They talk, talk, talk—to themselves, to adults, to siblings, to other children, to the dog and cat, or to their toys. All this talk bonds them to others in their world, distinguishes who they are becoming, propels learning, and lays a foundation for other language processes.

Laminack (1991) also documented his son's language development; this included Zachary's self-directed writing that aligned with all of the purposes for which Nigel used oral language, including ideational and interpersonal dimensions. Figure 3.1 shows how a kindergartener used writing for instrumental and regulatory purposes. He wanted to inform his teacher that he intended to behave (instrumental). He implies that, because of that change, she ought to allow him to select something from the surprise box (regulatory).

The examples of children's writing in this book—like that of Zachary and Nathan—reflect a wide range of purposes. Children are driven to learn and use language to express themselves in multiple modes (Wells, 1986). They engage with oral and written functions of language noticed in the world around them (Laminak, 1991). One expressive mode grows out of and supports the other.

Building Language Reservoirs

Engaging young children in social conversations, answering queries with sufficient information, and encouraging curiosity are natural ways to foster language development. They're also easy and enjoyable for all participants. Those around the child establish the expectation for language use; they ensure that it will flow effortlessly by responding respectfully and extending the exchanges. They also connect language use to daily activities—both social and functional.

---

ideational
expression of thinking on objects not present in the immediate surroundings or abstract

interpersonal
referring to a relationship between people

regulatory
serving to regulate, control, direct the behavior of another

instrumental
serving a useful, functional purpose

heuristic
serving to stimulate questioning that leads to further investigating and learning

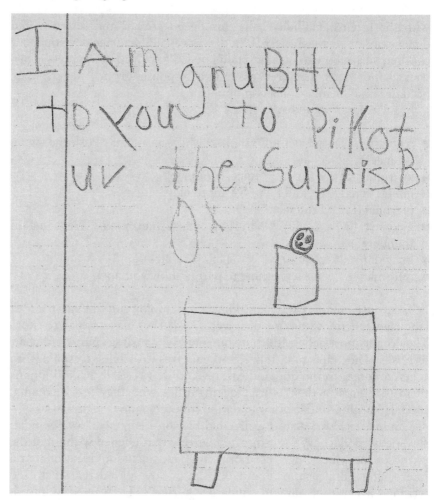

FIGURE 3.1
Nathan's Behavior Change

cadence
rhythm, beat, and pattern of spoken language

register of speech
form of speech accepted in different social situations (i.e. formal, casual, business)

meaning vocabulary or lexicon
all the words comprehended when heard; many also used in one's speaking vocabulary

The child learns the structure, cadence, and word meaning associated with his home language while immersed in using it—usually incorporating the informal *register* of a language for particular situations. The child builds a *meaning vocabulary* or *lexicon* in these conversations.

Words absorbed though the ears are processed in the brain to determine meaning using clues from context or explanations offered. The child soon begins to try them out. Sometimes he's successful on the first try; sometimes he needs clarification. Words that have been *in the ears and on the lips* are ones that the child will eventually find easier to read when first met in print. He will also use this language in his writing. Research has shown a high correlation between *meaning vocabulary* and reading performance, including success with both word recognition and comprehension (Anderson & Freebody, 1981). An extensive lexicon positively affects expressive language processes (speaking and writing) as well; children's word choice impacts the clarity and sophistication of their oral and written expression.

In literacy-rich environments, children are marinated in conversational language as well as the language structures used in other contexts.

Their lexicons expand with simple and sophisticated everyday words as well as technical and concept labeling ones. I'd wager that most everyone, at some time or other, has been amazed by a young child's correct use of a highly advanced term.

Adults introduce and explain items, situations, and events in the child's world, giving names and meaning to objects and concepts. Children seem to absorb language like sponges, especially when curiosity about terminology is piqued and the adult shares his enthusiasm for learning words. Parents read books and other printed material (e.g. forms, signs, comics, advertisements, and other environmental print) to children. And, they don't just say the words. They expand the child's horizon with deeper explanations and connection building by talking about the author's ideas; they build the child's reservoir of word knowledge, too. "The extensive vocabulary children need for complex tasks can be acquired if children have access to a bounty of good literature ... They must [also] be actively engaged with the reading material" (Cecil, 2007, p. 116).

Interesting Words and Lovely Language

Children's meaning vocabulary grows rapidly. A wealth of research on vocabulary development indicates that many children have acquired a reading vocabulary of approximately 5,000 words by the end of first grade and 50,000 by the time they graduate from high school (Graves, 2006). Graves, Juel, and Graves (2007) note that some words are learned through "rich and varied language experiences, teaching individual words, teaching word learning strategies, and [developing] word consciousness" (p. 20), but most are learned during wide reading and "real discussions—give and take conversations in which caretakers and later teachers give young learners the opportunity to think and discuss topics of interest in an open, positive, and supportive climate" (p. 207).

It's estimated that the average child learns about 3,000 words per year between grades 3 and 12, many related to content area topics (Graves, 2006; Nagy & Herman, 1985; Nagy, Herman, & Anderson, 1985; Nagy, Anderson, & Herman, 1987). That's about seven to ten new words a day—words are also learned incidentally and intentionally outside of school.

There's evidence that reading aloud to children and talking about the content of books increases their vocabulary and other language skills (Elley, 1989). It introduces children to interesting words and lovely language that soon becomes part of their *voice* when expressing meaning. Voice also adds life to their writing.

Voice personalizes writing, even at this early stage; it makes the message an extension of the writer. Even the youngest author can project voice that announces his ideas. Graves (1994) states that writing "has a driving force called voice ... Voice is the imprint of ourselves on our writing ... When voice is strong, writing improves along with the skills that help to improve writing" (p. 81). Broadening experiences, rich discussions, and quality literature introduce words and language patterns

voice (in writing)
writer communicates convictions, passion, personal feelings in an interesting manner

not often heard by young children in their daily lives. The child often tries them out, integrating appealing ones into oral and written expressions.

Language of Literature

decodable words
words that can be figured out by applying phonics, words with expected sound/letter matches

discourse
genuine two-way conversation, discussion

Angelina Ballerina books were my granddaughter's favorites when she was very young. An early favorite was *Angelina Ballerina's Colors* (Holabird, 2002a), a board-book with engaging illustrations and sparse text. Some of the words are simple and decodable, but ones like twirling, tutu, whirling, cartwheeling, and leaping caught Skylar's attention; they stimulated curiosity and questions. Our discourse included word talk; soon she was using such words in her own world. When her ability to attend progressed to more advanced Angelina stories, like *Angelina and Henry* (Holabird, 2002b), so too had the depth and breadth of vocabulary in the text. The language in this book includes such words as spun, encouraged, sigh, replied, shadowy, mouselings, whimpered, explorer, pelted, vanished, scampered, concertina, twitched, glinting, collapsed, bonfire, raged, howled, and loomed to name a few. Vocabulary learning is significantly impacted by story-time which incorporates such material; the child's word learning increases both expressive and receptive language skills (Doyle & Bramwell, 2006; Graves, 2006).

> Through stories and other genres of literature, children vicariously extend the range of their experience far beyond the limits of their immediate surroundings ... they develop a much richer model of the world and the vocabulary with which to talk [and later write] about it" (Wells, 1986, p. 152).

FIGURE 3.2
Skylar Reads to Emma

After listening to most books in the *Fairy Houses* series by Tracy Kane (2001), my granddaughters have carefully followed the detailed directions and constructed fairy houses in their backyard. They imagine the woods of Maine—the setting for the story—to be a magical fairyland and look forward to a summer vacation there. Significant others help children understand that life is full of stories to be told and information to be shared; interactions also demonstrate a range of genres for telling.

genres
kinds of text recognized by their structures (e.g. narrative, informational, poetry, letter, journalistic, essay)

Write Like That

Experiences with language have a cumulative effect. Children extrapolate from literature and grand conversations how authors and speakers craft engaging expressions of ideas. Bits of knowledge are stored; they're retrieved and adapted for personal applications whenever children perceive a fit with immediate situations.

Authors as Teachers of Writing

Exposure to literature builds children's awareness of the forms and functions of language used in writing (Fisher, Flood, Lapp, & Frey, 2004; Hedrick & Pearish, 2003). It also helps children discover the "power of language to create possible or imaginary worlds through words" (Wells, 1986, p. 156). Reading aloud to children is a time for collaborative conversation about content; it's also a context for emotional bonding. But, so much more is happening.

In each session, we are teaching writing. How else would children understand what writing should sound like if they had not heard it in a range of book forms (Ray, 2004)? Story reading becomes a stage, where children are exposed to and participate in book talk—words and structures they can apply in their own messages (Newkirk, 1989). Oral stories are important too; they're an effective bridge from literature to personal narratives. Wells (1986) called it *"storying"*; he considered the activity a "fundamental means of making meaning ... that pervades all aspects of learning" (p. 194). Horn & Giacobbe (2007) found that "writing begins with the oral telling of stories" (p. 8).

Storytelling: Another Model of Story Craft

My granddaughters also love oral stories. Their dad started this tradition by telling stories about his colleagues—slightly embellished tales about everyday happenings at school or about colleagues' families. The girls seem to absorb every detail and want to hear the stories repeated over and over. When I visit, they expect me to tell my stories. I had told my *At Rosemary's Beach* story at least 100 times before they actually went to the lake and met Rosemary. Meeting the characters and exploring all of the story settings was a great adventure. There was a stream of, "Show me where ...." What began as a night-time ritual to follow book reading has provided the girls with models for telling the stories of their lives—models of the content, structures, and language of telling in any genre.

Talk: Practicing How to Express Ideas

Talk provides an opportunity to communicate ideas as a coherent expression. Conversation helps us shape, clarify, refine, define, and revise them. Discourse is a mode of communicating as well as a stage for rehearsing ideas that can be crafted into a print form.

Discourse at Home

Talk at home is conversational whether it's for social purposes or associated with printed texts; the incidental teaching is natural rather than didactic. It differs from the talk children typically experience in school. Young children remind adults how simple and powerful incidental teaching can be when they question, "What's does … mean?" if the adult inadvertently adds a word or phrase into the conversation that is unfamiliar to them. The child usually remembers the definition offered because his curiosity was piqued. Simple, everyday conversation holds the potential for building word and concept knowledge—a basis for reading comprehension and writing vocabularies.

Talking in School

Silence in school is *not* golden. The classroom needs to be a place that nourishes the growth and expansion of conversational skills. Talk for learning can be a powerful instructional tool. "Children spend more time on-task when we encourage talking … they help each other [learn] … when we hear their voices we know a community exists" (Hansen, 1987, p. 79). When classrooms become communities, members model for each other, increasing learning exponentially (Graves, 1983). There's a purposeful hum in effective classrooms (Graves, 1983); it's a sound that signals learning is going on in here.

Sadly, talk as a learning tool has been grossly underused in classrooms. Fields, Groth, and Spangler (2008) note, "There are two ways of learning language: the natural way and the typical school way … The traditional school way … is to teach *about* it [language] rather than use it" (p. 78). An approach to language and literacy development that mimics the tenets of natural learning outside of school is reflected in classrooms with effective early childhood teachers. "The prescription is a massive dose of story time" (Fields et al., 2008, p. 92) for children who have missed this foundation for language success—and lots of talking (Wells, 1986). Early childhood classrooms that focus on oral language development are characterized by lots of meaningful talk, building a solid foundation for mastering written language (Hansen, 1987; Wells, 1986). In these classrooms, adults converse with children and children talk to each other (Fields et al., 2008; Hansen, 1987; Kirkland & Patterson, 2005; Newkirk, 1989). Sometimes, children talk to themselves—using inner speech or soft mumbling to rehearse. This is important talk too.

In *rehearsal* (by themselves or with others), children use conversation to narrate what they're thinking, guide what they're doing (e.g. when drawing, spelling, writing), or to clarify inner confusions (Bissex, 1984; Calkins, 1994; Gentry, 2005; Graves, 1983; Myhill & Jones, 2009; Whitmore et al., 2005). Besides self-talk, rehearsal for writing can also take the form of daydreaming, doodling, conversing with someone, sketching, outlining, or note making (Graves, 1983).

rehearsal talk
talk as a cognitive process to try out ideas and thinking as a way of learning, remembering, or guiding a task

Classrooms That Promote Talk

The functions that preschoolers have developed for oral and written language should be included in classroom interactions. Their strategies have served them well; in school, these should "be extended and developed, not suppressed by the imposition of routine learning tasks for which they [children] see neither a purpose nor a connection with what they already know and can do" (Wells, 1986, p. 68).

In preschool classrooms at a college campus early childhood center in a northeast state, activity stations are an integral part of the curriculum. Children visit various areas, set up with activities focused on the current theme study; they also visit generic ones that remain throughout the year. The latter include a dress-up area, painting place, block corner, book nook, kitchen, dollhouse, truck area, and a writing station. The writing station has as much traffic as other play areas; it's a hive of activity and learning. There's lots of talk about the how-to of literacy tasks at this station.

Writing stations are places where children begin to identify the tools, experiment with making marks, and assist one another in self-initiated writing tasks (Klenk, 2001). The teachers, Mrs. Thomas and Mrs. Little, usually direct one of the curricular stations before visiting with children around the room. They work and play with children engaged at stations;

FIGURE 3.3
Writing Center

there's a lot of conversation. All the while, the teachers make observations and note children's progress.

Mrs. Rodrigues greets her kindergarten students at the door each morning. An adult usually accompanies each child to the classroom in this urban bilingual class. At the door, Mrs. Rodrigues engages both the adult and child in a brief greeting; they speak in Spanish about the day, something they've brought, or news from their lives. At share time, children often expand on these initial exchanges. Although both English and Spanish labels are displayed in the room, Mrs. Rodrigues records children's words in the language in which they were spoken—Spanish. The oral-to-written language match scaffolds children as their words are read back. The language used is an extension of who they are; not using it would equate to rejecting them (Fields et al., 2008; Laliberty & Berzins, 2000). Classmates ask the teller questions; sometimes they share their story to compare experiences. These children recognize that others are interested in what they have to say; they want to keep talking.

Mrs. Smith has children begin the day with journaling. Seated at round tables, students talk, write, and, then, talk some more in low voices. She trusts that their conversations will lead to richer written work (Kempton, 2007). The talk helps children dig deeper into their ideas and feelings; it causes them to elaborate as they explain the message to their conversational partner. Mrs. Smith wants children to understand that authors write about the things *they* know and care about. "Helping children understand *why* we write belongs at the forefront of our instruction" (p. 100). Talking with others helps writers uncover details to include, appreciate what readers want to know, and consider a plan for getting started.

The children help each other to initiate writing; they help each other to keep going while Mrs. Smith takes attendance and lunch counts. With morning business completed, Mrs. Smith circulates and talks to writers; she sits with individuals to offer responses that support and nudge each

bilingual
ability to use two languages

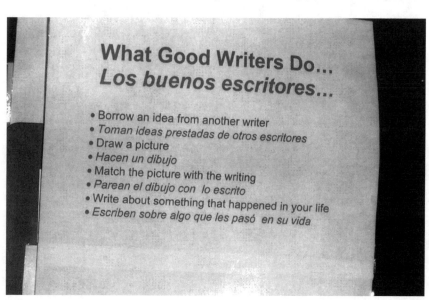

FIGURE 3.4
Good Writers Chart

one forward. Mrs. Smith mines a wealth of assessment data during these
brief conversations. At the same time, she guides emergent writers with
strategic questions—ones that spark more telling. In the beginning of the
year Mrs. Smith frames questions with who, what, when, where, why, or
how, helping children decide on additional details that clarify their narrative. As children finish their entry, they read it to Mrs. Smith and two
other classmates. The children benefit emotionally and cognitively from
these interactions. They are also motivated to increase text production
when their audience asks questions (Matthews & Kesner, 2003). Then,
everyone gathers for circle time that starts the day with additional conversation centered on the calendar, the schedule, news, and a new read-
aloud. This class includes several English as a Second Language (ESL)
students, but you'd never know it after the first few weeks of school.
Previously shy, quiet children begin to meet expectations for talk from
Mrs. Smith, their tablemates, and other classmates. Their transformation
from hesitant contributor to risk-taker is amazing.

assessment data
specific information related
to the quality of learner's
performance

These classrooms appreciate that, although spoken and written
languages are different, they're complementary resources for learning.
Expanding children's oral language fluency enables them to develop
thinking skills also associated with written language. Teachers who are
unaware of this symbiotic relationship are less likely to make provisions
that move young children toward written expression of what they want
to say (Horn & Giacobbe, 2007; Smith & Elley, 1997b; Wells, 1986;
Whitmore et al., 2005).

complementary resource
aligns well with, enhances
another resource

A Time and Place for Written Expression

Children with a lot to say, words to say it, and know-how for organizing
ideas realize that writing is another form of expression—one that makes
ideas permanent and available to a wider audience. But encoding ideas

FIGURE 3.5
Writers Share

into print requires effort, specific knowledge, feedback, and time. In successful writing classrooms, all ingredients are easily identified.

However, "writing has never taken hold in American education because it has been given so little time" (Graves, 1983, p. 90). Yet, *all* young children can write when they come to school even if only in a rudimentary way (Walshe, 1982; Wells, 1986); they want to write, too. When children are motivated to write and believe they can, they "invest more effort in it and learn more" (Hansen, 1987, p. 13). Writing brings them great "ah-ha"s of discovery; new understandings emerge as their ideas are expressed in print. Writing becomes another way of expressing what they think—a way that gives their ideas permanence (Graves, 1983). And, that's very, very rewarding; authorship motivates further production.

The next chapter describes the evolution of theory on learning and language acquisition; these findings lead to recognition of children's need for early writing opportunities—at home and in early childhood classrooms. Careful attention to aspects for building settings that nurture that learning, including field, tenor, and mode, ensures that children engage in literacy explorations and flourish as language learners (Cole, 2004) right from the start.

field
entire environment and physical surroundings

Elements that contribute positively to those aspects, making the environment optimal for such inquiry, are also described in Chapter 4. These are Cambourne's conditions (1999)—conditions that meet developmental needs for all learning and, in particular, learning about literacy.

tenor
climate, tone of emotional relationships

mode
materials and resources available

Extending the Discussion

- Think about personal experiences you've had in conversations with a young child. What did you notice about the child's use of language and ability to converse? How could you have expanded this conversation, mindful of the potential for incidental teaching?
- Examine a children's book for lovely language. Share your findings.
- Do a read-aloud with a child (or group of children). Allow the child to initiate the conversation about the story with comments or reactions. Describe what you learned in the session. Did the child's reactions surprise you in any way? Explain.
- Interview the parent of a young child. Ask her to reflect on the child's language development. What does she remember about her child's first words, first sentences or first initiation of questions about the world?
- Interview a children's librarian. Ask about book selection for read-alouds and methods for accommodating children's responses.

four
The Writing
We Need

At Home, At School

Big Ideas in Chapter 4

- Changing assumptions on literacy acquisition—beginnings, at home, in school
- Conditions for learning literacy and learning in general
- Moving toward a reading-writing classroom

Changing Assumptions

The perception that children follow a fixed order of skill acquisition for becoming literate becomes a self-fulfilling prophecy.

> The historic position that one has to learn to read words before one will be able to learn to write or spell them is still an assumption made by many teachers, and regrettably it turns out to be true when teachers assume it is so. (Clay, 2001a, p. 14)

It could—and should—be otherwise. Young children are constructive thinkers in their explorations with writing, just as they are with other learning. Ranges of appropriate achievement and spurts of growth are very common; both are highly influenced by physiological factors as well as the quality and quantity of the child's experiences during the early years (Caine & Caine, 1997; Jensen, 2001; Rushton, 2001).

Researchers have outlined broad stages in writing to make sense of observed behaviors, recognizing that children frequently exhibit behaviors out of expected sequences or characteristic of more than one stage.

"Development is a process not [merely] a series of stages nor a set of sequentially learned skills" (Dyson, 2003, p. 11). Durkin's stage theory, previously described, and Shulze's stages, outlined in the next chapter, provide a lens through which to view children's writing and recognize the thinking it reveals.

Simple Beginnings

As emphasized in this text, the language processes are symbiotic; they reinforce each other. Children choose to experiment with writing at a very early age; their self-initiated and sustained play with marking verifies that they all want to write when the setting is risk-free, comfortable, and supportive (Newman, 1984). This simple beginning has a powerful impact on literacy learning. "Writing can contribute to building almost every kind of inner control of literacy learning that is needed by the successful reader" (Clay, 2001a, p. 12). The young writer must

- think about the topic;
- gather his ideas;
- review the ideas;
- plan what he wants to say;
- decide how the telling will be organized;
- construct the text;
- revisit and refine the presentation; and
- determine if, how, when, and where he wants to share his message.

Parents as Teachers

Writing begins at home. Children of three to five years old are "already constructing understandings about what print looks like, how marks can be used to represent words, and how message content and writing forms are arranged for different social varieties of texts" (Rowe, 2008, p. 66). Parents play a key role in shaping the child's interest in writing and motivation to write through their soft teaching. Most of the time they're unaware of this teaching stance. That's how it should be—natural.

Adults respond to the child's request for information. They nudge learning forward when offering new information or experiences. The child may or may not be ready to absorb every detail, but repeated exposures ensure gradual assimilation. Bringing children to literacy is easier when the responsibility is shared. Parents who were considered active in fostering literacy development reported doing many of the following things (Nutbrown, 1999; Owocki, 1999). They

- drew children's attention to environmental print (e.g. signs, newspapers, magazines, mail) around them and talked about it;
- took children to museums, parks, zoos, and other special places and events;

- invited children to participate in writing for pragmatic and social purposes (e.g. lists, notes, party invitations, thank-you notes for gifts);
- involved children in using print for household tasks. For example, children observed adults use recipes for cooking and directions for assembling things;
- stimulated analysis of print on packaging as children helped with food preparation or accompanied them shopping;
- had letters (e.g. magnetic) for children to manipulate, examine, and arrange;
- provided frequent interactive read-alouds, encouraging conversation about characters, illustrations, and print. These included parent read-alouds as well as those at the library or a bookstore;
- stocked materials for drawing and writing (e.g. markers, paper, pencils, scissors, tape, glue, stickers), introducing them as tools for play. There was a place in the home designated for storage; children could easily access everything on their own and they kept it tidy (Figure 1.4). There was a consistent place for working on writing; children frequently had a child-sized desk, allowing greater independence when working;
- wrote notes to the child even before he could read—ones with a simple message like "I love you" or "You're a big helper." These shaped positive behavior while introducing the communicative purpose of print;
- played language games. Sometimes, these were commercial games; at other times they were spontaneously created ones.

Through these intricately woven activities as part of daily family life, young children begin to grasp the purpose, structures, and power of the written word—and so much more! A deep and abiding respect for parents as first teachers inspires school personnel to reach out to them—the parents of children in school as well as those whose children haven't yet begun formal education.

Newsletters from the teacher (Figure 4.1) can be vehicles for communicating classroom events and ways parents can be meaningfully involved in their child's learning. Some teachers send home copies of class books, story charts, and lists (i.e. *What we Learned*) of ideas contributed by children in discussions of a topic. This provides grist for extended conversations, writing and reading at home. One first-grade teacher regularly sends home a packet of poems introduced throughout the month. In this packet, there's also a summary of classroom activities that related to the poems. Children are very familiar with the poems since they've frequently read them chorally, discussed the content, and found letters, words, and punctuation within them. The packet encourages children to *show and tell* at home; it's also a guide for parent–child interactions that reinforce and strengthen literacy skills. During this quality time at home, the child builds self-confidence and self-esteem; parents recognize the potential of their contribution to the child's success in school. Such communications to the home acknowledge the vital role that parents play.

September 2008

Dear Parent(s)/Caregiver:

Your child learned a lot about writing before coming to school.
Your loving support with his/her efforts to write along with your praise
for each creation stimulated that learning. It also inspired your child's
self-confidence as a writer. At school, we're building on that wonderful
foundation.

Your child will have opportunities to write every day. Some of these
will be self-directed—at playtime or centers. Others will be generated in
response to teacher-given prompts—requests that don't have a single
correct answer. Early writing (from random marks to sound spelling) won't
look like adult writing, but skills in producing readable text will grow as
children learn more about sounds and the alphabetic code.

Learning about sounds and letters will help your child build
messages that are increasingly recognizable. Writing becomes one of
many gateways for understanding the reading process; constructing and
reading back one's own writing provides a safe experience with reading
while building numerous concepts about how print works.

I'm confident that the enthusiasm noticed in school for writing
activities extends outside of school. Your child will probably ask for
materials and tools for writing. A simple container with paper, washable
markers, pencils, ruler, letters, tape, glue stick, and other creative
items will keep your child happily engaged with literacy and artistic
development.

Let your child lead the way; respond to questions asked. Make
suggestions lightly to offer new possibilities in writing. However, the writer
decides whether to follow them. She/he may not be ready for that next
step right now. That's fine; with continued practice and positive feedback,
growth will come.

Please complete the *Checklist of At-Home Literacy Behaviors* and
have your child return it to school. You can add any additional information
in the **Comments** area. This will help us known more about your child's
interests and experiences.

I look forward to working with you this year, nurturing your child as
she/he blossoms in all areas of development. Feel free to contact me with
questions. You can visit or volunteer to assist in our classroom. Some
parents like to help by preparing materials for our projects at home. We
appreciate all of our helpers!

Sincerely,

Ms. _____

FIGURE 4.1
Parent Newsletter

Parents who are informed about the ways in which children
think and learn, and how they represent their thoughts in talk,
drawing and action are in a better position to support the
continuity and progression of their children's learning and
development (Nutbrown, 1999, p. 134)

The *Checklist of At-Home Literacy Behaviors* (Figure 4.2)—one that parents are asked to complete—generates valuable data for teachers; it also signifies the literacy development potential in simple activities that parents already do or can do with their child at home.

It's important to appreciate parents as partners when the child enters school. Families and schools need to participate in tandem; each plays a vital role.

Dear Parents:

Please check the items that relate to experiences your child has on a regular basis or behaviors you've observed.

Your child:

_____ sees you reading silently.

_____ sees you writing.

_____ listens to stories read aloud or told.

_____ can repeat nursery rhymes, songs, or finger plays.

_____ asks questions about the print or illustrations in books.

_____ notices and asks about print in the environment.

_____ likes to examine junk mail, magazines, or catalogs.

_____ likes to cook or bake with you as you follow a recipe.

_____ wants to help you follow directions when assembling things.

_____ likes to look for items in the store.

_____ likes to draw.

_____ comfortably uses pencils, markers, scissors, and other such tools.

_____ likes to write.

_____ likes to look at books.

_____ plays games that involve print.

Comments:

FIGURE 4.2
Checklist of At-home Literacy Behaviors

Adapted from Owocki, 1999

Classrooms That Acknowledge Changing Assumptions

Parents bring their child to school so that his continuing education can be influenced by a community of learners and guided by a professional teacher. They are not relinquishing responsibility, just establishing a long-term partnership. School partners need to accept children as they are in terms of developmental stage. It's especially important that children who've not had rich literacy experiences before coming to school receive extra infusions of them as soon as possible. These children are loved; they live in supportive family units. However, their parents may be unaware of the power they hold to plant the seeds of literacy.

Teachers sensitively make suggestions that are possible for parents to accomplish in any circumstance. They help every parent become a partner in the school's mission of building on literacy beginnings. Each child is on the journey of becoming; each has needs to be met before blossoming can occur. Successful teachers recognize that home–school partnerships make the journey smoother.

The writing samples in this text were created in child-centered classrooms where writing occurred daily for purposes that were relevant to children. When children arrive at school, they expect to maintain a degree of control (e.g. make decisions) over their learning and they "continue to seek the kinds of authentic tasks that they experienced at home" (Branscombe, Castle, Dorsey, Surbeck, & Taylor, 2003, p. 33). Writing represented in this text was an integral part of children's daily school experiences right from the start—in the earliest years. Children's literacy skills grew with increased scaffolded opportunities to write in personally meaningful ways. And, the classroom community expressed sincere interest, honoring first and foremost the intent and meaning behind the writer's work.

Writing with meaning flows when children are invested in the process. Writers must have a passion and purpose for communicating. This doesn't happen when they're directed to copy scripts. "When you teach children to write by copying they may come to believe that writing is only possible when there is a model to copy. This will block off discoveries" (Clay, 1987b, p. 50)—discoveries of personal purposes and voice.

Conditions for Becoming Literate

Recognizing the printed word introduces the concept that people, objects, and ideas can be represented in another form—one that doesn't look like what it names. Understanding the entire code for that representation takes time. Effective classrooms appreciate the general conditions outlined by Cambourne (1984) for all learning; they incorporate them in their writing program. "These conditions are many and complex but, I believe, there are seven that stand out" (p. 6). Cambourne (1999) also believed that these conditions were related to learning skills in one's home or second language. The seven conditions are the framework, the cornerstone, the theory that undergirds effective curricular design and daily lesson planning. They reflect a constructivist philosophy (Cambourne, 1999), suggesting "a concrete and viable means to enhance student development in literacy learning" (Rushton, Eitelgeorge, & Zickafoose, 2003, p. 11). When conditions are applied, learners grow as independent problem-solvers who have a repertoire of self-sustaining strategies. They become the litmus test when selecting activities. Meaningful ones fit in the framework—like the slipper on Cinderella; others do not. The theories, practices, and effective writing experiences for young children detailed throughout the chapters in this book are summed up with Cambourne's framework. They help us remember what's important—what we really need to do to support learners.

Condition 1: Immersion

Print is found in natural and strategic places in effective reading-writing classrooms. Cubbies (storage areas) are labeled with children's names; centers and play areas are identified with signs. A word wall grows as sight words are introduced and reinforced. But, the amount of print is never overwhelming. Too much becomes a distraction that will be ignored. Print is placed where it's needed and where it will be used pragmatically.

The classroom has a library of books on all kinds of topics, children's magazines, and charts depicting poetry, songs, or finger plays that are current favorites. Just like in a bookstore, the library and its contents are designed to lure in readers; it invites them to sit and browse a while.

Children's work is artistically displayed. Children like to review each other's drawing and writing, especially when pieces are attractively organized. More than praise, this peer approval verifies that their creations are valued.

Print is part of daily routines. As a student arrives, she searches for the cubby with her name; she stows items she won't need in the classroom (e.g. coat, boots, backpack). Then, she finds her name on the attendance list; she crosses it out or rewrites it. When she completes a task at a center, she'll do the same. The daily helper identifies who's absent as well as those who still need a turn at a center. Print continues to be part of routines and learning across the day.

Children have access to appropriate texts that stimulate interest in topics of study, problems to be solved, or stories to be heard. Supportive adults help them navigate this print and create their own—commensurate with their developmental stage. Such an environment with adult models is particularly important for children who lack such immersion at home.

Condition 2: Demonstration

Every day—at home, in the neighborhood, or on the way to school—children experience demonstrations of all kinds of behaviors; this includes good and bad models. Cambourne (1995) notes that models

FIGURE 4.3
Responses to
Literature
(The Big Toe)

"occur in the everyday ebb and flow" of daily life and are "always in a context that supports the meaning being transacted" (p. 185). Learning from demonstrations is something that comes naturally. In the classroom, teachers should capitalize on the instructional potential of demonstrations.

In Chapter 6, the importance of reading and writing to and with

FIGURE 4.4
Responses to
Literature (We Can
Write Letters)

children is discussed. Demonstrations present models of authentic literacy use; they show, rather than didactically tell, children what to know and how to respond. But, they "need to be meaningful and relevant to the child's life, not just an abstract concept" (Rushton et al., 2003, p. 15). When showing how writing is constructed, effective teachers verbalize their thinking and actions—even the most incidental ones—in order to make the whole process explicit.

Condition 3: Expectation

This is the most important condition; it centers on the "you can do this" messages that others communicate to the child. Emotions are closely linked to learning (Jensen, 1998). Attitude and self-confidence help learners maintain focus; positive emotions propel them over bumps in the journey (Caine & Caine, 1997). Camborne (1995) concluded, "expectations are subtle and powerful coercers of behavior" (p. 185). When a child believes he can communicate with print, motivation to persist is increased; his confidence is grounded in the fact that others assume he can and will do it. Effective teachers recognize a competent writer inside each child; they act on that belief and facilitate the unveiling of writers. "Simple words expressing genuine expectations of capability are powerful and have far reaching effects" (Shea, 1997, p. 57). Expectations must be realistic and developmentally appropriate; Rushton and Larkin (2001) propose that teachers "foster a learning context that builds trust, promotes self-direction, and encourages students to freely exchange their feelings and ideas so that the social/emotional realm is connected positively to cognitive and physical experiences" (p. 29).

Condition 4: Responsibility

If a child is to be held accountable—responsible for his learning—he must have a voice in it. This requires a degree of choice and decision-making on the part of the learner; the child should influence what, why, when, where, and how to learn about writing. Therefore, the learner will be able to accept the consequences of his decisions. A sense of empowerment—due partly to an increase in self-efficacy—accompanies the learner's acceptance of shared responsibility for learning (Bandura, 1998; Bredekamp & Copple, 1997).

Condition 5: Approximation

We don't hold off a child's speaking until he has mastered standard forms. We don't ask visitors to use simple words in front of the young child because he hasn't begun to utter long words or sentences. Children are allowed to approximate; we encourage and applaud it. We don't worry if the young child misarticulates certain words. We find it endearing; we know it will be straightened out in time, after he hears the word modeled over and over in natural situations. Children's oral language grows because we expect it to; we respect their attempts and engage them to talk. They get lots of practice.

Why then, would we ever hold back written language until the child can construct conventional text? That's illogical. Children want to write just as they want to talk. When they have abundant models and guided practice—when their written approximations are honored—children evolve as writers.

Condition 6: Employment

Children need to do more than comply with time for practice. They need to be engaged—involved with their heart and mind—for lasting learning to occur (Rushton et al., 2003). They need to think, explore, experiment, observe, talk, share, compare, discuss, reflect, conclude, and so much more. Such mental and physical investment guarantees learning (Bredekamp & Copple, 1997; Rushton et al., 2003); passivity cannot. Effective teachers create a safe, risk-free environment that's balanced with developmentally appropriate challenges. The result is increased inquisitiveness, enthusiasm, and engagement; children work productively, whether alone, with a partner, in a small group, or as a class. Silence isn't golden; nor is a useless cacophony. The classroom hums like a hive with the teacher as the lead bee.

There's considerable research that acknowledges the social aspect of meaningful learning—learning that's remembered over time because it's useful. This is discussed in Chapter 6. The need to relate to others is what makes us social beings. Both Vygotsky (1978) and Caine and Caine (1997) concluded that positive human relationships and interactions enhance learning.

Condition 7: Feedback

Feedback follows the performance. The teacher or audience of peers responds to the writer with compliments (praise) and comments (suggestions); these direct the writer to view his work through the lens of a reader. Response helps the young writer move away from an egocentric stance; he begins to appreciate how his message is received. Effective feedback is sensitively delivered, but it is specific. Generic compliments lose their veracity when the writer knows that the work contains areas that need improvement. Writers want feedback that identifies what's working and what's not. Cambourne (1995) emphasized that feedback should be "relevant, appropriate, timely, readily available, with no strings attached" (p. 33). Comments also direct further composing.

Responders can *feedforward* (Cole, 2004) when they capture a teachable moment. Well-delivered, timely comments nudge the writer to try something he hasn't yet attempted, but appears ready to try. Children find the courage to step into that unknown when they believe they have wings to flutter or someone to help them. Writing classrooms foster belief in self and the kindness of others in the community.

Toward a Writing Classroom

The classrooms described in this text bring Cambourne's conditions to life (1999) with curriculum designed to meet children's developmental needs. The writing samples presented—ones created at home and at school—reflect children's steady, supported growth. Many are in the book and numerous others are available at the companion website. These

Learning Need	Curricular Accommodation
Write through play	Centers and activities that stimulate self-initiated and self-driven writing
Opportunity to muck around with writing	Risk-free environment well-stocked with inviting writing materials that are easy to find and use
Authentic purposes to write	Self-initiated purposes as well as open-ended prompts for writing that relate to children's interests or units of study
Support from other writers	Adults and peers are available to respond to requests for help or information
Audience for writing	Adults and peers respectfully listen to writers sharing their work
Applause for writing	Adults and peers extend specific compliments to authors, noting the high points of the piece
Feedback on writing	Adults and peers sensitively express constructive comments to stretch the writer's thinking and skill

FIGURE 4.5
Curriculum Designed to Meet Developmental Writing Needs

Adapted from Rowe (2008)

writers got the right amount of the right stuff at the right time; their progress reflects that. Along the way, they grew in other language skills.

In an ideal writing classroom, children think about message first, but about sounds and letters too. When writers encode at the word level, they "focus on the constituent sounds of letters in words and how those letters map onto words" (Feldgus & Cardonick, 1999, p. 103); they're practicing phonemic awareness and phonics to get their ideas into print. Writers read back their message as they work and after they finish; they apply skills related to context, letters, and sounds to decode it.

In a writing classroom, children also talk about their work; they listen and respond to text written by others. Along with writing and reading, they're speaking, and listening. These expressive and receptive language processes are used as they are in the wider world outside of the classroom—interactively. That's when growth in one fosters growth in the others.

The next part of this text applies theory to practice, with descriptions of reading-writing pre-K, kindergarten, and grade 1 classrooms. Chapter 5 begins by looking at what's needed to get reading and writing started—at home and at school. It describes Schulze's stages of writing development; these provide benchmarks for determining where children are along a continuum of writing development. Chapter 5 also describes children's repertoire of meaning-making tools for expressing ideas, knowing, and wondering as they go about the business of building knowledge of their world, other people, and relationships.

Enriching environments for young children encourage expression and communication through multiple sign systems (i.e. drawing, writing, talking); children in such places have the materials, resources, physical setting, and support that encourage inquiry and creative language exploration. In these settings, parents and teachers mindfully mediate learning as they nurture and nudge in developmentally appropriate ways.

Extending the Discussion

- Discuss how Cambourne's conditions can be identified in a classroom.
- Suggest ways to enhance classroom activities to more prominently reflect Cambourne's conditions.
- Interview teachers about the home connections they've established. How do they elicit information on the child's literacy skills, interests, and experiences? How do they build home–school partnerships? How do they provide parents with guides for effective targeted reinforcement that's congruent with current classroom objectives?
- Interview parents of children in pre-K, kindergarten, and grade 1 classrooms. How does their child's teacher support a home–school partnership? Does the teacher keep them updated on classroom topics, learning goals, and lesson objectives? Does the teacher provide guidance for reinforcement of learning at home that's congruent with what's going on in the classroom?

part two
Mindfully Mediating Language Learning

five
Getting Writing Started

Tools for Drawing and Writing

Put a marking tool in a toddler's hand and it seems they know instinctively what to do with it—after first checking it out with their nose or mouth, that is! They've noticed significant people in their environment using these objects to change the landscape on a solid surface—typically, on paper. So, their logical response is to replicate that model. However, the nearest painted wall is not the solid surface we'd like them to transform. The pure delight registered on children's faces upon seeing the magical effect of any marking tool under their control is surely something to behold. What isn't as natural is a realization of the purpose for marking blank surfaces.

Making the Connection: Marking as Writing

Children's first marking appears to surprise them, as if it's a magical apparition. Their facial expression can be read as, "I did that?" The child repeats the behavior to test whether he'll get the same result or simply

FIGURE 5.1
Young Child Writes

kinesthetic
involving a physical
activity—doing something
tactile

to produce something that's aesthetically pleasing and kinesthetically enjoyable. Curiosity and pleasure seem to direct his action at this point.

The adult's response to the child's marking awakens him to the possibility of communicative intent. His marks carry meaning—ideas or a message. By addressing the marking as writing, adults attribute authorship to the child when they say, "Oh, you wrote something here. Will you read it to me?" For children who've been read to, the "ah-ha" from that request erupts with quiet majesty. Marking is how print messages are constructed.

Marking Can Mean

The connection that print marks are intended to stand for something readable—like a book—is a quantum leap into literacy; however, the seed of understanding must be planted, nurtured and given time to be linked to budding schema. Often, the child is astonished that we attribute meaning to this random display. We attribute intention and honor the creation when we ask about it—always using the language of communication.

The child wonders, "What *did* I write? (Or, what did I draw?) What *does* it say?" For, he hadn't realized he could *say* with marks (Clay, 1987a). We might gently scaffold an answer by suggesting a meaning. The writer either agrees or begins to attach his own meaning to these randomly created marks. And, that meaning might be totally different in the child's next reading. But, that's OK. Children's writing doesn't always begin with intention; the marks aren't always constant in the message they represent. Sometimes, the marking is done for an aesthetic quality and meaning is attached as the product unfolds or upon its completion. Examples are provided in the next section of this chapter.

When children say they can't read it, teachers ask, "What were you thinking about while writing? Maybe, it says that."

Asking children to read what they've authored reinforces the function and power of print to document what we want to say and communicate what we want to tell. At times, children use images to record their thinking or feelings; sometimes, they draw to say and tell.

Drawing to Communicate

Vygotsky (1978) argued that the child's drawing indicates the emergence of written expression. Research by Wells (1986) reaffirmed that belief; he concluded that drawing "is an important step on the way to writing" (p. 151). In drawing, the child attempts to directly represent an object— as it appears. Later, the child "discovers that the speech in which those objects are referred to can also be represented" (p. 151).

Drawing is different from writing, but intimately connected to it (Wells, 1986); both are *expressive language processes*. "Drawing is often the place where children's stories begin" (Kempton, 2007, p. 79). While they like to scribble intended messages because it looks like grown-up marking (cursive writing), children are also caught up with representing ideas ideographically—with drawing.

expressive language processes
language used for the output of ideas (i.e. speaking, writing)

receptive language processes
language used for the intake of ideas (i.e. listening, reading)

Drawing a Story

Children often communicate personal narratives and imaginary stories— those created from the fabric of their lives—through drawing. When asked about their production, the child's style may be one of *reportage* (Applebee, 1980) that elaborates with details unrepresented in the visual forms. The following excerpts demonstrate such exchanges.

reportage
techniques characteristic of news reporting

Example 1

   T: Oh, this looks interesting. Please, tell me about your drawing.
   C: It's a spider and the web. I was drawing a spider web because they're down in my basement. Yesterday, there was a big spider on my garage and it was scaring me. They scare me up.

Example 2

   T: You've used lovely shades of color. Please tell me about your drawing.
   C: It's a big ocean and waves.
   T: What about this part, right here.
   C: This is a fish—a big fish. A man caught this fish and it was big. It was Matt. It was big. Dad caught a big fish without Matt going with him. This big! (The child stretches out his arms to demonstrate.)

It isn't that one precedes the other; drawing and marking occur simultaneously. Young children often represent thoughts with images or ideographs because these more physically resemble the object(s) associated with the message. When a visual triggers pleasant memories, it might be notably repeated. Drawings of family, flowers, hearts, my house, my dog, my friend, my toy, my birthday cake, or holiday symbols are just a few of the constants. But not all drawings begin with communicative intention.

Constructing a Story From a Drawing

Sometimes, children are simply inspired to create a personally satisfying work of art with color and design. Or, they may be fascinated with experimenting in a particular medium (i.e. markers, paint). The following is an example that demonstrates this behavior.

When invited to draw, a preschooler traced his hands, one at a time. He started coloring in the fingers on one hand with a variety of bright colors. When asked to talk about his drawing, the child responded, "It's just my hand, but wait a minute until I do some more." Then, he proceeded to color in the palm and fingers on the other hand with a black crayon. The teacher asked why that hand was black. Without looking up, the child moved into storytelling about a good village, represented by the colorful hand, and a bad village represented by the hand that was black. "The people in the good village are nice and the people in the bad village are mean," he explained.

Drawing doesn't always have a story. Sometimes, children draw for aesthetic purposes just as adults do. The story and message are interpreted by the observer, as one does when visiting an art gallery. Sometimes there's a mix of ideas represented in the drawing—a stream of consciousness in image form. There may also be an infusion of marks amidst the images.

Mixing Drawing and Writing

Young children are typically ambivalent about the forms they use for messaging. They even call their drawing "writing." When creating the image displayed in Figure 5.2, the author vacillated between drawing and writing, but consistently identified her efforts as writing. Perhaps this was due to its story nature. She explained, "I'm writing a house. I'm writing people in the windows and a door right here. It says P, A, D, V, W, E. I am sad because grandma is going back to her home. Sandy [dog] made a mistake on the floor and Mom is cleaning it." This child is authoring a story in a mixed (visual and print) mode.

Drawing a Plan for Writing

Researchers have found that drawing helps both emergent and more fluent writers visualize what they want to tell; it helps them organize the big ideas and details in their message. It can be used at any point in the

Example 6

**FIGURE 5.2
People in the House
Window**

writing process; it's especially helpful in the planning stage. The writing that follows drawing has more words, sentences, and thoughts; it's richer and clearer (Norris, Mokhtari, & Reichard, 1998; Sidelnick & Svoboda, 2000). That's why tools for drawing should be included in the classroom along with tools for writing. Both are language processes that should be included in writers' workshop. As sign systems, each is used in its own way to communicate ideas, thoughts, and feelings.

Visuals as Language

In 1996, representatives of the International Reading Association (IRA) and the National Council of Teachers of English (NCTE), meeting to write the new standards for the English Language Arts (ELA), added *viewing* and *visually representing* to the traditional four language processes (listening, speaking, reading, and writing) and suggested that these new additions should be equally emphasized in children's literacy development.

Visually Representing and Viewing

viewing
a receptive language process involving the intake of information from any kind of visual (picture, graph, chart, symbol)

visually representing
an expressive language process involving the output of ideas using any kind of visual

Visually representing (e.g. drawing, sketching, making charts or diagrams) is an expressive process, while viewing (getting information from any kind of visual) is a receptive one. Development across all of these processes is important; growth in one supports growth in another. Irresistible materials that stimulate engagement across the full range of language use should be standard commodities in children's spaces.

Centers and Tools

Adults like to have a designated space in their environment (at work or at home) for writing—typically on the computer. We adorn that space with supplies that make writing easier; we decorate it to make working there a pleasant experience. Children appreciate the same ambiance and efficiency where they work, whether it's at home or at school.

Place for Writing at Home

Children's writing space doesn't need to be elaborate, but it must invite them in to work. Comfortable, well-equipped areas lead to extended time spent in writing activities. Start them early; provide simple props that say, "Write now; right here!" The portable *writing toolbox* (see Chapter 1, Figure 1.4) with its cache of supplies is an inexpensive way to have supplies ready. It can be created using a child's backpack or piece of wheeled luggage. Supplies can be purchased inexpensively at discount stores. As a pull-along or backpack, this toolbox can travel in the car, go to the coffee shop, or it can go outside for working in the playground or home deck. In a classroom, the toolbox can be used at a station or at a child's desk. Children could also take the toolbox home for an evening to finish a project. Some children don't have a wealth of writing supplies at home. The toolbox teaches organizational skills, since children are responsible for returning supplies to their proper place. Wheeled carts with several drawers are also handy in the classroom or home, but they don't travel as easily.

Place for Writing at School

In the classroom or at home, stationary writing areas (e.g. writing center, desk) say to the child, "Writing is what you do here." Figure 3.3 in Chapter 3 shows a writing center in use in a preschool classroom. Children work alone or together using the range of supplies offered at the center. They draw, write, stamp, and type to construct messages. Then, they mail, post, or deliver them to selected recipients.

Working together has rewards. Peers provide models and support; this creates a sense of community among authors, honoring each child's message making. Well-stocked, attractive classroom writing centers draw in participants who assist each other; sometimes, they even coauthor pieces.

Collaboration can also occur as children work side-by-side at tables. Figure 5.3 shows a child in a private, urban pre-K setting where drawing and writing is the first activity of the day. As they enter, they meet and greet the teacher and friends; then, they get their journals and begin constructing a message. They comfortably show their work to table-mates, ask friends for help, and respond to fellow authors. When their entry is completed, they "read" it to the teacher and classmates.

Rather than a designated place, the classroom can become the writing center at a predictable time in the schedule. Children working at tables find support and encouragement from surrounding peers. Writers have an instant audience; they also have models that nudge them to take new risks in their own writing. The preschool teacher at the urban northeast site reports that children love to work in their journals; sometimes, it's hard to move on to another activity. It's exciting to see how engrossed they are and how proud they are of their work. As they work, she circulates to assist and respond to writers.

FIGURE 5.3
Writing in Journal

Nurture Naturally

Effective teachers notice what young writers (or drawers) are doing well, what they're trying to do, but are confusing, and what they're not doing, but may be ready to learn. Teachers talk to children briefly about each point when conversing about the writing. Such discourse is an essential component in assessment of writing. Children learn to articulate their thinking and knowing as part of self-assessment. Such collaborative analysis is critical for targeted, differentiated instruction that begins "at the point of revealed need" (Walshe, 1982, p. 10).

Writers Lead

Let the child lead the discussion, focusing on her production as something that holds meaning. Encourage further additions; offer suggestions, but ensure her that she's in charge of where the writing goes. Answer questions with information the writer wants or needs at that moment—nothing more, nothing less. Be prepared to help her take a step forward when she's ready.

> T: How's your writing going? What are you working on here?
> C: I'm writing the first part, but I don't know what to write now.
> T: I noticed your drawing; it makes me curious about this story. Please read what you have to me.
> C: I went to a sleepover. It was fun.
> T: I'm wondering why it was fun? What did you do?
> C: We had popcorn and watched Tinkerbell. We laughed when her dog jumped for pieces of popcorn.
> T: That explains why it was fun. Who's this? (The teacher points to characters in drawing.)
> C: Emily and her dog, Riley. I was at her house.
> T: You could tell that. What do you want to write now?
> C: I'll tell what Emily and I did at the sleepover.
> T: That sounds like a good plan. Try that now.

It's often the gentle push that propels us to higher levels of performance when we were unaware of how to proceed or afraid to venture out of our safe zone.

Nudging Forward

Suggestions can be powerful. They imply your view of the writer's capability, while allowing him to remain in control. Remember, a child's decision not to use the advice is a valid choice. Interactive (collaborative) writing, gently peppered with modeled alternatives or examples of different writing formats, nudges collaborators forward (Johnston, 2004). There are infinite opportunities in any classroom for modeling authentic writing—writing with genuine communicative intent. Teachers write announcements, daily news, children's observations or responses as expressed in discussion, language experiences stories about something the class has done together, or directions for a task—all in front of children. As they write, teachers "give a running monologue of the thinking that goes with the writing" (Graves, 1983, p. 45).

The teacher writes slowly; the words recorded follow the statement, as it's identified collaboratively and, then, verbalized by the teacher to determine consensus. She pauses when stuck on a word or doesn't know what to write next.

> T: We have "Max felt lonely." What should we write next? What did he do?
> C: He went home after the wild rumpus.
> T: Yes; he did. Do you think he missed his family?
> C: Yes.
> T: He went home after the wild rumpus. (Teacher writes "He.") Mmmm. I'm stuck on this word—"went." He went home after the wild rumpus. I need to think about the sounds. /w/ /en/ /t/; w-en-t.

Such collaborative adventures with writing (such as class books, class lists, language experience charts or daily news) build the confidence and know-how for personal replication. This process—Language Experience Approach (LEA)—is described in Chapter 6; it begins by scribing young children's dictated stories and compiling pages into a book.

Bookmaking

Pop-up books are useful incentives to get young children into bookmaking. Parents and teachers discuss content with the child; they orally suggest an organization for ideas. When the writing is complete, pop-up pages are reread as the authors illustrate them. This engaging, creative learning activity holds children's attention for a long time and integrates abundant concept learning.

Children learn that one's telling can be recorded for repeated readings. They learn that the print on a page holds the message; illustrations represent and extend those words. This realization usually provides motivation for further pop-up productions. Having their stories in print is a powerful incentive for asking about words. Children frequently ask, "Where does it say?" Then, there's a quiet moment for examining the visual representation for a word or phrase. Soon children are ready to assume the role of writer—one step at a time.

Developmental Stages for Message Construction

Once children attach meaning to print, they become curious about how others make marks. They might ask, "How do you make mommy?" meaning "How do you spell mommy?" Durkin (1966) refers to this as *ask an expert* stage (Stage 4) explained in Chapter 2. Other researchers have offered similar descriptions for developmental stages of writing in early childhood (Dyson, 1985; Sulzby, 1985; Teale, 1986). There's consensus that these stages are not rigid.

Stages as a Framework

Schulze (2006) also outlined stages noted in young children's writing development. Movement across these is fluid and recursive; children's productions often reflect characteristics of more than one stage. The stages are useful as a framework for examining writers' knowledge related to the functions and forms of written text and what an appropriate next step for instruction might be. That instruction, accomplished in a mini lesson, might focus on what to tell in the writing, how to order the telling, how to order sounds heard and match them to letters when spelling words, how to locate a word needed in print around the room, or any other specific skills. Schulze's stages build on Durkin's historical ones by adding details; these elaborate and make each stage more distinct. Stages offer a guide for providing writers with targeted instruction at the teachable moment.

Teachers in a school or district collaboratively determine which stage model complements programs and approaches they're using. This provides consistency in conversations about children's progress across classrooms and grades.

Schulze's Stages

Schulze's (2006) and Durkin's (1966) stages are used to describe examples of children's writing across the pre-K and kindergarten classrooms visited for this text. Durkin's stages have been described in Chapter 2. Schulze's (2006) stages are described here (see also Figure 5.4).

Stage 1—Picture Drawing

Drawings take the form of the object they represent—a drawing of a dog is meant to look like a dog—at least in the eyes of the artist. The creation is an ideograph or a graphic image of the idea or concept; thus, drawing is an ideographic communication. Unlike drawing, scribbling (intended

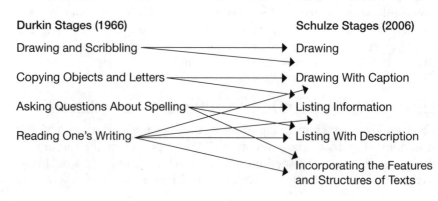

FIGURE 5.4
Overlap of Children's
Stages of Writing
Development

Durkin Stages (1966)

Drawing and Scribbling

Copying Objects and Letters

Asking Questions About Spelling

Reading One's Writing

Schulze Stages (2006)

Drawing

Drawing With Caption

Listing Information

Listing With Description

Incorporating the Features
and Structures of Texts

as writing) attempts to replicate writing; it's not intended to take the form of the object or idea represented. Like the word, the scribble for dog doesn't look like a dog. Scribbling as writing is *logographic*; the writer uses graphic symbols to construct the logos that stand for objects, words, or ideas. Thus, writing is a logographic communication (Harris & Hodges, 1981; Webster, 1996). There's freedom of form in both modes of expression, making either creation a risk-free endeavor.

logographic
graphic symbols are used as logos (symbols) to represent objects, words or ideas

However, ideographic communication is much easier for young children since the obvious visual clues support *reading* the message. Children draw what they want to tell. They can elaborate extensively on the creation with sensitive prompting and petitions such as, "Oh, I love your choice of color and design. And, you even used both crayons and markers. Please tell me about this picture." Ask, "What else can you add?" to stimulate further meaning making.

If you notice something in the child's work that will be a *teachable moment* (perfect time for learning) for others in the class, point it out publicly with the creator's permission. "Billy, can we do a *quick share* (Fisher, 1991) right now with everyone? I'd like the class to see how you … ." Or, after children share their work with a partner, a few selections could be shared with the whole class to point out unique features that others might want to try next time. This pays off with a boost to self-esteem for the artist and helpful hints for other children. The next stage elaborates on drawing.

Stage 2—Drawing With Caption

Children begin to add labels to their drawings. The labels are formed with mock letters and words, random letters and words, print in the room, or with known words. This process occurs in any language, as Figure 5.5 from a bilingual kindergarten in an urban school reflects.

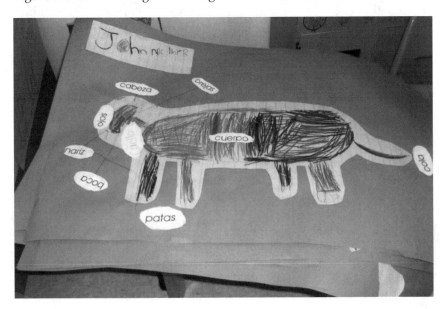

FIGURE 5.5
Animal With Labels

Children typically use the labels as cues to direct their telling; they point to them as guides for others who might "read" their drawing. Through their pictures and labels children reveal their favorite things and activities, the members of their family (immediate and extended), or memorable experiences. The emphasis is on communication, but adding a label also starts children thinking about word construction. Simple word labels interject *voice* (Graves, 1994) in the meaning that's been constructed. The words selected are powerful ones for the writer; typically they identify the heart of the message. It's important to nurture voice (word choice and expressive language patterns) in its budding stage as previously discussed in Chapter 3.

To reward the use of voice and encourage further development, let the child know you've noticed and attended to what he's written. Teachers, as mentors to novice writers, have the power to influence. "The way a teacher talks can position students differently in relation to what they are doing, learning, or studying [or writing]" (Johnston, 2004, p. 9). The goal is to be sensitively and constructively supportive. You might say, "___ I noticed you've written names by these people and by the dog and cat too. Can you tell me more about the dog?" When the child responds with dog anecdotes that reflect his passion—his voice—you could reply, "I love dogs too. Can you write what you told me? Readers would want to hear about ... ." (Then, repeat something he told you that adds voice to the writing.) The development of voice propels writers to the next stage. Simple labels become insufficient for bearing the weight of extending voice. Children need to expand labels to phrases and sentences where the sequencing of words becomes important for message constructing.

Stage 3—Listing Information

This stage is identifiable by children's free flow in writing—ideas are connected, loosely connected, or a potpourri of thoughts about things they like, people in their lives, things they want or want to do, what they know, or experiences they've had. It often takes the form of listing (see Figure 5.6). The lists serve as categorical inventories. Newkirk (1989) considers young children's list writing as a first foray into expository writing. Phrases or sentences are very simple and are directly associated with the picture drawn. Talking about the drawing and text helps the writer realize how he can elaborate—what more he has to say. As writers go beyond the simple sentence to expand ideas in writing, they move to the next stage.

expository writing
informational writing

Stage 4—Listing With Description

This stage is a small step beyond stage 3. The added descriptions expand on the simple sentences offered as captions for drawings. Typically, what's added is related to the picture, but not always represented in the drawing. It might tell something more or reveal the author's feelings about the object, person, or situation depicted (see Figure 5.7).

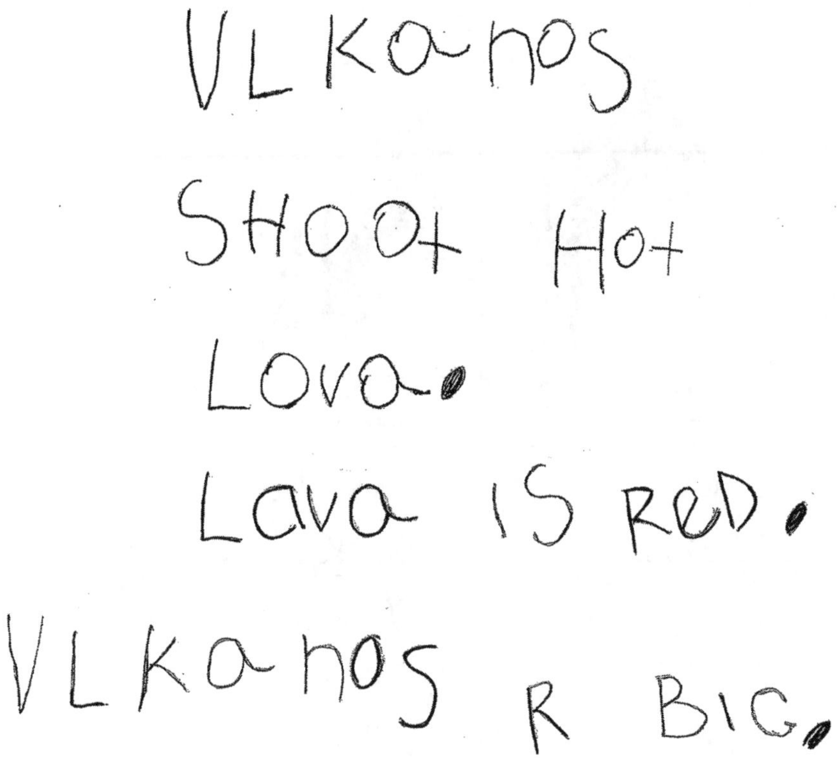

VL Kanos

SHOOt Hot

Lova

Lava IS ReD.

VLKanos R BiG.

FIGURE 5.6
Volcano Facts

Stage 5—Incorporating the Features and Structures of Texts

Just like anyone else, children write best when the focus is something they know and care about. Voice comes naturally with such topics, whether the content is developed as a personal narrative or an exposition of the writer's knowledge.

Obviously, stage 5 goes on indefinitely, as writers refine what they say and how they say it. Children's writing shows they're capable of producing many types of texts (Graves, 1994; Temple et al., 1993). The array of literature and models shared in the classroom inspires young writers to stretch their wings and try something new. Figure 5.8 shows an example of early stage 5 writing. Sensitive adults recognize these fledgling attempts and expand writers' knowledge of new structures.

expository writing
informational writing

exposition
discourse for the purpose of sharing information

Stage-by-Stage Demonstrations

Model, model, model—and continue to model! Modeling how to begin and expand on kernel sentences, step by step, is the best way to get children started and moving from stage 1 to stage 5. Teachers can do a write-aloud for each stage, as children appear ready to take the next step. Figures 5.9–5.13 illustrate this activity for stages 1 through 5 as a narrative is developed about my dog, Storm.

On a large sheet of chart paper I make a drawing (stage 1). Then, I label my drawing (stage 2). I give children time (some weeks) to practice.

Dingo

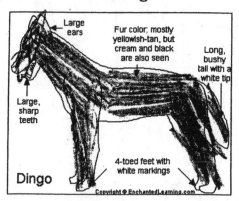

A Dingo c a wild dog
Aboriginals used them for
hunting. They were as living
blankele They are noctarnol
They are meat eaters They
eat kangarnoo and rats
lisards

FIGURE 5.7
Dingo Report

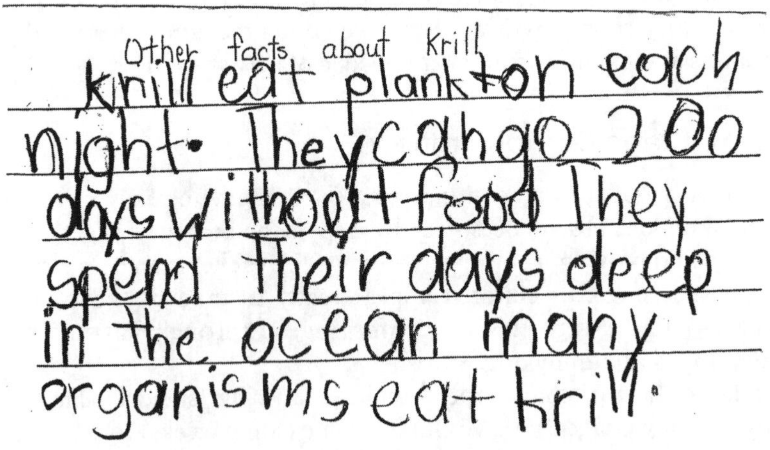

Other facts about Krill
krill eat plankton each
night. They can go 200
days withoelt food They
spend their days deep
in the ocean many
organisms eat krill.

FIGURE 5.8
Report on Krill

Storm

FIGURE 5.9
Drawing—Stage 1

FIGURE 5.10
Drawing With Label—
Stage 2

Storm is my dog.

Storm is my dog.
We go for walks.
He's friendly.

FIGURE 5.11
Drawing with
Sentence Listing
Information—Stage 3

FIGURE 5.12
Drawing with Short
Sentences As
Description—Stage 4

FIGURE 5.13
Drawing with
Narrative—Stage 5

Storm is usually a good dog. Sometimes he chews up papers and makes a mess. He likes me to call him Good Dog when he behaves. Storm knows I always love him.

When they're ready to move beyond labels (stage 3), I demonstrate writing a sentence caption for my drawing. I invite children to ask wonder questions based on the caption, "Is there something else you'd like me to tell with my words?" Then, I expand my writing (stage 4) in response to their questions. I explain that sometimes I have to think to myself, "What else would someone want me to tell about this picture? That helps me decide what words I could add (stage 5). You can do that too."

"Demonstrating, listening, praising, and questioning can help children ... progress through these stages of written language development ... encourage each child to write about personal experiences ... so his or her voice emerges" (Schulze, 2006, p. 79). The final stage demonstrates budding awareness of specific traits and structures of good writing. Of course, this awakening doesn't occur in a vacuum. Children learn to recognize these aspects of writing when we mindfully introduce a variety of genres and draw their attention to them during shared reading, shared writing, and read-alouds (Calkins, 1994; Graves, 1994). They take the next step in their writing, attending to quality and structures—just like the models they've enjoyed.

Writing in Pre-K, Kindergarten, and Grade 1 Classrooms

The next three chapters (Chapters 6, 7, and 8) examine writing in particular pre-K, kindergarten, and grade 1 classrooms in different SES and demographic areas in the United States—environments that support and extend children's development as writers. The teachers in these specific schools incorporate the right amount of previously described ingredients, allowing children to weave a strong tapestry of literacy competence. The sites selected were highly recommended as ones exemplary of the emergent literacy perspective described in this book. The teachers who participated are well-respected by colleagues and their immediate supervisor or principal as competent professionals. Quality teaching and joyful learning aligned with theory characterize classroom interactions in each.

It's important to note that the visits to these classrooms occurred over two academic years. A relationship was established with the sites, teachers, and children in each classroom. The process was ethnographic in nature; I was a "participant observer" (Denzin & Lincoln, 1994, p. 1). Classroom descriptions are intended as "detailed [enough] so that if a reader of the case were suddenly to be transported to the site, he or she would experience a feeling of déjà vu" (Lincoln & Guba, 1985, p. 365). Data were analyzed for patterns and themes related to the theories outlined in previous chapters; information was condensed, clustered, and sorted (Huberman & Miles, 1994) before reporting. Participants were ensured that the text would tell the stories of their learning communities, but not attempt to compare or evaluate instruction, activities, or achievement within or across sites (Lincoln & Guba, 1985). It's expected that readers will draw further inferences from data.

Chapters 6, 7, and 8 also include selected vignettes from other reading-writing classrooms; these offer additional insights on the nexus of theory and practice. In addition, each chapter describes instructional practice that supports successful literacy learning. Along with an examination of writing in pre-K, Chapter 6 outlines *non-negotiable* ingredients (those which cannot be eliminated or substituted) for literacy acquisition. These include reading and writing to, with, and by children.

ethnography
a research strategy often used in the social sciences for gathering data on societies or cultures. This type of research may also be called a field study or case report

participant observer
researcher who enters a setting to gather data and interact casually and non-directively with subjects while observing

---

Extending the Discussion

- Interview a child about his drawing. Discuss the drawing and intentionality behind it with colleagues. What does it reveal about this child's ability to communicate ideographically?
- Interview a young child about his writing that takes the form of marking (i.e. scribbles, forms, letter-like forms, random letters). Discuss the writing and intentionality behind it with colleagues. What does it reveal about this child's ability to communicate logographically?
- Interview a teacher in a pre-K or kindergarten classroom. Ask her how she invites children to write. How does she encourage anyone who might be reluctant to try?
- Think about how you would set up a writing center in an early childhood classroom. Share your ideas. What would it look like? Where would you place it? What supplies would be available? How would you schedule its use? How would you assess the work completed there?

six
Writing in Pre-K

Big Ideas in Chapter 6

- Developmentally appropriate practice
- Sulzby's stages for word construction
- Scaffolding for literacy learning
- Writing in pre-K classrooms at each site
- Analysis of writing samples from the sites
- Common patterns in pre-K classrooms that foster literacy
- Approaches for engaging children in reading and writing
- Assessment of children's writing
- Classrooms of diversity

Playful With Intention

Graves (1981) noted that young children's writing "resembles spontaneous play" (p. 7). Play writing demonstrates children's confidence in an ability to communicate in print long before they use writing conventions. As demonstrated with writing samples, intentional writing—writing with a focus on function or purpose—comes well before attention to form or conventions (Rowe, 2008; Wohlwend, 2008). In fact, Calkins (1994) reports "ninety percent of children come to school believing they can write" (p. 62).

However, some children's early attempts at message creation are unrecognized; the efforts are regarded as random scribble (Beaty, 2009) and "dismissed as insignificant and inconsequential" (Vukelich et al., 2002, p. 73). Too often, the suggestion that children in pre-K should engage in reading and writing is met with resistance. It's considered an attempt to push down curriculum that belongs kindergarten or grade 1.

But, that's not what's intended. Developmentally appropriate literacy practice is what's advocated.

> Developmental learning is highly individual and non-competitive; it is short on teaching and long on learning; it is self regulated rather than adult regulated; it goes hand-in-hand with the fulfillment of real life purposes; it emulates the behavior of people who model the skill in natural use (Holdaway, 1979, p. 14).

Environments that support exploration into writing, stimulate engagement with books and print, and provide young children with time, voice, and choice *are* developmentally appropriate. Children grow socially, emotionally, *and* cognitively.

Developmentally Appropriate Practice (DAP) Includes Literacy

Writing and reading to, with, and by children constitutes *developmentally appropriate practice* (DAP) because it's what they naturally want to do, and do on their own. This differs from highly didactic, scripted programs for young children. The latter are typically *developmentally inappropriate* in content, pacing, and mode of instruction; they create significant inequities. Research shows that children's cognitive, social, and emotional development are positively affected by DAP, such as the literacy activities described, regardless of their culture, race, or demographics. On the other hand, there are significant inequities in the programs delivered to or withheld from children (Kostelnik, Soderman, & Whiren, 2007).

Sometimes, instruction in letter names and sounds is detached from using skills for authentic purposes; the focus is on phonemic awareness, phonetic knowledge, and word learning as isolated skills. These bits and pieces of information are abstract for the young child. Learning and remembering them is harder when the child doesn't fully appreciate their function. At other times, instruction in alphabet knowledge and word learning is held off altogether because it's deemed to be developmentally inappropriate content for pre-K curriculum. When that happens, children's natural curiosity can be eroded.

A recent review of a long-awaited report from the What Works Clearinghouse concluded that few of the popular commercial programs—including comprehensive and supplemental ones—showed evidence of positively impacting student achievement. Most programs had little rigorous research to support claims; many of the studies failed (Manzo, 2007). Highly scripted programs fail to accommodate areas of differences, including learners' culture, interests, readiness, or ability. Such programs typically outline a one-size-fits-all curriculum, sequence of instruction, format for assessment, and timeline for mastery, as if children could all be treated the same. To treat young children "as if they

scripted programs
publishers' programs for
instruction that provide a
script for teacher, direct
instruction sequence, and
acceptable responses from
children

differentiated instruction
teaching that
accommodates individual
needs, interests, or
strengths of children

were objects on a conveyer belt to the future goes against the American grain" (Ohanian, 1999, p. 19). Prepared lessons and materials make programs appear efficient, but they usually fall short in providing ideas for *differentiating* (Tomlinson, 2001) instruction.

At home and at school, children are quite busy with literacy experimenting—emulating models they've observed. They initiate the writing. Evidence of children's messaging can be found on a variety of surfaces (including paper, books, junk mail, old forms, chalkboard, refrigerator, pavement, or sand). And children use all kinds of writing tools (such as chalk, pencils, pens, markers, sticks, stones, magnetic letters, or paintbrushes).

Soderman and Farrell (2008) state, "As soon as children discover that what we think can be saved by writing it down for others to see, development follows swiftly if frequent opportunity and modeling are provided" (p. 70). These children have made a connection with print in their world and texts read to them. They know that the marks (print) carry the message (Beaty, 2009). They begin to ask, "Where does it say … ?" They have listened to the sound of language in books as well as the content of stories. They know the message for each page and won't let an adult reader miss any part or word on it. I know; little listeners have corrected my miscues! Children also repeat captivating words and phrases they've heard over and over in favorite stories.

It may be the meaning that makes particular words appealing; sometimes, it's simply their sound or the way they roll off the tongue. Children's growing meaning vocabulary reflects input from favorite authors as well as adults who have discussed texts (and other things) with them. Based on such observations, pre-K teachers plan for literacy activities that are

FIGURE 6.1
Manipulating
Magnetic Letters

collaborative (children participate in planning), *social* (children work with others), and *playful* (children engage in enjoyable, risk-free, interesting tasks), as well as *cognitively enriching* (children learn). Literacy explorations *are* developmentally appropriate practices (DAP) when provided in developmentally appropriate ways. In other words, activities across the spectrum of language processes (listening, speaking, writing, reading, viewing, and visually representing) are appropriate in early childhood classrooms when designed with child-centered guidance, materials, and expectations. Young children are taking the first steps on a journey toward becoming literate; they're approximating literate behaviors that take time to refine. Effort needs to be accepted, respected, and encouraged with each performance.

cognitively enriching
stimulates thinking activity and learning

child-centered
focused on, attentive to the identified needs, interests, and strengths of children

Effective pre-K classrooms are places that invite *playing to learn*; they're well-supplied with materials that attract attention and stimulate inquiry (Owocki, 1999; Whitmore et al., 2005). They foster experimentation, including risk-free play with drawing and writing; they expect and respect the range of children's literacy levels; they welcome children into the literacy club (Smith, 1983). When teachers arrange such an environment, gently nudge, and offer lots of support, children learn.

Begin With Free Writing

Children come to school with different amounts and types of literacy experiences; they know different parts of a complex whole. It's as if they have pieces of a jigsaw puzzle—some have more pieces than others—and aren't sure how they fit together or what's missing (Clay, 2001a). This makes early literacy instruction particularly challenging. Assessment of what's known by whom needs to be carefully conducted before moving forward. Effective teachers are continuously observing and taking notes on performances as children engage in daily classroom activities. Careful examination of children's writing against checklists of stages helps teachers determine where children are in their achievement, the best next step, and appropriate instruction for continued progress. Analysis of writing samples collected in pre-K classrooms at two sites is provided in this chapter.

Sulzby's Stages of Word Construction

Sulzby (1985; 1990) outlined seven broad stages for young children's writing that include attention to message and word constructions (these are not intended to reflect a rigid hierarchical order).

- Stages 1 and 2, drawing and scribbling, align with the Durkin (1966) and Schulze (2006) stages previously described.
- Stage 3, letter-like units, is distinguished by separate marks that approach the shape of letters with vertical, horizontal, and circular motions. Gradually, the young writer begins noticing how "experts" use various combinations of letters to create print.

- Stage 4 is characterized by children's use of random strings of letters to represent a message. Usually these are letters they know or those most important to them—like letters in names. Their forays into writing lead children to begin noticing print all around them. They examine the construction of print in the environment.
- Stage 5 involves children's use of environmental (including classroom) print; they typically replicate it in their writing. Sometimes children ask for conventional spellings—"How do you make?" Their efforts stimulate interest in the details; children are exploring with letters and the sounds they represent. They're also forming their own phonetic hypotheses and using sound spelling when they don't know the word or have a model to copy.
- Stage 6 involves sound spelling.
- Stage 7 is distinguished by a message written with conventional forms.

The lines between stages are fluid; there's a great deal of overlap. Teachers begin where each child is in his personal learning journey. The goal is to engage children in free writing—writing without pressure. This extends what some children have already begun to do at home; it initiates a new mode of communication for those who, for whatever reason, have not tried to write, even though there have been models of writing all around them. Effective early childhood classrooms do not follow artificial mandates or benchmarks for writing. Children's interest and development guide the *scaffolding* that's offered for emerging writing skills. Teachers simply respond to what children are trying to do; it's natural and intuitive. But, doing this in classrooms of diversity requires sound knowledge of child and literacy development, as well as thoughtful curricular planning based on efficient assessment.

classroom of diversity group of students that reflects multiple populations, interest areas, ability levels, and other dimensions

The term "scaffolding", attributed to Bruner (Wood, Bruner, & Ross, 1976), describes the kind of help provided to the learner who is attempting to perform a task that cannot be completed independently, but can be accomplished with some assistance. Mindfully scaffolding children's efforts in writing as well as with other developmental milestones is consistent with the Vygotskian concept of a Zone of Proximal Development (ZPD) (Vygotsky, 1978). The following exchange exemplifies a scaffolding exercise that helped a writer move past his writer's block.

> T: Billy, you haven't started. What are you going to write about?
> C: (Child shrugs his shoulders.)
> T: Mmmm. I remember when John talked about using a gift card at Target, you told everyone that you had a gift card too. Have you used it?
> C: Yes. (Pause) I got an action figure.
> T: It must have been fun picking it out.
> C: Yeah. My brother was there. He wanted me to get a different one.
> T: Can you draw a picture that shows what happened?

C: Yeah.

T: Do that and I'll come back to see it.

(A few minutes later:)

T: Great picture Billy. There's a lot of detail. That means you drew lots of things that help me understand your ideas. Please tell me about your picture.

C: That's me. That's mom and my brother Timmy. We're looking at action figures on the shelf.

T: Do you think you could write names by the people in your picture?

C: Yeah. (Child writes a name by each person in the picture.)

T: You could write what you just told me here; it would help readers understand what your picture shows. You said, "We are looking at action figures." Listen for sounds and use the letters you know. Can you get started?

C: Yeah. I know how to write "we" and "at".

T: Great. Write "we". Listen for sounds in the words after that; write down letters for each sound. I'll come back in a few minutes to help some more.

Scaffold for Learning

A learner's ZPD is that area between what he can do by himself (independent level) and what he cannot yet do, even with help (frustrational level); it includes all the performances the leaner can do with maximum to minimal assistance (instructional level) (Bodrova & Leong, 1996; Vygotsky, 1978). Scaffolding does not change the difficulty level of the task; it only makes it possible for the learner to accomplish it (Bodrova & Leong, 1998). With each performance of a scaffolded task, less assistance is necessary. Any support (scaffold) is gradually *faded* as the target behavior, once in the ZPD, becomes independent. Vygotsky (1987) states, "What the child is able to do in collaboration today he will be able to do independently tomorrow" (p. 211). Of course, support can be reestablished whenever the learner falters in initial tries.

Think of a child first trying to swim. The assistant holds on to that child, who's usually wearing all kinds of floating aids. When he appears buoyant, the assistant lets go, but remains ready to scoop him up should the swimmer start to submerge. In this case scaffolding comes from human and material sources. Although scaffolding provides security with new challenges, it should not become a permanent structure. Effective and timely *fading* with any scaffold is critical. When fading, the assistant gradually hands over responsibility for independent performance to the learner. First, the helper steps away; she allows the child to swim supported with floating devices. Gradually, the floating aids are also shed until, one day, the child is swimming without any at all. Without fading, learners remain dependent; *learned helplessness* solidifies (Bodrova & Leong, 1998). Effective scaffolding guides the learner to

learned helplessness learner becomes dependent on help even after he's capable of the performance

take ownership of writing tasks—and even do challenging ones herself with limited assistance.

Guiding Early Revision in Writing

As described in earlier chapters, responding to the child's marking as authorship stimulates awareness of message making and self-reflection; the writer considers, "What did I say?" She analyzes the construction for clarity; she rereads and checks whether the marking is sufficient for the intended message.

Early in the academic year in the preschool study described in Chapter 2 (Shea, 1992), one preschool writer used scribble, letter-like forms, and letters to record a message. She expressed an understanding that extended messages required more marks. She revised by adding more print. An exchange that supported her efforts went something like this.

> C: This says something interesting. I wrote Lyle the Crocodile here.
> T: I know you like Lyle stories. I can't wait to hear what it says. Please read it for me.
> C: I can't read very well on my paper so you have to help me.
> T: Sure. Do you remember what you were thinking about when you wrote it?
> C: I can show this to my mom and tell her what it says.
> T: Yes, you can do that. What were you planning to tell in this writing? Please read what you wrote?
> C: Lyle went back to his real home, not the regular house. He stayed with the owners who were scared about him.
> T: Can you show me where it says that?
> C: Right here. I have to write one more thing. (Child continues marking.)
> T: What did you just write?
> C: I can't tell you yet. I have to make more. (Child continues marking.)
> T: Can you read it to me now?
> C: This says Lyle the Crocodile didn't want to stay with his real owners. They didn't want him anymore. Then, he stayed with the owners who were scared about him.
> T: Who didn't want him anymore?
> C: Mr. Valenti.
> T: I didn't remember that about Lyle. I'm glad you wrote it down. You used several letters. Now, you can read this to mom when she comes.
> C: And I'll read it to my Dad too. I wrote an "i" because Lyle has /i/. I made "l" too; Lyle has an "l". And, I made "h" for "he," and "t" for "to," and even "d" like in "dad" for two "didn'ts"— and lots more "i"s and "l"s all around for all the other words.

The teacher's responses in this conversation were genuine queries meant

FIGURE 6.2
Lyle the Crocodile

to direct the child's analysis of the print while respecting her expressed intent and flow of the story. Effective pre-K classrooms are designed to invite, stimulate, and support early writing; teachers in these settings encourage, scaffold differentially, and respectfully respond to each author.

Writing in a Private Urban Pre-K

A small, private, and well-established urban school includes pre-K classrooms. It's located in a large city in New England. The director/teacher, Mrs. Linden, builds on the foundational knowledge children bring to school. Years of experience at this level validate her beliefs in children's ability and desire to engage in writing and reading. This teacher commented, "Children get their journals right away when they come in.

They talk to each other and to me as they work. They love to write. They're so proud when we read it back together." The teacher constantly reinforces the connection between writing and reading; children read back what they've encoded—with assistance as needed.

This teacher's enthusiastic comments and generous "oohs" and "aahs" demonstrate her appreciation of their effort and product. Mayer (2007) points out "journal writing is not just for kindergartens. With encouragement, preschoolers can write in journals on a daily basis and choose their own topics" (p. 38).

To reinforce the concept that these marks carry meaning, Mrs. Linden asks each child to read his message to her once it's completed. Later, Mrs. Linden underwrites (Behymer, 2003; Johnson, 1999; Newman, 2004) the child's words below his kid writing, using adult writing (Feldgus & Cardonick, 1999). She does this before the message is forgotten. It's the teacher's note-taking—the way adults write. The children understand that; they know they can use their way of writing, because it's encouraged, accepted, and respected in this classroom. But, the children naturally begin to make connections and draw from previous underwriting—much as they do with adult writing in the room. They work at figuring out the underwriting—often asking for help to read it or have it read back to them. Then, they use selected bits and pieces from it when constructing a new journal entry. They also use the alphabet on the journal paper provided. It's a constant reminder that letters are used to construct words.

While their early attempts to write at home may have been regarded as random scribbling, children in this classroom are positioned as writers—right from the start. At first, children may be unsure or reluctant when asked to read their message. Rowe (2008) suggests offering tentative readings, expecting the child to accept it or reject the interpretation and come up with one of his own.

underwrite
writing conventional form below the child's message

FIGURE 6.3
Journal Writing in Pre-K

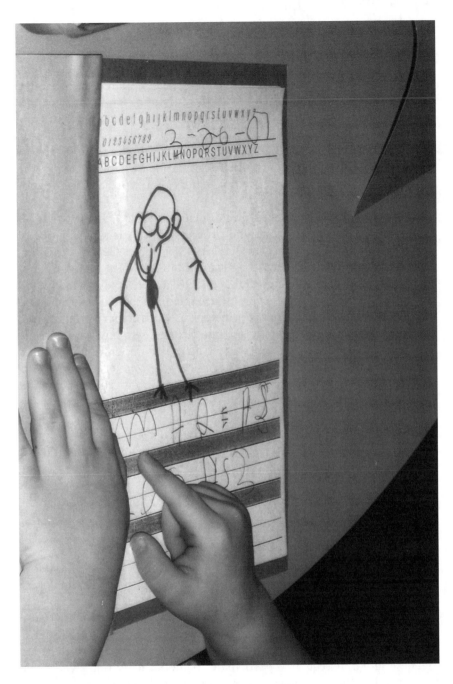

FIGURE 6.4
Child Reads His
Message

Children new to this school quickly get caught up in the flow. Writing as a common element in the day's activities helps newcomers quickly catch up to their writing peers. Writing samples from this site demonstrate children's initial forays and their amazing growth in concepts about how writing works. The features of Sulzby's continuum are revealed in each writing sample for both pre-K sites. These, as well as Durkin's and Schulze's stages, can also be identified in the samples. In Chapter 5, Figures 5.7–5.13 report these details.

As expected, there's a wide range of developmental levels represented in these writing samples. Some children write longer pieces so there's more to analyze and talk about. As previously noted, young children's writing pieces can reflect more than one stage; children's work often reveals several points on Sulzby's (1996) continuum.

They aren't conventional in form, but each production *is* writing because it communicates ideas (Calkins, 1994; Graves, 1994; Schulze, 2006). These children use *kid writing*. Writing samples from this classroom reflect an array of modes for encoding ideas—from drawing and scribbling to *sound spelling* (writing letters that represent the sounds heard).

sound spelling
spelling words by matching sounds to letters used to represent them, phonetic spelling

Most children in this class began with scribbles. These scribbles demonstrate linearity or horizontal progression; this is typically one of the first features that appear in children's writing (Gentry & Gillet, 1993). Eventually, most used a typical mix of scribbles, random letter strings, and invented spellings (Sulzby, 1996) as reflected in the samples on the companion website. Several journal entries reveal quantum leaps of understanding in the alphabet principle, as word constructions moved from scribbles to semi-phonetic spelling (using one or two appropriate letters to spell the word) (Gentry & Gillet, 1993). Semi-phonetic and phonetic word constructions have been characterized as *sound spelling* (Sulzby, 1990). Teachers seem to prefer this term to invented spelling; it recognizes what children are actually doing

The Gentry and Gillet's (1993) spelling stages are outlined in Chapter 7 when talking about writing in kindergarten because they are more significantly present in writing at that level. Although sound spelling is not typically found in writing produced by four-year-olds, a few writing samples from this pre-K classroom did reflect the Gentry and Gillet (1993) spelling stages. These are reported in Chapter 7 following the introduction of the stages.

Expectations in this pre-K classroom empower children. The teacher continuously reinforces a "can do" attitude about communicating with picture and print. It's an activity the children engage in willingly and joyfully. Maybe, that's why some advance to sound spellings. Rudimentary sound spellings, as noted in Figures 6.5–6.7 and other writing samples at the companion website, reflect children's knowledge of and ability to use letters and sounds. These children write every day as they enter the classroom. They also enjoy, discuss, and respond to books read by the teacher.

These children regularly participate in modeled writing, where the teacher talks aloud, verbalizing her thinking as she constructs text (e.g. Morning Message or The News). Children observe as messages are encoded, absorbing something about the writing process with each experience. Figure 6.8 shows a Morning Message that introduces new props in the kitchen area. The teacher read and reread the illustrated message; the pictures helped children "reread" it later with a friend. Figure 6.9 is an example of the News. Space is provided for each reporter to add an illustration.

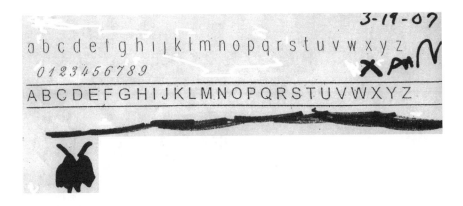

FIGURE 6.5
Max's Journal Entry

Collaborative writing (language experience) activities engage children in the planning part of message construction in this classroom. For example, children planned what to say and how to order the telling when writing a report of their trip to the apple farm, a class story, and an adapted book. The teacher wrote down the message according to the class consensus—again talking through the encoding process. Children were encouraged to give follow-up writing a try in their journal, expressing personal comments about the experience or topic.

The teacher/director of the facility always celebrates their work, graciously asking children to read what they've written. As children start

collaborative writing (language experience) teacher and children plan the text orally before the teacher scribes the words with or without help from children

FIGURE 6.6
Adam's Journal Entry

to use beginning letters, the teacher excitedly lets them know that she can read their kid writing all by herself! Writing in this pre-K is a developmentally appropriate practice (DAP). The teacher's acceptance of children's entry points, the nature of her response to their queries, the environment she's prepared, and the activities that occur there make it so.

Writing in a Campus Early Childhood Center Pre-K

Two pre-K classrooms, located in an Early Childhood Center on the campus of a private college in a northeastern state were visited periodically over two academic years. The Director, who is also a member of the college faculty, coordinates the Center; two certified, experienced Early

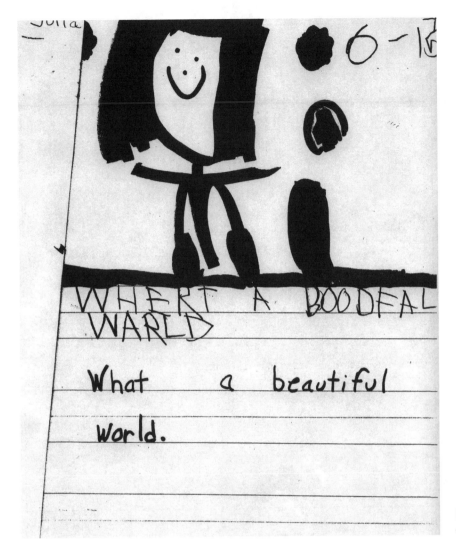

FIGURE 6.7
Julia's Journal Entry

Dear boys and girls

There's something new in the dress-up
center. It's a chef's hat and apron.
You'll look just like the chef in our story
when you wear it.
Cook a special meal in the kitchen area.
Please write your recipe down for us.

FIGURE 6.8
Morning Message

The News
January 19, 200_

Mason went skating with his dad. He went
fast and didn't fall down.

Julie had a play date at her friend's house. They
played with Barbie dolls.

Carrie's dog likes to play in the snow. He looks
funny jumping in it.

FIGURE 6.9
The News

Childhood teachers work directly with the children. There's a great deal of collaboration and co-planning. College students enrolled in early childhood courses complete participation hours, assisting in the classroom with centers and free play. Participation at the Center fulfills college students' requirements for observation and practicum hours.

Writers in these pre-K classrooms have lots of opportunities to ask for help; several messages demonstrate Durkin's (1966) *asking the expert* stage or copying from print in the room. Other writing samples reflect independent free writing as well as responses to prompts associated with theme studies. Writing samples from these classrooms are also found on the companion website.

At this site, children engage in a variety of free-choice activities. Adults facilitate free play, interacting with children and making observations about their growth in multiple areas. The classroom has a well-stocked library; there are stories, informational books, poetry books, picture books, concept books (e.g. alphabet or number books), magazines, and

FIGURE 6.10
Book Rack

other genres of text. Children read alone, with a friend, or are read to by a college student.

The writing center offers several options for materials and purposes. Children can paint, draw, write, cut, paste, and package their message in an envelope for later delivery. Each day, there are theme-based activities for small groups and whole group lessons.

While at the centers, teachers and college assistants work with children in small groups; the teachers conduct whole group mini lessons. Children gather for circle time each day; this includes the Morning Message, the News, read-alouds, theme discussions, collaborative writing, singing, and a variety of other community building and collaborative learning activities. Figure 6.11 shows a class quilt story. The teacher scribed each contribution; then, authors illustrated their words and the pieces were "quilted". Children read the finished quilt with peers, college helpers, teachers, and parents.

In these classroom communities, writers help each other as they construct messages; they also learn from each other. The daily literate activities continuously draw children's attention to their environment, resources in the classroom, the people around them, and demonstrations of literacy. Children build specific knowledge and apply it in their own efforts to communicate.

When constructing personal messages or responding to prompts, children at this site explore and experiment. When children ask questions (for example, "How do you make?"), these young writers receive assistance from college students, but it only comes at the child's request. Not all pre-K classrooms have the benefit of assistance from pre-service teachers, but parents, grandparents, and retired people are often willing to volunteer time to assist young writers.

FIGURE 6.11
Class Quilt Story

Recording dictated spellings or copying available print resources rein-forces children's awareness that words—like their name—have a specific sequence of letters. Eventually, children begin to make phonemic/phonetic connections—association of sounds heard and letters used. But, when highly motivated to get it all down, eager young writers do not ask for help or work through each word; they often revert to creative forms and sound spellings to increase the content and length of their message (Clay, 1987a). This was also noted in these classrooms; such efforts were celebrated and encouraged.

Children in both classrooms at this site see themselves as writers—as part of a writing community where others offer support and encourage-ment. Their movement across established stages is fluid and recursive; productions often reflect characteristics of more than one stage. *Journey books* (portfolios) now used at this site document children's writing development, validating each step.

portfolio
collection of work samples that reflect progress and skill development

Analyzing Writing Samples From the Pre-K Sites

Figures 6.12–6.14 provide an excerpt of analysis of writing samples from both pre-K sites. Each sample is described; levels are determined for Durkin's, Schulze's, and Sulzby's Stage Theories. (Full analysis of writing samples and templates can be found on the companion website.)

Most writing samples from these pre-K sites show characteristics of more than one stage. The literacy growth represented in these samples is the result of the mindfully mediated, developmentally appropriate soft teaching that was planned as well as spontaneously initiated at "teach-able moments." These children have many, many opportunities to write; they engage in the functions of print using the forms they know.

From Private Urban Pre-K

Madison

In November, Madison experimented with writing; she created forms intentionally, expecting that the "marks" expressed her meaning. She used a scribble stream and letter-like, separate forms to write about her drawing. Madison wrote "Mama" in the writing area after labeling her drawing. In March, Madison was writing a sentence fragment—Monkey swinging on a branch—by appropriately representing the first letter of key words as well as the last sound (E) of "monkey".

Emily

Emily uses writing to record what she's learned—Moons are floating in space. Her intended message takes the form of a sentence. She attempted to use spacing. Several sounds are appropriately encoded. Emily confused the /n/ sound in moons with /m/—a continuous sound that is somewhat similar in its formation. She started writing "are" with r, using the letter name heard for spelling. Emily began floating—FLO; then, she added letters to create a longer word. Again, she used the letter name heard to spell; Emily wrote N for "in". When segmenting sounds, Emily heard (and perhaps felt in her mouth) a sound close to /b/ for the /p/ in "space" and wrote B; she represented the sound at the end of the word with S. In response to a story, Emily wrote a sentence that expressed her conclusion. Again, she attempted to use spacing and appropriately encoded several sounds. Emily's sentence included two known writing words—A and "is". Emily repeated known writing words in "A flower is pretty." She correctly spelled the first and last sound in "flower"; she represented the first syllable of "pretty" with P and the last syllable with TE.

From Campus Early Childhood Center Pre-K

Mackenna

McKenna had a sense of story. Although there's no solution, she clearly identified characters, problems, and an event in her Chipmunk story. She used the drawing to convey the story that's dictated; there was no attempt to create printed text. In response to a prompt, "Over Thanksgiving, my family…" Mackenna answers, "Ate Turkey" with scribble writing and her picture of a turkey on a platter. Following a read-aloud of *The Three Bears*, Mackenna draws them in her journal. She copies the word BEARS from the book cover and used a backward numeral for the word three. Mackenna wrote her name on a second try. Her message was reported as, "Do not leave the front door unlocked."

Aidan

Aidan constructed a statement that started with scribbles and continued, "My S…A… is LookiNG FAR PENGUiNS." (My seal (?) is looking for penguins.) He may have copied the word penguins from a source in the room. Aidan drew a picture to show what he liked to do on rainy days and wrote, "jump in puddles" to complete the sentence starter. He most likely asked an expert for these spellings. Aidan's chick says, "Peep. LTs GT 3 GO 3 TAE. MOVES." Although he read back line two, Aidan's intended message was not recorded. Aidan used words and a picture to record his prediction; the worm will …"GO INTO THE (picture of hole)." Aidan had done a lot of writing this year in school and at home.

FIGURE 6.12
Description of Writing Samples

From Private Urban Pre-K

Stage	Madison		Emily		
	Mama	Moons	Princess	Flower	Monkey
D 1–4 (Durkin, 1966)					
1. Drawing and Scribbling	X	X (D)	X (D)	X (D)	X (D)
2. Copying Objects and Letters					
3. Asking Questions About Spelling		X (? about sounding)	X (? about sounding)	X (? about sounding)	X (? about sounding)
4. Reading One's Writing	X	X	X	X	X
S1–5 (Schulze, 2006)					
1. Drawing	X	X	X	X	X
2. Drawing With Caption/Extended Caption—C/EC	X (scribbled C)	X—w/EC	X—w/EC	X—w/EC	X (EC using letters)
3. Listing Information		X—explanation	X—explanation	X—explanation	
4. Listing With Description					
5. Incorporating the Features and Structures of Texts		X—uses letters to represent sounds w/several appropriate matches	X—uses letters to represent sounds w/several appropriate matches; uses known words	X—uses letters to represent sounds w/several appropriate matches; uses known words	X—sentence fragment to describe picture; uses beginning and ending sounds

From Campus Early Childhood Center Pre-K

Stage	Mackenna			Aidan			
	Chipmunks	Thanksgiving	Bears	Penguins	Rainy	Chicks	Worm
D1–4 (Durkin, 1966)					X (D only)	X	X
1. Drawing and Scribbling	X (D only)	X	X (D only)	X			
2. Copying Objects and Letters			X		X		
3. Asking Questions About Spelling				X	X	X	X
4. Reading One's Writing		X	X				
S1–5 (Schulze, 2006)					X	X	X
1. Drawing			X				
2. Drawing With Caption/Extended Caption—C/EC			X—C	X	X		X
3. Listing Information							
4. Listing With Description						X—dialog	
5. Incorporating the Features and Structures of Texts	X Drawing = Ideograph for the story scribed by adult		X Adult scribed her dictated moral for the story				

FIGURE 6.13 Analysis of Writing Samples

Private Urban Pre-K

Level Sample	Drawing as Writing	Scribble Writing	Letter-like Units	Random Letter Strings	Copying Available Print Print or Asked for Spelling	Sound Spelling	Some Conventional words
Madison—Mama	X	X					
Madison—Monkey	X					X	
Emily—Moons	X			X		X	
Emily—Princess	X					X	X
Emily—Flower	X					X	X

Campus Early Childhood Center Pre-K

Level Sample	Drawing as Writing	Scribble Writing	Letter-like Units	Random Letter Strings	Copying Available Print Print or Asked for Spelling	Sound Spelling	Conventional
Mackenna—Chipmunks	X						
Mackenna—Thanksgiving	X	X					
Mackenna—Bears	X				X		
Aiden—Penguins					X		
Aiden—Rainy	X				X		
Aiden—Chicks	X			X	X		
Aiden—Worm	X				X		

FIGURE 6.14 Determining Placement Along Sulzby's (1990) Continuum of Emergent Writing

Common Threads in Pre-K Classrooms That Foster Literacy Growth

At both of these pre-K sites, literacy-learning principles outlined by Rowe (2008) were evident. The budding ability of some children to segment sounds and represent them appropriately with letters is quite amazing when compared to what's typically found in pre-K classrooms.

Too often, one of two things happens. Sometimes, instruction in letter names and sounds is detached from using them for authentic purposes; the focus is on learning such elements as isolated skills. These bits and pieces of information are abstract for the young child. Learning and remembering them is harder when he doesn't fully appreciate their function. On the other hand, letter-sound instruction and sight word learning is postponed—when it's determined to be developmentally inappropriate content for pre-K curriculum. When that happens, children's natural curiosity can erode.

Pre-K classrooms that foster literacy teach essential literacy components and guide transfer of literacy skills and knowledge to applications with personally relevant and authentic purposes. In the classrooms described, children applied phonemic awareness to *rubber-band* words (stretch them out to hear the sounds) and sound spell; they increased phonemic awareness through their writing (Richgels, 2001). Not all children came as far in the journey during pre-K, but all were learning about the functions and forms of print by using it for their own purposes. However, the journey was always positive and the travelers enthusiastic. The operational literacy-learning principles that set the stage for learning in these classrooms include the following:

- literacy concepts can be learned through play activities;
- "risk-free" opportunities for experimentation and exploration with writing foster learning;
- young children can create a message independently. It's intentional even when it's not conventional. Each construction reveals the child's current level of understanding about writing;
- authentic purposes for writing stimulate increase engagement;
- "expert" models of writing inform and motivate;
- collaborating with others about writing fosters growth and community;
- writers need to realize that others value their work.

The curriculum at these sites is mindfully based on guided discovery; the environments draw children into webs of experiences where they uncover information. Children co-direct the spin of investigative threads, taking ownership for their learning adventures. Units of study take on the personality of the class as children offer questions and wonderings that lead investigations. The teacher's role as *sage on stage* is critical; telling and showing still occurs, but, mostly, the teacher is a *guide on the side*—coaching children. Instruction at this level can be referred to as *soft teaching*—teaching that's incidental and scaffolds what children are trying to do. Soft teaching works best in a comfortable, *watching-the-expert* studio. The audience is engrossed; there's no pressure. It's *over-my-shoulder teaching*—like invited eavesdropping topped with a tad of advice.

It's like watching a TV cook, or designers on a daytime make-over show transforming a dull room into one that pops. I sit back and take everything in as the experts talk through what they're doing; soon I begin to believe, "I can do that." At that point, I'm ready for *asking the expert*—seeking specific help where I need it. Young children feel empowered in the same way. We immerse them in language experiences right from the start as an interactive audience. Children are constantly observing experienced language users (older siblings, parents, teachers, authors) model why and how we read, write, listen, talk, view, and visually represent—how we communicate. They become totally immersed in literate activities; they learn language, about language (its forms), and how to use language (its functions). "When teaching emergent literacy, teachers should *saturate*, or immerse children in and expose them to meaningful print in the classroom through reading and writing" (Schulze, 2006, p. 22). Children need to be exploring and experimenting with both writing and reading on a daily basis (Morrow, 2009).

sage on stage
knowledgeable mentor demonstrates or teaches the skill

guide on the side
knowledgeable mentor supports and facilitates the learner's performance

watching the expert studio
environment where the learner is offered multiple demonstrations of the target skill

over-my-shoulder teaching
spontaneous mini lessons provided as needs or interests are recognized

Saturated in Language Experiences

A great book is one that appeals to the head and heart—with no priority for either. For children, it's the same. Great books are not always award winners or on any particular list for recommended reading. Children's favorites may not be books we'd choose. But, something about them appeals to the child. Great books don't get used up; children want to hear them over and over. We introduce classic pieces of literature whenever we can. But, despite our own preferences, we don't mind reading children's favorites over and over when we know they really enjoy them. Their choices are important. The reader and listener find something new to appreciate and talk about in each repetition; ideas for writing are also planted. Schemata keep growing.

Approaches for Engaging Young Writers and Readers

To begin the process of saturation in print, include reading *to*, *with*, and *by* children as well as writing *to*, *with*, and *by* children *every* day—even if it needs to be in smaller doses on particular days because of scheduling conflicts (Mooney, 1990).

> Children will be helped to learn to read and write as success-
> fully and as naturally as they learned to talk if they experience
> a program which includes ... reading to, with, and by children
> and writing to with and by children (p. 9).

At the same time, mix in listening, speaking, viewing, and drawing. Allow lots of time to practice each.

These essentials aren't just for the youngest learners; they should continue throughout the grades. If we include *to*, *with*, and *by* every day in every classroom, there'd be a huge reduction in the number of struggling learners. Children's reading experiences would reinforce and inform all the other language processes; their writing experiences would too.

Writing *to* Children: Morning Message, Signs

Even when children are not yet reading conventionally, it's useful to place messages, labels, and directions in strategic places in the room. Research has shown that children attempt to read print embedded in their environment; they use *historic* (Figure 2.5) or *immediate* (Figure 2.6) clues in the print context as aids (Shea, 1992). As previously described, historic clues are ones associated with the child's previous personal experiences; immediate clues relate to the context of the situation or print examined.

Children expect print to be meaningful and associated with the context in which it's found. Their responses repeatedly demonstrate this. Teachers often place messages with sparse print in highly contextualized situations. They read them often while touching the words.

Teachers might start with a message as concise and pleasant as "Good morning." This remains constant for quite a while. Very, very gradually, more is added. "Good morning boys and girls." Then, "Good morning boys and girls. Today is …" Labels and signs are used in the classroom right from the beginning. Personal cubbies—where children keep their coats, papers, snacks, and other personal things—have name labels. Centers and special areas (e.g. book nook, fish tank, gerbil cage, writing area, kitchen, dress-up) have signs. Storage places are identified. For example, the teacher might say, "Here are the sand toys. It says 'sand toys' on this cover. You can use them today, but please return them to this box—sand toys (touching and pointing to the words written on the cover). Someone can help you." The teacher expects children to be informed and directed by the print displayed; and, they are. The teacher also lets children know that she believes they can begin to contribute to print constructions.

Writing *with* Children: Language Experience, Interactive Writing:

The Language Experience Approach (LEA) has been used for decades to introduce children to basic concepts about print (Allen, 1976; Hall, 1976; Veatch, Sawicki, Elliot, Barnett, & Blackey, 1973). Holdaway (1979) states, "This approach also brought reading and the production of written language together for the first time in natural and helpful ways" (29). Children see their words recorded. It can be personal experiences they're sharing as in the News (Figure 6.9). LEA verifies that what children say is valued—respected enough to be written down and read back. Children learn how print is mapped onto the page—the directionality in English of top to bottom, left to right with a return sweep that creates horizontal lines of print.

To encourage this learning, it's important for the teacher to think out loud while encoding; she talks about spellings, punctuation, and other conventions. Children eavesdrop or listen over her shoulder. After several LEA sessions, children start to help write out messages. They offer letters for spelling or tell the teacher where to go next on the paper. The behaviors celebrated identify what's desired. Soon, more voices are contributing.

Figure 6.8, previously discussed, is an example of a Morning Message with somewhat extended content—one from later in the school year. Over time, the message is expanded with brief details; illustrations support children's independent rereading.

Teachers often use LEA to construct a class chart of personal news or common experiences. It begins with discussion to organize, reflect on, and recall ideas. This strengthens expressive language and thinking skills, as well as community. Collaboratively, the teacher and children decide on what they want to say and how they want to organize it. The teacher writes down the personal anecdote, report (for instance, a class trip to the apple farm), or collection of thoughts on a topic (i.e. signs of fall). The News (Figure 6.9) is an example of reporting personal stories. The teacher records children's expanded ideas with as few words as possible—ones that capture the central message; this keeps the content manageable, allowing children to understand how their idea was encoded for permanence and later rereading. Too much print at this point can overwhelm children. Simple sketches are added to illustrate the words; these act as cues, supporting children's rereading. LEA charts remain in the room for a reasonable period of time, especially while a unit of study is in progress. Figure 6.15 shows a chart created in this way.

Children expressed what they've learned about caring for pets. As their ideas were recorded, the teacher verbalized her own thinking, chatting about how to format print on the page (numbering, directionality, punctuation, capitalization), high frequency words needed, sounds heard in words, and letters needed to spell the sounds heard. Children contributed assistance as they listened in on the teacher's thinking; they spoke out, telling the teacher what she needed to do.

In both pre-K classrooms in the Early Childhood Center at the college campus site described earlier, children contribute to class compositions in book form or as wall or quilt stories. These are proudly displayed in the room and hall. Parents are seen reading them as they wait for dismissal. Children are eager to show the part they contributed. Figure 6.16 shows

Taking Care of Pets

1. You need to love your pet.

2. Pets need food every day. People need to feed them.

3. Dogs need to go for a walk.

4. Sometimes dogs need a bath.

5. Pets like to have toys.

6. Animals need a place to sleep.

7. You need to clean up after your pet.

8. Pets need to go to the doctor too. They go to the vet.

9. When you go away, take your pet to the kennel. She can stay there.

FIGURE 6.15
Learning About Pets

a class book, *Snowy Owl Lives in the Arctic*. Figure 6.17 shows a class-created mural retelling of the Little Red Hen. One day, Thomas contributed an initial kernel for a story and others carried the theme with each addition (Figure 6.18). The beginning is in the upper right. When the paper is folded in half, the story starts at the left in the first rectangular box, "Once upon a time there was a rich King." The story continues left-to-right, one side then the other when not on the wall.

All this collaborative writing inspires children; they begin to write on their own at school and at home. They often bring writing done at home into school for sharing.

FIGURE 6.16
Class Book: Snowy
Owl Lives in the Arctic

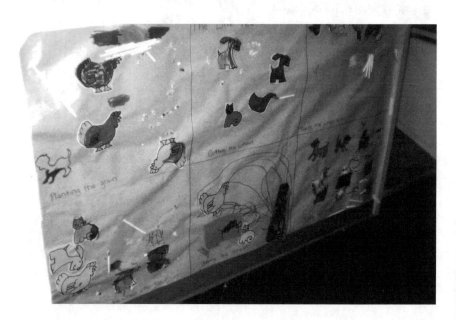

FIGURE 6.17
Class Mural of
Retelling of Little
Red Hen

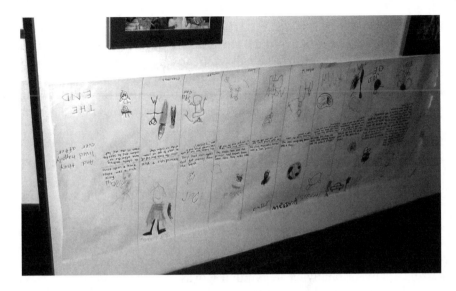

FIGURE 6.18
Thomas Starts a Story

Writing *by* Children: Independent Writing

Convinced they are capable of writing meaningful pieces and buoyed by the models presented, children launch into independent writing with enthusiasm and conviction.

Writing props placed in play areas are irresistible. Ray (2004) suggests that "the first thing we need to do is get writing tools in their [children's] hands, paper in front of them ... We call whatever they do with those tools *writing*" (p. 49). We don't allow them to think they can't write; we make it clear that approximations are accepted. Ray (2004) stresses that young children need the freedom to record ideas in their own way. Tell them "just to pretend to write if they like" (p. 50). That takes away any hesitation or worry about correctness.

Literacy props are simple and inexpensive items transformed by adult suggestions and the child's imagination. A pad of paper in the kitchen play area is used to construct a shopping list; when the kitchen becomes a restaurant, it's a waiter's pad. The car and truck area has paper for making signs and garage work order pads to list repairs needed and completed. Specialty pads are available at any office supply store. The mailbox area has stamps and inkpads for posting letters and packages. Children like to compose letters in the writing area, stamp them, and file them in their cubbies before taking this mail home to parents. The animal area has a tablet for recording observations. Children draw and/or write down what the fish, gerbil, or bunny are doing at the moment; they're acting like scientists. Often, they work in pairs or small groups and collaboratively direct the recorder. Whiteboards with erasable markers are also a favorite free time choice. Children practice writing and drawing, erase, and start again. They partner up, "Let's make our names. Let's make Spiderman." Sometimes, children's writing is gently directed toward a purpose.

Children in the campus pre-K created playbills at a center for a

writing props
items in the environment that stimulate interest in and activity with writing (i.e. notebooks, forms, markers)

performance in the dress-up area. Those in the dress-up area worked on signs for audience seating and the stage before dictating the play's script to a college student helper. When all was ready, a command performance was given! Throughout this playwriting process, children looked on as their words were written and read back to verify the accuracy of recording. In such experiences they were nudged toward Durkin's (1966) final stage; writing was taking them into reading.

- They were encoding their ideas in print form, mapping print onto the paper in directionally appropriate ways.
- They listened to words in their message; they listened for the sounds in those words.
- They tried to match as many sounds as they could to letters that represented those sounds.
- They used words found in print in the room, asked for help, and sometimes conventionally wrote familiar words.
- And, they *read* what they wrote to themselves and others. That's *reading*.

Reading *to* Children: Reading Aloud

Parents and teachers read aloud to children before, while, and after they begin to write. Each process fuels growth in the other (Rasinski & Padak, 2009). Reading aloud to children reveals why we read; it brings pleasure and fulfills basic needs for information. Stories entertain and informational books answer wonderings. We read to children because "children who haven't heard words sing, who have not experienced words that made them laugh and cry, words that make them stomp and holler and words that make them go suddenly quiet, even pensive, are not going to be readers, no matter how adept they are at decoding" (Ohanian, 1999, p. 55). Neither will they become writers, inspired to construct messages that deeply affect readers.

Reading aloud increases children's understanding of others, the world, and themselves. Through books, children broaden their horizon beyond the neighborhood as they visit new places and learn new things. But the benefits are local too; books help children make sense of situations in their lives. Learning from listening requires focused attention. And, this attending supports development in meaning-making skills. In fact, most comprehension strategies can be practiced while listening (Miller, 2002; Owocki, 2003). It's a great time to begin practicing strategies for deeper comprehension since children aren't burdened with having to decode the words too.

We scaffold children's efforts to visualize, make connections (to other books, the world, or themselves), ask questions, make inferences, determine a theme, or retell (Zimmermann & Hutchins, 2003); they're focused on thinking—on understanding—with each task. Starting this way puts comprehension front and center—where it belongs. Right from the start, children should know that we read to understand the message. The author puts words on paper to share ideas, just as the children do when they write. If they haven't understood, they didn't read—or listen. It was a babble (meaningless utterance) of words.

Since it's easier to remain attentive when the material and the presentation are interesting, choosing the right text and *performing* the read-aloud enthusiastically is critical. If you've ever tried to separate a child from a water puddle made by a rainstorm, you know that there's no limit to attention span when the activity holds interest. Forget about attention deficit at those times! So catch and hold children's attention with texts that captivate and inspire. The content will establish a reservoir of material and models for writing.

attention deficit
inability to remained
focused for prolonged time

Determine children's interests and choose quality literature accordingly. Length is also important. Start with high-interest, short books or magazine articles to gage children's ability to absorb information and maintain focus. Gradually, widen your choices to longer selections. *Ladybug* (Cobblestone trademark) is one of several wonderful magazines for preschoolers. There are teacher guides at www.cobblestonepub. com/resources_lyb_tgs.html for each issue; these incorporate a range of language activities that can be adapted for any classroom and integrated into thematic units.

First and foremost, allow children to enjoy the experience and text. This may sound quite obvious and not worthy of mention. However, I've been a victim of *didactic talk seizure* (long instructional monolog) that suddenly creeps into book conversations when I wasn't on guard for its symptoms. Try to guide deeper comprehension with soft teaching at story time. But also plan to mine examples that will impact what children are doing or trying to do in their writing (or drawing). Talk about interesting words the author uses, "I liked that word *rumpus* too. It helped me know how noisy those monsters were. I bet you've had a wild rumpus when playing with friends." The website includes a plan for a read-aloud of *Where the Wild Things Are*.

Or, you might say, "I've heard you say interesting words; try to use some of those in your writing today." Draw children's attention to illustrations that are good models of what they could do, "I noticed that this illustrator used lots of very bright colors. Each page has only one or two things on it." Aloud, notice captions and their purpose, "And, there are names by each picture for me to read. I think you could write something like this in your journal today." Emulating the model propels children into Durkin's (1966) and Schulze's (2006) Stage 1—and, Stage 2 if they add print.

As children notice print and ask about words, include read-alouds with sparse print on each page. But, don't stop reading longer books; you want to keep the flow of benefits from that experience. Books like *Where's Spot* (Hill, 1980) are a good first choice in the sparse text category. Point to the words and invite children to chorally read (or echo read) with you. Those who are ready will eagerly participate, reading "Not here." as you pick up the flaps. Others will continue to follow along silently, but they're often seen rereading these easy books during free time.

Over time—with lots of interactions like this—most children begin to learn basic linguistic principles, including

- print represents speech;
- print has constant features—a set of letters is used;
- units of letters stand for a word;
- words are repeated;
- some words have parts that sound alike;
- some words have similar letters.

Some children come to school knowing these principles or catch on faster than others; these are the ones who've been read to regularly and are already using print. Just ask any pre-K teacher after a few weeks—or less—of school, "Who's had lots of literacy experiences before coming here?" They can readily identify the group of children who

- gravitate toward books, knowing that they'll find interesting information and wonderful stories within the pages;
- have longer attention spans—since they've learned to maintain focus when read to at home;
- like to verbally express their thinking about stories, the world, and experiences;
- have an expanded meaning vocabulary;
- make connections with life situations and stories, saying something like, "That's like when Curious George had to go to the hospital";
- are relatively uninhibited about drawing and writing in their own way.

Teachers reinforce emerging understandings of linguistic principles—which some children already have—with word labels in the room, signs, name cards, magnetic letters, and alphabet books. These and other literacy props cause children to pay attention to print, ask questions about it, and move toward Durkin's (1966) *ask the expert* stage. This simple format for reading aloud also establishes protocols for reading *with* children.

Reading *with* Children: Shared Reading

Shared reading takes read-aloud to a next step by inviting children to chorally read during successive rereads. To replicate the intimacy of reading at home—in a setting where the child can see the illustrations and print as the text is read—teachers use enlarged print with children seated in a cozy gathering place where everyone has a clear view (Holdaway, 1979). At the pre-K level, the length of text is brief. Since the goal is to have children move from listener to participatory rereading, it's important not to overwhelm them. Books with few words per page are appropriate. Songs, finger plays, and poetry are also great choices for shared reading at this level. For now—for this purpose—less is more. The words can be written on chart paper and simple, colorful illustrations can be added to connect visuals with the words. The pictures serve as anchors, helping children differentiate the charts and remember the content when charts are later displayed for rereading. With materials ready, invite children into the comfortable space, explain the procedure and expectations, and enjoy the collaboration.

It's useful to introduce the text by talking about the title and author. For example, after copying a short part of the poem *Tiptoe* by Karla Kuskin (1971, p. 33) onto chart paper, you could say, "Today we are going to read a poem about walking on tiptoes. Can someone show us how to do that?" After the demonstration, reveal a picture you've added to the chart. "Emily tiptoed just like this (pointing to the picture). Let's all try it. Stand up in your place, tiptoe around in a little circle, and sit right back down ready to listen." When everyone's ready, congratulate the children, "How wonderful that all of you can balance on tiptoe; you did that so well. Walking on tiptoes can be difficult. Why might someone want to do it?" Talk about coming up to someone quietly—possibly to surprise that person. Say, "I'm going to read this poem about walking on tiptoe while you listen." Read the poem aloud while *tracking the print* with a pointer (touch under each word as it's read). Invite children to respond or comment when you're finished reading. It's a very open petition, "What are you thinking about after listening to this? Please share your ideas." Enjoyment, understanding, and making connections come first. Now, it's time for children to participate.

track print
move finger along under each word while reading, demonstrating the speech-to-print match

Let them know that you have no doubt that they can be readers along with you. One particularly creative teacher (not at the sites described in this book) had children use magic glasses to read along at the beginning of the year. These were colorful sunglasses she purchased at the dollar store. When the children felt they had the reading power—when the magic was inside of them—they could take their glasses off and read on their own. It worked like training wheels on a two-wheeler. These were magic glasses; they bestowed confidence! Expectations are powerful. Sometimes, they make us believe ourselves capable when we couldn't have imagined it on our own.

Say, "I'm going to read the poem again. This time, I'd really like you to help me. We'll read out loud—that's oral. We'll read together—that's choral. Let's call it our *choral oral*—together, out loud reading. I'll touch each word as we read it to help us keep the place—and pace. Here we go." Reread the text with a few timid, faint voices accompanying you. Don't be discouraged. Know that others will come along; just continue the process—and believe it will happen. Thank collaborators for their help and say, "I like how it sounds when we read together. Let's try it one more time." During this rereading, give children a listening task. "This girl told us about two other ways she moves. She also told us where she goes on tiptoes. When you're reading with me listen for these two things—another way she moves and where she goes." Reread the poem; children share that the girl also skips and runs. She goes down the stairs,

choral oral
reading together (choral) out loud (oral)

through the door, and to the living room. Tell children, "Tomorrow we'll take turns; some people will choral oral read while others move like this girl. Then, we'll switch so everyone has a turn. That'll be fun!" Leave on a high note. It also sets a new purpose for rereading and listening.

Dramatic responses are a wonderful way to extend enjoyment and engagement with a particular text. These activities are a favorite at all ages because of their inherent playfulness. Children act out the content of a text as it's read aloud.

Another activity is to reread the whole poem (or any shared text) aloud to see what interesting things children notice in the print. Pre-K isn't too early for directing attention to print; research has shown that, on their own, young children notice print in their environment and draw conclusions about its significance (Harste, Woodward, & Burke, 1984; Shea, 1992).

The discussion starts with; "I noticed the word 'day'. Here it is—d-a-y. That word is on our calendar—d-a-y. It's at the end of every day's name, like Mon-day, Tues-day, Wednes-day, Thurs-day, Fri-day, Satur-day, and Sun-day—d-a-y. What did you notice?" A response may not be offered or someone might share what she noticed in the picture. That's all right. Just keep modeling *noticing*. As children's knowledge about print grows, they'll notice too. As it's offered, shortened versions of children's noticing are recorded on chart paper. Although economized, recorded "noticings" use the child's words. Too much print overwhelms very young children. Keep it simple and playful; there's no pressure. They will learn.

Recording offers opportunities to model encoding. Verbalize (think out loud), figuring out some of the letters needed to spell words. Write out the other letters without belaboring the task and losing children's attention—a little goes a long way. The teacher's effort reinforces that what we say can be recorded for permanence. Even when children can't remember what they said, they know which line of print represents their contribution.

Children ask, "What did you write for me here? What did I say?" until they can read it. They tell their friend or parent, "That's mine; that's the one I said. I can read it. It says … ." The child moves a finger under the print, just as the teacher did. At first, he isn't tracking with a word-to-word match, but he is maintaining left-to-right directionality. Often, early read-backs don't have a word-to-word match, but the child is accurately engaging in *reading-like* behavior and believes he's a reader. That's a solid foundational stone. Enlist parents' help to reinforce and extend the learning.

When you've completed three or four shared readings with poetry charts, compile copies of them into a booklet. These are sent home with a letter (Figure 6.19).

Teachers who do home visits when working in a pre-K program report that parents appreciate clear suggestions for simple, enjoyable activities. Most parents want to be involved, but don't know just what to do. A big fear that parents express is that they're worried about creating confusion

Dear Parents:

The children are taking home a collection of favorite poems, songs, and finger plays. We have read these together several times. We call it our *choral oral* (together, out loud) reading. Your child will enjoy partner reading them with you. She/he's not expected to read them alone.

Sometimes we act out what the words are saying. This dramatic play is always great fun! Your child can direct these performances. You might want to include other family members as well.

As you're reading together, slide a finger under each word as it's read. This reinforces the *speech-to-print* match that's developing. It helps your child notice words as well as the spaces between them as markers.

Most of all, have lots of fun. I'd love to hear about your experiences with this activity.

Sincerely,

………..

FIGURE 6.19
Parent Letter

with the school's methodologies if they did try to help. Keep sharing; the alliance benefits everyone. Soon children display more and more self-initiated reading-like and reading behaviors.

Reading *by* Children: Independent Reading

With abundant demonstrations and immersions (marinating), children begin to mimic literate behaviors. Teachers provide them with time to practice reading even when the performance is *reading-like* (telling the story from memory or the pictures as the pages are turned). Figure 6.20 outlines steps for a guided *reading-like* activity with very young children. The steps are explained each time the teacher meets with a group; key words identifying before, during, and after reading behavior are emphasized (survey, predict, read, retell, and respond). The pictures represent what to do at each point. Even young children can eventually follow the steps with peers; they know how to interact with books.

The pre-K classrooms described in this chapter had a cozy book nook. Visiting the book area was a choice during the day's first time block for

S P 3R: Survey, Predict, Read, Retell, Respond

Survey
(Explain: Survey the book. Look at the cover and pictures inside.)

Predict
(Explain: Predict what the book will be all about. Think about what you see and what you know.)

Read
(Explain: Read the book. Look at every page and decide what the author is telling.)

Retell
(Explain: Tell someone all about the book.)

Respond
(Explain: Draw a picture of something in the book. Write down what the picture shows.)

FIGURE 6.20
Reading by Children in Pre-K (adapted from Owocki, 2007)

center activities and free time. Children at the book nook read alone, read with a friend, or had an adult helper read to them. In the on-campus pre-K, this adult was a college student; in the other pre-K classrooms it was the teacher or a parent helper. In these pre-K classrooms, there's a lot of *familiar text time* since shared texts (texts that have been introduced and read to the class) are placed in the book area for children to use. This includes the previously described teacher-created charts for shared reading. It also includes collaboratively written class books.

familiar text time
time to engage with text/ books that have been shared

Putting It Together

Combined, to, with, and by reading excursions create warp threads (strong long threads that run lengthways in a piece of cloth). Children construct woof threads (threads that run across) during to, with, and by writing experiences. Interwoven, the threads create a sturdy fabric.

Writing and reading to, with, and by children continues through the grades with increasingly more sophisticated texts and responses. Given quality materials and the guidance of an expert weaver, all children are capable of designing a personalized literacy tapestry—one that grows with additional threads and details as language knowledge expands.

Assessing Children's Writing

Teachers use checklists when analyzing writing samples. They consider stages outlined in the Durkin (1966) and Schulze (2006) models for message creation; these were described in Chapters 2 and 5. Each writing sample is further analyzed for placement within seven broad categories for word construction outlined by Sulzby (1985; 1990) and found earlier in this chapter. The results are reflected in Figures 6.12–6.14. Pre-K writing samples that demonstrate spelling attempts matched to the Gentry and Gillet (1993) stages are analyzed in the next chapter, where those stages are introduced, since writing in kindergarten is more often where early spelling experimentation is identified. Checklists help teachers identify small groups for targeted instruction on a common need or where individualized instruction is more appropriate.

The writing samples from these pre-K sites show characteristics of more than one stage. The literacy growth represented in these samples is the result of the mindfully mediated, developmentally appropriate soft teaching that was planned as well as spontaneously initiated at teachable moments. These students have many, many opportunities to write; they engage in the functions of print using the forms they know.

Classrooms of Diversity

Children have constructed a contextual understanding of how to communicate in their home language; this includes idiosyncratic word usage, grammatical structures, and dialectal patterns. Jago (1999) stresses the importance of knowing which languages the child speaks, reads, writes, and understands. "A society that seeks to address the needs of all children is one that recognizes linguistic individuality" (p. 165). When this differs from the language of instruction used in school, children need to learn how to reconstruct their ideas in new ways (Laliberty & Berzins, 2000; Rubin & Carlan, 2005). Sharing literature, discussing its content, and engaging in grand discussions across the day present opportunities for children to learn the standard language without devaluing their *home register*. Along with these opportunities, other conditions need to be met.

Learning a second language takes time. Learners need lots of opportunity to practice in a setting that's safe and comfortable—one that accepts and encourages their efforts. Classrooms where children abundantly talk and listen to each other—as well as to the teacher—support ESL children's development of basic communicative skills in the second language. However, their proficiency with academic language may take five to eight years (Cummins, 1979).

idiosyncratic word usage
personal word usage or speech pattern

dialectal speech
speech that reflects a regional variety of a language

home register
form of speech acceptable in the setting

Analyzing bilingual children's writing is the best way to assess their development in the two languages; their compositions reflect growth in each as well as connections they've made (Laliberty & Berzins, 2000; Rubin & Carlan, 2005). In Chapter 7 writing samples from an urban ESL classroom are analyzed. For most of the children in this classroom, kindergarten was their first school experience.

When initial school experiences (in pre-K or kindergarten) are risk-free and meaningful, children jump into literacy and learning. Hopefully, this happens in a garden that welcomes their playful approach to learning—one that nurtures development in social, emotional, and cognitive domains. Literacy learning positively impacts all of these areas.

Moving Into Kindergarten

The children from pre-K classrooms like the ones described in this chapter have amassed a lot of literacy beginnings. But, many children come to kindergarten without preschool experience; other entrants attended a preschool that didn't expect them to write. Some children had limited opportunities to read and write at home. When provided with the conditions that others have had, these children quickly join in as authors.

In the next chapter the Gentry and Gillet (1993) levels are discussed. As previously mentioned, some of these pre-K writers have already moved along the Gentry and Gillet (1993) developmental continuum for spelling. Although these pre-K writers and kindergarten authors in Chapter 7 had lots to say, they typically abbreviated printed messages, writing a gist idea to label, explain, or describe their drawing with writing.

Chapter 7 will introduce a strategy for scaffolded support—one that helps emergent writers expand message and refine form. Although children's approximations are accepted and respected, we do have expectations. With positive coaching, they gradually move toward conventional forms. However, too often, children "encounter an emphasis on correctness of form that casts doubt on the integrity of their personally invented messages" when they enter kindergarten (Wohlwend, 2008, p. 43). An inappropriate focus on correctness over communication in early writing inhibits young children's experimentation with print for all of its functions (purposes) (Larson, 2002; Morrow, 1989).

In the pre-K settings described in this chapter and the kindergarten classrooms introduced in Chapter 7, teachers respect the communicative intent of children's early marking. They understand that children seek to refine their writing, striving to construct a message that's readable by others. Writers accomplish that goal as they gain knowledge about the alphabetic code. Conventions are not forgotten; they're held in balance—introduced developmentally. In this atmosphere, writers thrive and grow into readers.

Extending the Discussion

■ Examine the pre-K writing samples at the website with course members or colleagues. Partner up to examine all samples from a particular child. Be prepared to discuss this child's development with the group.

■ Collect writing samples from a local pre-K or your own classroom. Discuss each with peers. Determine where these writers fall on the continuum. What would you recommend for scaffolding these learners, nudging them forward?

■ Visit a pre-K classroom or consider the sequence of activities in your own classroom. Look for instances of writing to, with, and by children. Look for time planned for reading to, with, and by children. Discuss how each was mindfully woven into daily activities.

■ Create a writing center or *writing toolbox* for a pre-K classroom. Donate it to a pre-K or use it in your own pre-K classroom.

seven
Writing in Kindergarten

Accommodating a Range of Literacy Beginnings

Children who've had rich literacy experiences at home and at pre-K come to kindergarten interested in and motivated to continue engagement in such activities. One child told the teacher that he expected to learn how to write longer stories and read bigger books when he went to kindergarten in the "big school"—on the first day of big school!

For other children, kindergarten is an initial foray into literacy. They've been observers of print in the environment, but have limitedly explored or used it. The range of differences in children's linguistic knowledge at the beginning of kindergarten can be wide. Teachers strive to meet children where they are, challenging some further or introducing literacy (e.g. in ways described in previous chapters) to others. Although the appropriate next step differs, each child takes it when instruction's on

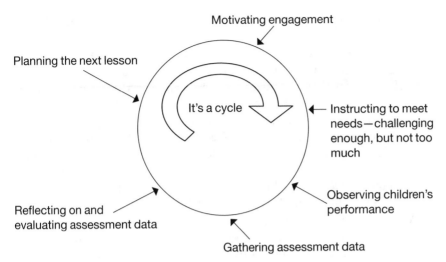

Motivating engagement

Planning the next lesson

It's a cycle

Instructing to meet needs—challenging enough, but not too much

Observing children's performance

Reflecting on and evaluating assessment data

Gathering assessment data

FIGURE 7.1
Teaching–Learning
Cycle

target, meeting his immediate needs. Knowledgeable early childhood teachers are child-centered in their approach to instruction, following an *instructional cycle* that attends to individual interests, abilities, confidence, and motivation. Their teaching is data-driven. It's not a performance of sequenced, one-lesson-fits-all scripts that become the curriculum in some kindergarten classrooms. Learning is essential. But, building children's confidence, motivation, and perseverance comes first; developing these qualities ensures that learning will occur. Early childhood teachers work hard to design environments that nurture all of these, appreciating that growth is personal in nature and gradual in speed.

Becoming Literate: A Journey Not a Race

Continuously setting challenges seems to be a very human condition. We briefly savor each accomplishment before imagining, "What's next?" Learning is a journey; it takes time to arrive at levels of competence. And, there are places where we rest for a while and build new steam for the effort ahead. We may take time to enjoy the view or explore the surroundings where we are—like growing horizontally. Getting to the next plateau brings satisfaction and builds genuine self-esteem—a feeling of, "I did it!"

Of course, intellectual accomplishments are the result of personal effort and a little help from others because learning is inherently a social process. Vygotsky (1978) concluded that all higher mental functions had social origins that appear *between* individuals before they exist *within* the individual. He believed that the Zone of Proximal Developmental (ZPD), discussed in Chapter 6, is created by social collaboration (Vygotsky, 1986). As the child's performance is scaffolded within and through his ZPD, the social use of language in the process is a significant contributor to his learning (Owocki, 1999). As described in Chapter 3, children learn language and its functions—in oral and written modes—through interactions that take place in a social context (Halliday, 1975; Laminack, 1991).

The most effective way to assess the learning that's acquired is to watch and listen to the child in a social context (Goodman, 1985), take careful notes on their performances, and analyze the information for strengths and needs. Teachers determine which areas on stage level checklists relate to observed behaviors and work products; they keep in mind that growth occurs over time (Beaty & Pratt, 2011). Instruction tied to data collected is more likely to be differentially appropriate, addressing identified needs, nudging learners toward the next step, or challenging them to try new things—whichever is most appropriate for the situation (Dodge, 2005; Tobin, 2008; Tomlinson, 1999).

We challenge learners to try something new—to step forward—when they've demonstrated readiness, knowing that even small accomplishments build confidence and motivation to persevere. Effective teachers provide children with a safe, supportive environment for stretching their wings. Young children are comfortable with appropriate challenges—ones they believe they can accomplish. This is evidenced in challenges they set for themselves; sometimes the tasks seem quite difficult.

Kindergarten writers and readers also provide peers with support and encouragement; their demonstrations say to others, "I like to do this. You will too!" When the activity is enticing and the community supportive, children willingly participate. They see it as achievable when others are there to assist and show the way.

Young children *want* to participate in literacy activities just like significant others in their world (Ferreiro & Teberosky, 1989). Growing into literacy is a challenge children set on their own; they work at it willingly. Offering support and gently nudging while walking beside them allows it to happen. Literacy activities don't detract from play and social time in kindergarten; they are part of it.

Developmentally Appropriate Practices as Literacy Play in Kindergarten

Developmentally appropriate literacy play makes the garden of children lush rather than a testy, skills driven *garden of thorns* (Brodsky-Chenfield, 2007). Owocki (1999) offers tips for designing a literacy-rich play environment. To accomplish this the teacher:

- establishes expectations for behavior, personal responsibility for learning, and care of materials;
- establishes an atmosphere that promotes risk-free exploration with print;
- invites children to use print in their own way for authentic (real-life) literacy functions;
- provides an environment rich in genres of and contexts for print;
- stages classroom centers and play areas with creative literacy props (Chapter 5); and

- allows for open-ended print exploration while directing children's discoveries of print's functions and forms.

DAP emphasizes interactive curriculum, based on content that's concrete, real, and relevant (Bredekamp, 1987). "Children are provided with many opportunities to see how reading and writing are useful before they are instructed in letter names, sounds, and word identification" (p. 55). Teachers begin literacy play with print that's meaningful to the child.

The Importance of a Name

The first conventional word formations that most children recognize and create are their names (Clay, 2001b; Temple et al., 1993). A name holds great importance (Clay, 2001b; Perlmutter et al., 2009; Trushell, 1998). Children want to form their name legibly so they and others can recognize it and identify what belongs to them (Bodrova & Leong, 2007). In the course of accomplishing that, "children learn to focus attention on specific aspects of print, and they get practice in remembering deliberately" (p. 160). Name writing also provides the child with a repertoire of known letters (Temple et al., 1993); he rearranges letters of his name randomly or aesthetically to form other words. Clay (1987a) describes such creative word construction as reflective of the child's emerging appreciation of the *generative principle*.

generative principle
writers create new words by reordering a limited set of letters

This makes name identification and name writing powerful tools for starting a discussion about print forms (Campbell, 2004; Clay, 2001b). "Their [children's] names tell them, and us, who they are and where they come from" (McGill-Franzen, 2006, p. 163). Teachers write children's names on their work, cubbies, and on center lists for turn taking. They draw attention to the distinctive features of each name, helping children identify their own and the names of others. This makes everyone feel important (Clay, 1991). Teachers design engaging activities that use name recognition as a venue for learning features of print and all about classmates. Having children sign-in for daily attendance or sign off when they've completed work at a center are very common tasks; they create a data trail of progress toward accuracy and legibility. Name recognition is creatively used for literacy learning in the urban kindergarten classroom described in this chapter.

The teacher in the bilingual kindergarten uses children's names to teach phonemic awareness and letter recognition. Each day a different child is the special helper. One duty is to assist with morning activities, including the News. But, before the weather and calendar are completed, this special helper is given pompoms. The child's name is also clearly written on the board.

One day, Damon called out each letter in his name while shaking pompoms. He shouted, "Give me a D. Give me an A." etc. as the teacher pointed to the letters. The class repeated his cheer. After spelling the full name, everyone repeated it in syllables to count the number they heard. Names are the first words on the word wall, using beginning letters of each to categorize. Soon children are writing their own name to identify their work; they're using names when drawing and writing about friends.

Clay (1975) noted that children are also naturally motivated to recognize and write the names of special people; they often create lists of family and friends' names. They analyze and talk about the components of different names, determining whose name has more syllables or which names have similar letters. Names are used as a basis for introducing and reinforcing syllables, letter recognition, and letter sounds. Name games, word hunts, word sorts, and letter hunts are additional activities that reinforce concepts with meaningful content (McGill-Franzen, 2006). All the while, this knowledge is applied to creating messages; it's not just for letter practice in isolation. Beyond names, children gradually absorb other words presented in meaningful contexts; they add them to their repertoire for reading and writing.

The News as Literacy Practice in Kindergarten

The kindergarten classrooms visited use the News as a daily event just as the pre-K classrooms did. However, as learners' knowledge grows, recordings are extended and the teacher's verbalizations become more detailed. Children, who already know the protocol for the News, usually jump right in with stories to tell. The kindergarten teachers visited regularly used the News as a teaching tool to expand children's print awareness and knowledge; it was always a community building experience as well.

While recording News, the teachers selectively exaggerate letters and their sounds in words; consonant sounds are first emphasized during this phase. Words that need to be spelled automatically (such as "in", "to", "I", "the", "at") are recorded with, "Oh that's t-h-e for the." Other words are phonemically segmented first (for example, "/c/, /a/, /t/"). Then, the letters needed for spelling each phoneme are given. "That's c-a-t for cat." Some children rapidly absorb—like sponges—information about phonemic segmentation and phonetic constancy (and inconsistency) with this soft teaching. Others need more exposure and support, but they also come to know.

Children in these kindergarten classrooms begin to recognize patterns for representing words; understanding that it isn't a personal choice or random. They conclude, "This is how the experts do it." Sometimes teachers highlight high frequency (HF) words in the News—ones that children can begin to write automatically and conventionally. The teacher writes HF words without sounding, saying, "Oh, I write this word a lot. I know how to spell it. I don't have to stretch sounds. Some words are tricky; you can't match all their sounds to letters." The teacher emphasizes the tricky factor with a word like "of". Attention is also drawn to selected print conventions. For example, she notes that capital letters are used for the names of people and places; periods are used at the end of sentences that tell and question marks come at the end of questions.

In Figure 7.2 the teacher circled HF words when the News was reread.

high frequency words common words that appear in printed text with high frequency (i.e. I, was, to, in, on, of, the)

FIGURE 7.2
Our News

Each HF word was also rewritten at the end of the News in a shape children had learned (reinforcing a mathematics concept). Daily News charts are hung in the classroom. Children frequently refer to them for specific words when writing. A copy of the News is sent home daily. Parents reread the News with their child; they reinforce HF word and shape identification. The messages also stimulate lots of family talk. Children often mimic the creation of newsy pages at home. They bring these in for the class to read and discuss.

Talk during News time strengthens children's expressive language skills; it also reinforces the concept that writers share what they know about and care about. The stories of children's daily lives are outlined, organized, and elaborated through talk; they become the content for further writing. Class-created charts, lists, books, letters, or Language Experience Stories (Chapter 6) provide similar opportunities for lessons about word and message construction. Such activities generate insights into the literacy process in situations that are motivating, meaningful, and non-threatening. As children go about recording their stories in the kindergarten classrooms described in this chapter, they use what they've taken from all these models—applying what they know at the moment. Conversations about this writing initially focus on understanding the message—communicating their meaning.

Reading What's Written

To remember the intended message, the kindergarten teacher at the urban school also underwrites what the child read; the kindergarten teachers at the rural school record what the child said on the back of the paper. Children regularly reread their writing; they also begin to notice and ask about features in adult writing.

The desire to write so others can read the message drives development; children attend closely to and emulate processes modeled for word construction. They work on segmenting sounds and spelling what they hear—or think they hear. This is the Sound Spelling Stage. A *phonic phone*, made from PCB piping, is a magical tool for work at this stage (Figure 7.3). It directs articulated sounds to the speaker's ear, making it easier to isolate and identify sounds at the phonemic (separate sounds) and phonological level (sound chunks—syllables, rimes). Phonic phones can be made or purchased from a school supplier for a nominal price. Some conventional spellings are also incorporated into children's writing at this time. These are familiar words that are written automatically or that children have copied from a resource in the room.

Children look back at translations on the back of their journal pages (adult writing for their kid writing). They ask the teacher to read it for them, "What did I write? What did you write here?" They know the teacher's writing repeats their message. With the younger child, this process suggested the possibility of an intended message. In this case, the writer encoded with self-recognized intention, but has difficulty decoding

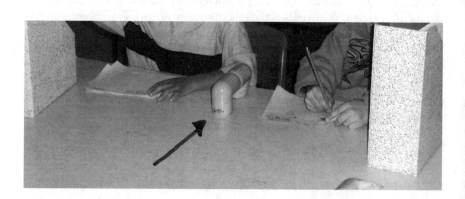

FIGURE 7.3
Phonic Phone

when trying to read it back. He wants to know where each word is represented. The teacher points to each word and slowly reads what she wrote. "Hmmm," is their typical response and off they go.

Strategically, children use pieces of that print in a new message. If they ask the teacher how to spell, she segments the sounds for them and asks, "What do you hear?" With a question mark hanging on his nose, one child responded, "b?"—for b-a-t. "OK," the teacher said, "Put that down. Anything else?" "A /t/?" he responds. "Great! Put that down. We'll both know that's 'bat' when we read it with the beginning and ending sounds you wrote."

At early stages, teachers don't worry if the child can't isolate and identify all the sounds. Children record what they know and it's celebrated. However, teachers know to be a little on guard during this routine scaffolding; some children try to get the teacher to do their work! When the teacher asked him what he heard with her sound segmenting, Josh responded, "What do *you* hear?" The teacher didn't fall for it. She answered, "It's your writing. Put down the letters for what *you* hear. I'll stretch the sounds again; I know you can do this."

Don't worry about vowels at this point. That comes later. Although they accurately place vowels in *automatic writing words* and copied words, children use vowels randomly in many words at this point—as placeholders between the sounds they confidently represent. Or, they confuse the short vowel sound heard when stretching the phonemes in the word with the name of another vowel. In this case, short /e/ ... /e/ ... /e/ begins to sound close to the name of letter *A*. The mouth is in a similar position. Other common substitutions related to short vowel sounds with the names of other letters include: short /i/ spelled with *E*, short /o/ spelled with *I*, and short /u/ spelled with *O* (Scanlon et al., 2010). Such spellings are not random; they reflect focused attention to segmented phonemes (sounds) and letter names; these are logical confusions.

automatic writing words words the child can write automatically without having to segment sounds and think of letter matches

placeholder object used to temporarily hold the place for another one (in this case a random vowel for the appropriate one)

In the kindergarten classrooms described in this chapter, teachers are usually able to read children's writing with consonant skeletons, a few automatic writing words, and pictures or context for support. Experience with young writers has honed their ability to decode these messages. However, there are times when they puzzle over a creative sound spelling. But, most often, there's a logical explanation from the child when he's asked about it.

As discussed, creating the motivation to engage, setting achievable challenges, allowing practice in a risk-free environment, and scaffolding at the point of need promotes literacy learning. Throughout the process, teachers observe, collect and analyze data, reflect, and plan future lessons. What children know, what they're able to do, and the extent of their literacy exploration are instructionally useful information for kindergarten teachers. In fact, it's more helpful than much of the typical data collected before kindergarten entry. Developmentally appropriate, authentic literacy tasks—ones that engage young children in reading and writing—provide kindergarten teachers with data for targeting instruction at the start of school.

Measuring Achievement: Teacher-created Assessments

Two tasks are proposed here as useful components in a school's pre-K screening procedures. Or, kindergarten teachers can use them at the beginning of the year to assess children's literacy knowledge. Both tasks provide valuable information with instructional utility. The tasks meet criteria of DAP and the first part of Morrow's (2009) suggestion that assessment include "observations of children engaged in authentic classroom reading and writing tasks and on more formal tests as well" (p. 43). The first task assesses the child's recall of story; the second stimulates a demonstration of the child's concepts about print, including its functions and forms.

In the reading-related task, the teacher greets the child with, "I'm going to read a story to you. When I finish, you can tell me what you remember—who was in the story, what happened, and why it happened." These are very short stories with simple plots. As the child independently retells the story, the teacher notes his *unassisted* retelling on the checklist.

retelling
relating the events or information absorbed from the reading (or listening event) as well as inferences, connections, and conclusions

To expand incomplete retelling, the teacher first asks, "Anything else?" When the teller appears finished, the teacher prompts by asking about unaddressed areas. If the child adds appropriate information, the teacher checks it off in the *assisted* retelling column. It's assisted because the expression wasn't self-initiated. When the child can't remember or retell, the teacher takes him back into the story to look at pictures and reread. If the child responds appropriately, the teacher makes a note in the *look back* column for that story element.

When children come to the writing station, the teacher invites them to use markers to write. Free writing is the first option. However, if that produces a blank stare and non-response, the teacher says, "Maybe, you want to help Harry." The teacher picks up a monkey puppet—the kind that wraps his limbs around you. She tells the child that Harry is Curious George's cousin. The teacher explains, "Harry told me he's tired of doing monkey tricks all day. He came here from the zoo to see what boys and girls do in school. He wants to tell his monkey friends all about it, but he's worried he'll forget. Can you tell him what they do and write it here (on a piece of paper)? And, put your name down too so he'll remember that it's from you."

Children usually write their name with confidence. Then, the teacher asks, "What should we tell Harry first. What do children do in school?" When this procedure was used in a school district (not one associated with classrooms visited), Stephanie responded, "Read books." "That's right," the teacher responded. "Of course! Write that down for Harry." Stephanie responded, "But I don't know how to write." The teacher assured her, "You can write it your way. He can read kid writing if you tell him what it says because he's just a little monkey." Stephanie wrote PHN. She added ITD for "eat lunch" and DOE for they "go when they hear a ring".

Most of these writing samples were like Stephanie's. But, a few children had no idea what the teacher meant by kid writing; some were reluctant to use it. When Joey didn't understand what kid writing meant, the

Name _____ date _____

Text read _____

Child predicted during story reading .... Yes ____ No ____

Child discussed illustrations during story reading .... Yes ____ No ____

Area	Unassisted retelling	Assisted retelling	Look back/ reread
Identified setting			
Identified main characters			
Identified the problem			
Described events to solve problem			
Described solution			
Retold story in correct sequence			
Described main character's reaction to the problem			
Made inferences and/or connections			

Level of comprehension: ____ Full and detailed

____ Partial, but satisfactory

____ Fragmented

Comments:

_____

FIGURE 7.4
Comprehension Checklist Kindergarten Screening

teacher used the suggestion offered by Ray (2004) for hesitant, inexperienced writers (Chapter 6). Joey visualized a writer, thinking about how writing is done.

"Joey, kid writing is like pretend writing. When you play fireman, you're pretending. You do the things you think a real fireman would do. Pretend writing is just like that. You can write however you think it goes; you're in charge of this pretending." A few writers incorporated automatically known words; some just scribbled. But, there's always an outlier!

One child in this district's pre-K screening assessment responded nonchalantly and confidently to the free writing option. Jeremy wrote, "The time I like is summer"—perfectly. He read back every word. The teacher invited him to write more and he did—using conventional spellings. Jeremy's reading was evaluated; he was also a reader—at lower levels!

The retelling and writing screening activities provide useful data—evidence of children's book experience, writing level, fine motor skills, and confidence. These two literacy stations are the only informal assessments in the district's pre-K screening procedure, but not the only measures used.

A third and fourth station used formal commercial measures—ones with scripts for directions and standardized scoring. These tests assessed children's gross motor skills and expressive/receptive language. The information was charted and shared with the kindergarten teachers. Not surprisingly, the teachers found that a combination of formal and informal measures was valuable.

standardized scoring
raw (actual) scores are
translated to standard
scores (i.e. percentiles,
stanines)

Although family circumstances and cultural factors impact the amount and nature of children's preschool literacy experiences, all children have acquired literacy knowledge in their home language (Laliberty & Berzins, 2000; Rubin & Carlan, 2005; Whitmore et al., 2005). Knowing what children bring allows teachers to start where they are in the process of decoding and encoding a message.

Encoding at the Word Level: Stages of Spelling Development

Skill in word construction grows gradually. Children who've had opportunities to experiment with print and use it functionally are more motivated to learn about its forms. Appreciative audiences stimulate young writers' interest in knowing more about the standard forms of writing. Children grow beyond the personal nature of kid writing that uses sound spelling and seek to make their ideas readable by conforming to a consistent code everyone understands. "Rather that mastering the parts (letters) first, children do just the opposite. They attend to the whole (written lines) first and much later to the parts" (Beaty, 2009, p. 59). Gentry and Gillet (1993) outline five stages of spelling development.

precommunicative stage
earliest stage of writing
characterized by scribbling,
shapes, forms, random
letters

The first stage in the Gentry and Gillet model for development in spelling is called the *precommunicative* stage, although it's more like an *early communicative* stage. The term "precommunicative" fails to recognize that even the most primitive scribble forms can have intention. Even when a message isn't apparent, the intention could have simply been to be recognized for the creation—communicating "look at what I made". Gentry and Gillet (1993) note that one of the first features that makes children's marking look like writing is its linearity or horizontal direction. Marking at this stage is characterized by:

- free-form, random-looking scribble;
- letter-like forms, random letters, and/or copied letters (as the child progresses);
- the repeated use of known letters or ones the child is able to write;
- indiscriminate inclusion of upper and lower case letters—usually the form that's easier to write. The use of upper case letters within sentences may continue as children move into the next stages. This is noted across the writing samples in this text;
- beginning attention to directional consistency (Schulze, 2006).

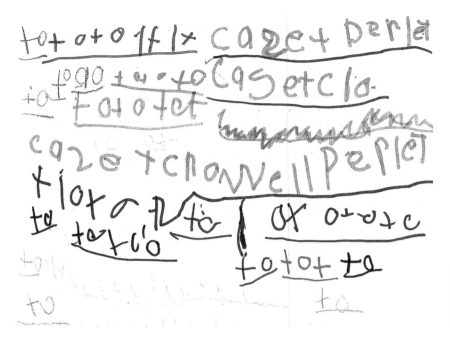

FIGURE 7.5
Random Letters,
Scribble, Copied
Letters

As children participate in interactive writing and transfer that learning to their own work, they begin to understand that writing is connected to the words said (or planned). Speech-to-print matching draws attention to words and, specifically, the sequential sounds (phonemes) that are heard as words are stretched. This takes years with very young children; kindergarteners may transition to the next stage in a few months. Bear, Invernizzi, Templeton, and Johnston, (2000) state, "The movement from this stage [precommunicative] to the next [semi-phonetic] hinges on learning the alphabetic principle; letters represent sounds and words can be segmented into sounds" (p. 18).

The *semi-phonetic* stage is characterized by a budding understanding of phonics. Children's writing reflects the associations they're beginning to make with the sounds they hear and the letters used to represent those sounds. Writing at the semi-phonetic stage:

semi-phonetic stage
the writer spells words with
one or two appropriate
letters for sounds heard

- is more readable with the contextual support of the writer's illustrations;
- often includes a few known words;
- uses an appropriate letter to spell the beginning sound of words—this is usually the most prominent sound;
- reflects emerging understanding of sound segmentation; more sounds (usually beginning and ending) in words are represented;
- shows awareness of standard directionality for the language;
- reflects confusion of letter names with sounds in words; children might write *u* when spelling *you*. One speller at this stage wrote *w* for the first sound in *dog*; he matched the /d/ heard at the beginning of *dog* with the /d/ heard when saying *w*. Even older struggling writers confuse letter names with letter sounds; a fifth grader spelled *was* as

yus. He heard the first sound of the letter name *y* when saying *was.* Although included in the semi-phonetic stage by Gentry and Gillet (1993), other researchers have isolated this characteristic as *letter name* stage (Bear et al., 2000);

■ is influenced by how sounds feel as they're produced in the mouth (Schulze, 2006). Children confuse letters that have similar tongue placement or mouth formation; writing jr for /dr/ is a common error.

Effective kindergarten teachers observe what children are doing, what they're using but confusing, and what they want to know. Based on conclusions, they plan what to emphasize when modeling sound matches and patterns that will move writers forward and increase their confidence, motivation, and production. All the practice with sound

FIGURE 7.6
I Was Going Slow

I was going slow.

segmenting that writing provides increases the likelihood that children will begin to wonder about how to represent more and more of the sounds they hear. This propels them to the next stage.

Children in the *phonetic* stage represent most (in long words) or all (in short words) of the sounds they hear in words. Writers at this stage:

- include letters to represent all (or most) of the sounds heard in the word;
- spell sounds in a fairly sequential manner;
- spell sounds heard (e.g. the *oa* in boat with *o*, the *kn* in knee with *n*, the *ph* in phone with *f*, or the *er* in player with *r*);
- attempt to spell medial sounds (e.g. vowels), letter combinations (e.g. consonant blends and digraphs), and multi-syllable words; and
- produce readable text.

phonetic stage
the writer spells most or all sounds in the word with letters that can represent the sounds

As writers at this stage progress, children begin to incorporate linguistic knowledge gained from immersion in and demonstrations with print; they begin to notice words and develop a mental image of the way words look in print. This is the beginning of visual strategies for spelling. Children notice patterns and linguistic structures in the language that do not hold true to the sounds of letters separately. For example, they notice that the past tense ending on verbs is spelled *ed* whether sounded as /d/, /t/, or /id/. As children incorporate this linguistic knowledge, they move into the next stage.

In the *transitional* stage, writers consider what they hear, what they understand about the meaning of a word or its parts, what they know about word patterns, and their memory of how a word looks in print. They are getting closer and closer to correct spelling; they're developing *spelling consciousness*, but their products aren't always conventional (correct or standard spelling). Spelling consciousness involves curiosity about the structure of words, knowledge of the language system (linguistic knowledge), awareness of social expectations for spelling, and a habit of consistently applying spelling knowledge (Shea & Murray, 2000). All this takes nurturing and practice to develop. Teachers talk through the thinking needed to revise spellings; they connect the revised word to other words that follow the same pattern. Spelling in English is such a complex process; there's a lot to learn. "English spelling requires attention to three overlapping aspects; knowledge of discrete letter sounds and the letters associated with these, knowledge of letter patterns and their corresponding pronunciation, and a visual memory for words" (Shea & Murray, 2000, p. 38). Writers at this stage:

transitional stage
writers spell with an awareness of silent letters, spelling patterns, and multiple spellings for specific sounds

spelling consciousness
curiosity about spelling, attention to word structure

- attempt to revise their spelling;
- use a vowel in every syllable;
- incorporate visual strategies with sound spelling;
- demonstrate an understanding of morphemic (meaning) units (e.g. prefix, suffix) and inflectional endings ('s, s, ing, er, est) in the language;

they add these to root words to modify word meaning and grammatical function; and

- use an increasing number of automatic writing words—words they know how to spell correctly without having to sound them out.

Bissex (1980) offers a notable example of the transitional stage in her son's writing. Paul spelled *makers* (people who make) in a way that overrode straight phonetics. Spelling by sounds, he would have written *makrz*. Instead, Paul applied knowledge of the morphemic system to spell *makeer's*. He understood that /r/ in this case was spelled *er*, meaning one who makes, just as work*er* means one who works. He didn't realize a

FIGURE 7.7
How to Climb a Tree

need to drop *e* from the base word before adding *er*. Paul heard /z/, but knew that the sound is spelled with *s* to mean more than one. And, once children learn about apostrophes, they're inserted for good measure everywhere! Paul's transitional spelling reveals an expanding awareness of principles of English orthography.

Instruction at this stage is focused on the *spelling demons* that children appear to have. What words or word patterns trip them up? What are they trying to use, but continually confuse? Teachers develop a class *core word list* that includes HF words, common demons (most confused words) and individual demons (Routman, 2000).

spelling demons
words that present difficulty when trying to spell them

The last stage is *conventional*. Conventional spelling is relative to a writer's developmental level. Writers at this stage correctly spell most of the words they use. But, a five-year-old at the conventional stage cannot spell what conventional stage spellers at 15 years old or 25 years old can

FIGURE 7.8
Rachel's Thank-you

spell; it's developmental. As the writer expands ideas with more sophisticated words and sentence structures, knowledge demands increase for spelling. Children need to be supported as risk takers; teachers encourage them to improve their message with interesting word choices.

Position *conventional* as the place we want our writing to be after it's edited. That honors attention to multiple elements of style—message quality, spelling consciousness, and the perseverance to make one's work ready for an audience of readers.

At this stage:

- help writers to notice unusual and interesting words when reading. This builds meaning vocabulary and visual memory of particular words and word patterns;
- develop children's proficiency with a pictionary (containing scenes with labels for individual items) for word selection and spelling;
- teach skills and strategies for efficient proofreading and editing;
- encourage writers to use wonderful words rather than safe ones; they'll be able to edit their work; and
- focus on increasing children's repertoire of automatic writing words.

As noted in Chapter 6, some pre-K writers moved toward these spelling stages when encoding messages. Spelling that approaches semi-phonetic and phonetic stages is more the exception than the norm in pre-K. What creates such exceptions? The classrooms described in Chapter 6 provided daily modeling and scaffolded support in writing. The youngest writers in these settings had time to write on topics they knew and cared about; they were allowed to grow at their own rate. Figure 7.9 reflects an analysis of pre-K writing samples that reflected the Gentry and Gillett (1993) spelling stages. It's placed in this chapter where the spelling stages are outlined.

A Caveat on Conventions

There's an important caveat to mention here. Too much emphasis on spelling correctness negatively impacts message quality and fluency in writing (Larson, 2002). Although conventions are important, and children do need to learn about them, conventions need to be put in their "proper place" (Temple et al., 2008, p. 284) in the curriculum for instruction to be relevant. Young writers who've had an opportunity to record messages and stories—to explore functions of language for their own purposes—appreciate the need for conventions, have a basis for attaching meaning to the information, and recognize personal relevance for the knowing how to construct readable print (Temple et al., 2008). Morrow (1989) notes that, "Problems arise when the developmental, social, and natural environments in which literacy flourishes are exchanged for a systematic presentation of skills that do not reflect a child's stage of development socially, emotionally, physically, or intellectually" (p. 15).

Writer's Name	Sample's Title	Grade	Pre-communicative	Semi-phonetic	Phonetic	Transitional	Conventional
Madison	Monkey	Pre-K			X		
Max	Sinking	Pre-K			X		
Nicholas	Dog	Pre-K			X		
	Mountains				X		X
Andrew	Family	Pre-K			X		
	Cookie				X		
Chase	Rock	Pre-K			X		X
Emily	Moons	Pre-K			X		
	Princess				X		X
	Flower				X		X
Julia	Boat	Pre-K			X		X
	Garden				X		X
	World				X		X
Liam	Penguins	Pre-K			X		
	Bouncing				X		
Adam	Silly	Pre-K			X		X
Joseph	Thankful	Pre-K			X		
	Tracks				X		

FIGURE 7.9 Overall Stage of Spelling Development Represented in the Pre-K Samples

There's more sense than nonsense in English spelling (Scott, 1993). Developing young writers' curiosity about words with a *spirit of inquiry* (Schulze, 2006) makes spelling a puzzle- or problem-solving process—one that's engaging and lifelong! As children in kindergarten classrooms read and write together in ways that are meaningful to them, they learn about the language systems and grow in their ability to express ideas with voice, clarity, and increasing accuracy—even when that expression is simple. When writers worry about taking risks or fear venturing beyond what they know, they need sensitive scaffolding from parents and teachers.

Ask students if you can use their writing to show wonderful spelling attempts that are close, but not correct. Showing the intricacies of literacy is a tenet of effective instruction and far more powerful that merely talking about it (Weaver, 1998). It also gives the child who shares time to shine. All writers are transitional with words infrequently used—ones with complex letter patterns, and words with unexpected letter combinations based on their derivation. Movement to the final stage is a lifelong journey that begins in the early years.

Observations of Writing in an Urban Kindergarten Classroom

Children write right from the start in kindergarten classrooms (English and bilingual) in an inner city northeastern state. Here too, there are wide differences in children's background experience and prior literacy opportunities. Writing samples available at the companion website reflect the range of development across message and spelling stages.

Word-for-word transcriptions (scripts) for English samples are included on the website. Approximation translations are embedded in the description for the bilingual samples. Descriptions for all samples are on the website and some excerpts appear in Figure 7.10. Each sample described has been analyzed for stage level (Schulze, 2006) and spelling development (Gentry & Gillet, 1993) (Figures 7.11 and 7.12).

English Samples

Angela

Early in the school year, Angela writes a simple sentence to accompany her leaf tracing technique. She correctly writes high frequency words (the, is) and very likely effectively used words displayed in the room (leaf, yellow). She uses a period at the end of the sentence. In October, she relates what she knows about the farm. She uses words provided in class discussion to carefully construct sentences that end with a period. She has reversals of h and s in her writing. The illustrations are detailed; they add content to the message. Angela expresses what she is thankful for with her completion of a sentence prompt and ends her sentence with a floating period. Her Winter Time book reflects that she is venturing beyond words provided and experimentation with sound spelling. She uses a period at the end of the first sentence; she begins the last sentence with a capital letter—perhaps unintentionally. Capital letters (B and D) are used inappropriately; a strategy often used by children who confuse b and d. Angels identifies a discriminatory practice that Martin Luther King worked hard to change. "All people can sit anywhere on the bus." She uses sounds to phonetically spell people (pepl) and anywhere (in war), although she breaks anywhere into two words. Again, she reverses the letter s. In her book on spiders she reports facts known. She punctuates sentences with periods; she sometimes reverses her s, but also writes them correctly. In June, Angela describes what she likes at the beach. She spells most words correctly and phonetically spells cream, boat, and watermelon. She uses punctuation on one page; there's a period at the end of a line rather than at the end of the sentence.

Carmen

All words in Carmen's book, Day and Night, are spelled correctly. She uses periods to end each sentence—one per page. Carmen doesn't uses spaces between words.

Bilingual Samples

Note: In some cases, a best translation to English has been determined based on the writer's use of words. However, word choice may be representative of local usage. Forms may relate to syntactic changes of base words. Translations were accomplished with the assistance of a translator as well as an online Spanish/English dictionary (www.spanishdict.com).

**FIGURE 7.10
Description of Urban Kindergarten Writing Samples**

Carlos

In November, Carlos explained how his family celebrated Thanksgiving with an illustration and a random string of letters—Mommy cooked rice and turkey. By March, he has created a readable message that consists of a full sentence; Carlos offers a logical conclusion—The bats go out at night. In the illustration, he accents letters in his spelling murclelago (for murcielagos), but not in his sentence. He hears /k/ and spells casa with a k at the beginning. He writes salen for salir (go out); he writes dei, presumably for de (at; of). He also uses k for the beginning of canguro and for the second /k/ sound hocico in his drawing and labeling of a kangaroo (April sample). He may have seen the English spelling of kangaroo and has incorporated that beginning. In May, Carlos constructs a readable sentence; it's confusing with the illustration—I help my dad wash the baby. He writes guagua (baby) with backwards g in each place, but I expected it would say wash the car. He's inserted a y in ayudo to revise his spelling. Carlos places an accent in papa. In June, his full sentence with a period explains his detailed drawing—I like to jump into my swimming pool.

Nayshira

In February, Nayshira works on expressing facts learned on a topic. She writes, "A cow gives milk. A cow gives us meat." Nayshira spelled carne (meat) as kare. She writes, "I [am] sad (riste for triste) here (esta). Here. Mommy has (tenia for tiene) two books." It seems each sibling got a book and she didn't. In her response to *Happy Birthday Martin Luther King* (March) she writes, "Everybody goes to the same school." She spells todos (everybody) as todo, mismo (same) as misma, and escuela (school) as eskesla—again using k for the /k/ sound. In May, Nayshira explains how music makes her feel. "I feel happy." She has both yo and me for I; she writes senta for se siente (feels) and felis for feliz (happy).

FIGURE 7.10
Continued

English Samples (Schulze, 2006)

Name	Title	Grade	Drawing	Drawing With Caption/ Extended Caption—C/EC	Listing Information	Listing With Description	Incorporating the Features and Structures of Texts
Angela	Leaf	K	X				X—sentence expressing complete idea about the drawing
	The Farm	K	X		X—fact sentence for each page		X—created a book
	Thankful	K	X				X—sentence expressing complete idea about the drawing
	Winter Time	K	X		X—sentence for each page		X—created a book
	Response to HB Martin LK	K	X				X—sentence expressing complete idea about the drawing
	Spiders	K	X		X—fact sentence for each page		X—created a book *Continued overleaf*

FIGURE 7.11 Assessment of Message in Urban Kindergarten Writing Samples

Name	Title	Grade	Drawing	Drawing With Caption/ Extended Caption—C/EC	Listing Information	Listing With Description	Incorporating the Features and Structures of Texts
	At the Beach	K	X		X—sentence for each page		X—created a book
Carmen	Day and Night	K	X				X—created a book

Bilingual Samples (Schulze, 2006)

Name	Title	Grade	Drawing	Drawing With Caption/ Extended Caption—C/EC	Listing Information (personal, opinion, or fact)	Listing With Description (elaboration)	Incorporating the Features and Structures of Texts
Carlos	Thanks-giving	K	X				X—random letters to express idea
	Bats	K	X				X—sentence expressing complete idea about the drawing
	Kangaroo	K	X	X—labels			
	Helping Papa	K	X				X—sentence expressing complete idea about the drawing
	Swimming Pool	K	X				X—sentence expressing complete idea about the drawing
Nayshira	A Cow	K	X		X—listing facts		
	Martin Luther	K	X				X—sentence expressing complete idea about the drawing
	Music						X—sentence expressing complete idea about the drawing

FIGURE 7.11 *Continued*

English Samples

Writer's Name	Sample's Title	Grade	Pre-communicative	Semi-phonetic	Phonetic	Transitional	Conventional
Angela	Leaf	K					X
	The Farm	K					X
	Thankful	K					X
	Winter Time	K		X (thrao for throw, bos for balls)	X (sno, war for wear)		
	Response to HB Martin Luther King	K			X (pepl, iny war)		X (HF words—all, can, sit, on, the, bus)
	Spiders	K					X
	At the Beach	K			X (bowt, watrmelin, crème)		X
Carmen	Day and Night	K					X

FIGURE 7.12 Overall Stage of Spelling Development Represented in the Urban Kindergarten Writing Samples

Bilingual Samples

Note: In some cases, a best translation to English has been determined based on the writer's use of words. However, word choice may be representative of local usage. Translations were accomplished with the assistance of a translator as well as an online Spanish/English dictionary (www.spanishdict.com).

Writer's Name	Sample's Title	Grade	Pre-communicative	Semi-phonetic	Phonetic	Transitional	Conventional
Carlos	Thanksgiving	K	X (random letters)				
	Bats (Response to Literature)	K			X		
	Kangaroo	K			X		
	Helping Papa	K				X	
	Swimming Pool	K					X
Nayshira	A Cow	K				X	
	Martin Luther	K			X		
	Music				X		

FIGURE 7.12 *Continued*

Many children at this school have not attended a pre-K; kindergarten is their first school experience. Two of the classrooms are bilingual classes. Children are grouped for instruction; they change classrooms to work with peers with a similar level of English proficiency. Wall print in the bilingual classrooms is mostly Spanish; children write in Spanish. Of course, their "writing" begins with the full range of random marks that require translation for others to understand—from scribble, to letter-like forms and random letters (Figures 7.13–7.16).

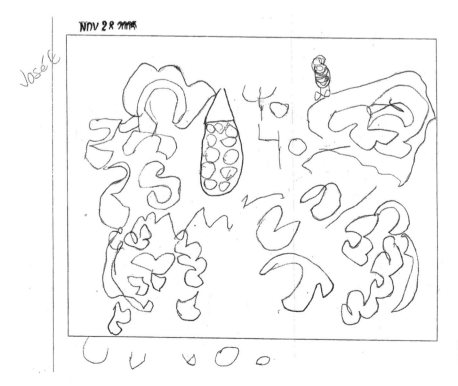

FIGURE 7.13
Letter-like Forms

FIGURE 7.14
Scribble, Letter-like Forms, Random Letters

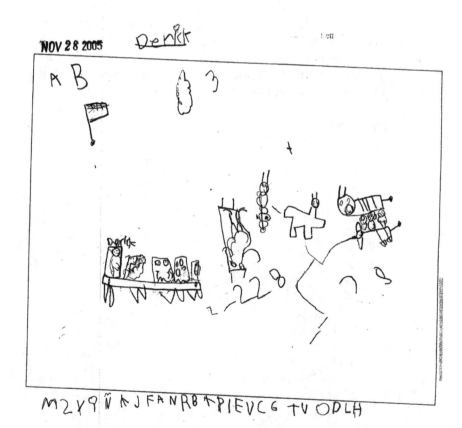

FIGURE 7.15
Random Letters

FIGURE 7.16
Readable Sound
Spelling

Although the answer appears to be spelled with random letters, Joshua begins his response with words from a prompt, "What do you like to play?" He writes, "I like (gusta) to play (jugar)" (Figure 7.17).

Children's writing in these classrooms follows the Sulzby (1990) stages previously discussed. Grand conversations (in both Spanish and English) are characteristic in these classrooms—conversation that's centered on responding to story, morning business (attendance and lunch count), sharing personal news, singing, talking about letters-sounds-words, playing together, and working together on projects. Literacy instruction is seamlessly embedded within thematic studies; there are multiple moments of soft teaching as children go about the business of learning. Writing is connected to content as children use it to respond to literature and construct informational books connected to theme studies in the classroom. Nayshira records her scientific observations in a journal entry; she's observed five big ones (caterpillars) and reports that, "The caterpillars are climbing" (Figure 7.18).

FIGURE 7.17
Joshua Likes . . .

Observations of Kindergarten Writing in a Rural Northwest Community

Armed with ideas from multiple sources and aided by expert guides (i.e. resource teachers, conference speakers) for bringing writing, drawing, and conversation into primary classrooms, two teachers in a rural northwest community provide their kindergarten authors with a highly productive writers' workshop environment. They've examined a wide range of research and programs associated with the topic and have synthesized core beliefs that guide their practice. Writing is a daily event in these classrooms—one that occurs in the workshop as well as across content areas.

Every workshop session includes a mini lesson; these are based on identified needs or a determination that children are ready to be nudged forward—forward to a new writing concept, format, or purpose. Brief lessons revolve around procedures, strategies, organization, skills, or writing craftsmanship (Figure 7.19).

These kindergartners are marinated in quality literature in the form of picture books that inform, tell stories, and create images. Exemplary literature inspires them and presents possibilities. Children write using the range of genres that they have enjoyed as models.

The teachers also model by writing to and with children across the day, emphasizing the importance of writing as a tool for thinking, learning, responding, and sharing ideas. Children collaborate as writers

FIGURE 7.18
Recording
Observations

- ■ Procedures (Where do we get materials? Where can we work?)
- ■ Strategies (How do I decide on a topic or what to tell? How do I add information?)
- ■ Organization (What goes on each page? How should I illustrate my message?)
- ■ Skills (How do I spell words? Which punctuation do I need? What do I do when I edit?)
- ■ Qualities of good writing (What interesting words did the author use? What structure did the author use to share his message?)

FIGURE 7.19
Categories for Mini
Lessons

and learners; they ask each other for help, talk about their work in progress, and present final versions. Through their efforts, children build an appreciation of the functions and forms of writing. Empowered to make decisions about content and format, these kindergartners are highly motivated to problem-solve their way through the process of encoding a readable message. There's also evidence of spelling stage development (Gentry & Gillet, 1993) in their writing (see the companion website for full examples). Writing samples from all the kindergarten classrooms are available at the website, along with word-for-word transcriptions and descriptions. When particular children in these kindergarten classrooms have difficulty getting started with writing, teachers scaffold them sensitively and strategically into authorship.

A Scaffolding Process for Writing

protocol
set of rules (established plan) for carrying out an action

materialization
using a concrete object and physical action to guide the learning of a concept

inner speech
silent or softly spoken self-talk used to guide one's performance of a task

distinctive features
the characteristics of a word that help the child distinguish it and remember how to construct it

Bodrova and Leong (1998) outline a protocol for *Scaffolded Writing*—a temporary support for reluctant or overwhelmed emergent writers that combines materialization, inner speech, and sound segmenting skills. Of course, extensive teacher modeling precedes the introduction of this approach. Bodrova and Leong's (1998) scaffolding process for emergent writing is based on Vygotskian theory of ZPD. The protocol utilizes the two components of *materialization* and *inner speech*. The slide viewer or word window that allows children to isolate a single word is an example. The child adjusts the slide to show a designated word in the window; he analyzes the word for *distinctive features* (Kibby, 1989) that will help him remember it when reading and writing (directions of how to make this can be found on the companion website). Children can also *frame* a word with their fingers; this works well with large print on charts (Figure 7.20).

FIGURE 7.20
Making a Word Frame

Materialization must be accompanied by the child's inner speech that provides rehearsal, direction, and guidance through the task (Galperin, 1992). The speech is often subvocalized (spoken softly). Inner speech and materialization fade once the skill is internalized. Both components draw children's attention to the discrete, sequenced sounds in words. However, some children may need a separate scaffold for segmenting, sequencing, and representing sounds in words. Teachers use *Elkonin boxes* to problem-solve how to spell particular words.

Elkonin's (1963) research showed that children who used sound boxes for identifying phonemes in a word scored higher on measures of meta-linguistic awareness. For example, the strip of three boxes is set out for words with three phonemes. The child moves a penny into a box for each phoneme spoken as the word is articulated (Figure 7.21). Then, he thinks of the letter(s) needed to spell each sound.

Phonemic Awareness — Identifying Sounds in Words

Elkonin boxes for word with **three** phonemes

Target word: cat:

The child moves a penny into the first box as he says /c/. He moves a penny into the next box as he says /a/. Finally, he moves a penny into the third box as he says /t/.

Target word: boat

The child moves a penny into the first box as he says /b/. He moves a penny into the next box as he says /o/. Finally, he moves a penny into the third box as he says /t/. (Let go of the letters! At this point, the child is *matching sounds* to boxes — *not* letters.)

Later, when letters are introduced, the child learns that the medial sound /o/ in boat is spelled with two letters.

| b | oa | t |

FIGURE 7.21 Phonemic Awareness— Identifying Sounds in Words

The teacher models how to use lines on the page that have been high-lighted with color. In demonstrations, she uses various strategies for word construction. These include listening for sounds and representing them with appropriate letters, using known letter patterns, spelling automatic writing words (such as "the" and "of"), and using resources in the room (for example, word wall, charts, books, and signs). She also models—by thinking out loud—how inner speech guides her through the task. With this preparation in place, the teacher initiates Scaffolded Writing step by step.

1. The writer verbalizes his message. The teacher repeats the message to confirm what was said; she may help the writer refine or simplify the statement.
2. The teacher and writer repeat the message together as the teacher makes a highlighted line on the paper for each word. This may be

done before or after the child illustrates. However, drawing first often helps the writer gather and organize ideas.

3. The child is given the paper with highlighted lines. He constructs the message by writing a word on each line. As he writes, the child repeats the message; he verbalizes plans, uses strategies, and problem-solves throughout the process. (He uses Elkonin boxes on scrap paper to problem-solve tricky words.)

4. The procedure is repeated as the message increases in length.

Some Scaffolded Writing interventions are individualized while others are planned as mini lessons for small groups or the class. Effective topics for mini lessons are determined from an analysis of children's reading and writing performances; they make use of teachable moments that target immediate needs.

Mini Lessons: Small Bites for Big Learning

There are many, mini lessons in the kindergarten classrooms visited (see Figure 7.22 for examples). Some are for the whole class; they're presented at the beginning of the writing session. Others are for a small group or an individual; they can occur at any time during the day. These are better described as a brief conversation between teacher and learner(s) during which the teacher clarifies a point of knowledge. One teacher calls them her "FYIs". These are powerful teaching moments because they're targeted and limited to what the learner needs to know.

The teacher tells the children, "FYI are letters that stand for the words *for your information*. People say FYI when they want you to know that the information might be important; it means—here's a little something you need to know." The teacher uses FYIs to share small bits of knowledge that children need right away. For example, she might call a group together to remind children when and how to use particular punctuation forms. Or, someone may need to be reminded about where to use capital letters; they have a place and purpose.

Such lessons evolve from observations of what children are doing—particularly what they're using, but confusing. They're not derived from programs with scripts, worksheets, and arbitrary benchmarks. Children respond because they recognize the immediate relevance of the information. FYIs are shared throughout the day—across the range of classroom interactions. The topics for FYIs are the same as those for mini lessons.

Procedural FYIs are always very important in the beginning of the year; they establish the protocols for behavior and expectations for productivity. The kindergarten teachers visited take time to make classroom protocols clear and habit forming. Procedures are also reintroduced whenever children forget the dos and don'ts associated with independent writing time. Good intentions have a way of slipping sometimes! But, they're easily righted when the groundwork is solid. Skill and strategy FYIs cover a wide range of options, but the choice of what to teach is always based on assessment. For example, when children are having difficulty leaving spaces between words, teachers provide a strategy FYI; they emphasize *wordness* and spacing during Shared Reading and collaborative writing (e.g. the News, class charts). Mrs. Linden (teacher in the private urban pre-K described in Chapter 6) shows children how to use Mr. Spaceman (Figure 6.3)—a Popsicle stick with a face at one end. The writer sets the stick at the end of a finished word and begins the next word right after the stick.

Another strategy that an FYI might address is how to find words you need in various resources in the room (i.e. on a chart, in a book, on the wall, or on a previous journal page). The teachers want children to realize that their fellow writers are resources too; children can also ask a friend

wordness
characteristics (i.e. spaces between) that define separate words in print messages

---

Procedural Mini Lessons
1. What we do during writing time
2. Where we work; how we work
3. How we organize materials
4. Where we get help when it's needed
5. How we help each other

Strategy Mini Lessons
1. How writers show with words (e.g. *The blowing snow hurt my face*)
2. How we decide on a topic and what to tell
3. How information can be added, deleted, or rearranged in the draft
4. Finding words needed in the room (e.g. on charts, in books); asking classmates for help
5. How to read your writing
6. How we illustrate—matching pictures to text; choosing medium; where to place illustration for best effect

Organization Mini Lessons
1. How kinds of writing are structured (e.g. story, information, poetry)
2. How much should go on a page
3. Where to put print on page; where to illustrate
4. Using word balloons, charts, maps, etc. for information
5. How to order pages (e.g. title page, dedication, table of contents)

Mini Lesson on a Skill
1. Spelling by sound—as much as you can; spell the best you can
2. How to form letters
3. Spacing words
4. When to use capital letters
5. Where to use punctuation

Qualities of Good Writing Mini Lessons
1. Pointing out effective *leads* (opening) in read-aloud texts
2. Drawing attention to lovely language in read-aloud texts
3. Noticing structures in read-aloud texts
4. Examining good endings in read-aloud texts
5. Discussing what appeals in favorite poems, stories, or informational books

FIGURE 7.22
Topics for Mini Lessons

for help. To casually model how a friend can assist, teachers stage such a request while team teaching. One teacher shared examples of how she's done that.

During independent writing time, the teacher asked her colleague in a voice that all could hear, "Mrs. Blake how do you spell 'cat'? I need that word right here in my story." Mrs. Blake responded, "Mmmm. I better stretch it. /c/ ... /a/ ... /t/ . It sounds like *c* for /c/, *a* for /a/, and *t* for /t/." Another day, the teacher asked her colleague for a word, creating a demonstration on using resources in the room.

She said, "Mrs. Blake how do you spell 'night'?" Mrs. Blake responded, "I know. One handprint on the wall has the word right on it. Let's check it. There's r-i-g-h-t. Maybe, 'night' is like 'right.' Just change the first letter; take off the *r* and put *n*." Such demonstrations arrived at accurate spellings, but the emphasis was more on the process.

Another teacher shared a story about Tommy, a child in her class who had difficulty articulating certain words. This was not one of the kindergarten teachers described in this chapter, but the story is important here. It reflects the power of writers helping each other; it could happen anywhere when the writing community is a supportive one. Tommy realized that his spellings reflected the way he said pesky words, but were more conventional when he matched how someone else said them. Tommy also knew that his teacher approved of asking a friend for help. Whenever he had to write a tricky word, he'd ask a tablemate, "Billy, please say 'wabbit' for me. And, say it vawe slow. (Pause as he starts to write, then stops) Say it again; stwetch it this time—weally long. (Pause while he finishes the word) Thanks." His peers always assisted as requested with casual grace and sensitivity since that was the tone in the classroom.

Teachers in the classrooms visited remind children, "If you get the sounds down for a word, we'll be able to read it back even when some letters are missing. Fixing up words here and there is a job that comes at the end of writing and all writers need to do that." They add, "As we learn more about sounds and letters that go together, you'll be able to spell more and more words." Sometimes a child provides a strategy FYI, explaining how he figured out the spelling for a word. Literary FYIs can be incorporated into story reading as well as writing time.

When responding to texts, these kindergarten teachers include discussion of author's (and illustrator's) craft (style)—how the author expressed ideas (story or expository), interesting words he used, or the medium and content of his illustrations. The teachers think aloud (verbalize) how one might incorporate similar styles when writing. They keep it simple—centered on one big idea from the selection that would be possible to emulate. The grist for literary FYIs can also come right from children's work. This is wonderful when it happens. The writer has a moment in the sunshine; the model is always age appropriate.

When Jamie wrote about fishing with Grandpa, his teacher had him share his sentence with the class. Jamie read, "We woke up fish with our bait." Children talked about how his sentence created a picture in their mind and made them want to know more—Why? When? How? What's bait? They noticed how his picture offers more information. Children's repertoire of what to say and how to say it grows exponentially with quality input and demonstrations as well as lots of time for supported practice. Jamie was exposed to a wide range of wonderful literature and had lots of time to engage with it. Jamie's teacher realized the importance of a well-supplied classroom library where children have easy access to books. The content of Jamie's reading was reflected in his experimentation with writing style and word choice.

Multi Genre Read-alouds

Morrow (2009) suggests about five to eight books per child in a classroom library. These include both narrative and expository selections with three to four levels of difficulty. Too often, book collections in primary classrooms are primarily narrative. Moss, Leone, and Dipillo (1997) conclude that nonfiction should comprise one-third to one-half of the total number of books in the collection. To ensure engagement with books in the classroom, teachers introduce them, read them, discuss the content and authors with children, re-circulate old favorites, and prominently display them. Morrow (2009) recommends, "Approximately 25 new books should be introduced every two weeks, replacing 25 that have been there for a while. In this way, 'old' books will be greeted as new friends a few months later" (p. 291). Although some contend that the number is too high, Moustafa (1997) concludes that a primary classroom should stock 1,500 books for reading aloud and independent reading. That number may be excessive, but any classroom that intends to foster independent reading, must be well-stocked with a variety of high-interest books that are easily accessed by children (Fields et al., 2008). Children become better readers when books that engage them in reading are readily available (Neuman & Celano, 2001).

An abundant supply of books is obvious in the kindergarten classrooms visited. Books are tasted, savored, and repeated; they're accessible to children—to enjoy and use. In the bilingual urban kindergarten, the teacher skillfully translated into Spanish the English version of a picture book as she read. It was amazing; she didn't miss a beat! The children saw the illustrations and heard the text in their first language. Books of all genres were shared in this way.

An inviting book nook draws children in at free time as well as independent reading time in these classrooms. Books are selected for the opportunities they offer for building children's meaning vocabulary (especially *tier two* and *tier three* words), background knowledge, and interest in reading.

Tier one words are the most common, high frequency words in the language. Most children are fluent with these. Tier two words are more descriptive ones appropriately used by some children (such as shrieked, enormous, flap); they have usually heard and used them in their speech. Such words are in the child's meaning vocabulary—words that have been in her ears and on her lips (Beck, McKeown, & Kucan, 2002). Children

tier one words
basic, easy words most children understand and use in speech

tier two words
more sophisticated words that some children understand and use in speech

tier three words
words associated with a specific domain, content, or topic

with large meaning vocabularies are able to articulately express their ideas, using precise and appropriate words. Hart and Risely (2003) found a significant difference in vocabulary for children starting school. Those from lower SES homes typically had a much smaller repertoire of meaning vocabulary and delayed expressive language skills (Hart & Risely, 2003).

Tier three words are content-specific words that build background knowledge related to a topic of study (such as hibernation, temperature, evaporate). These are typically new words for most children, although the child who's amassed a large body of knowledge on a topic will know tier three words related to it. Reading aloud followed by grand conversations expands both tier two and tier three words for all listeners (Beck et al., 2002). Soon the most memorable and useful words find their way into children's writing.

Moving Forward

First grade teachers can immediately distinguish the literacy advanced from the literacy novices—and those somewhere in between. The curricular focus of children's kindergarten classroom is clearly reflected in their familiarity with the content of and protocol for literacy-related activities. The range of development in any first grade is typically very broad in the beginning of the year, but narrows when children are provided rich opportunities to grow and lots of sensitive support. The next chapter describes writing in first grade classrooms where children continue to write for all the authentic reasons literate people do. First grade writers also begin to *process* some of their writing—refine it for publication. The steps for processed writing are also described in the next chapter.

Extending the Discussion

■ Examine the kindergarten writing samples available at the companion website with colleagues or course members. Partner up to examine all samples from a particular child. Be prepared to discuss this child's development with the group.

■ Collect writing samples from a local kindergarten or your own classroom. Discuss each with colleagues. Determine where these writers fall on the continuum. What would you recommend for scaffolding these learners—nudging them forward?

■ Visit a kindergarten where creative writing is done every day or consider the sequence of activities in your own writing kindergarten classroom. What protocols are followed? How does the teacher scaffold writers? Describe children's level of enthusiasm, confidence, and purpose when writing.

■ Design a possible mini lesson for the kindergarten classroom you visited or for your own kindergarten classroom. Explain why you planned this lesson. Ask for reactions, comments, and suggestions.

eight
Writing in
First Grade

Big Ideas in Chapter 8

- A curricular emphasis on writing
- Small city grade 1 classroom
- Urban charter school grade 1 classroom
- Research-based practices for writing
- Writers' workshop approach in grade 1
- Managing the workshop beyond the first publication
- Assessment during writers' workshop

A Curricular Emphasis on Writing

Writing continues to flourish in first grade classrooms that exemplify the basic tenets for effective teaching discussed in previous chapters. It becomes progressively sophisticated in message quality, length, and use of conventions as writers practice the craft. But, it's important to remember that first grade writers aren't expected to be at the end of the writing journey in June. Learning to compose is a lifelong process.

There's no rigid timeline or sequenced exposure to skills in effective writing classrooms. In such settings, learning to write is a continuous process of refining the sophistication (e.g. clarity, word use, voice, style) of one's message. Basic skills used to encode a three-word, readable sentence are used to construct a longer message. Children absorb information, ask questions, and experiment when they're cognitively and emotionally ready.

In the exemplary first grade classrooms visited, writing occurs during workshop time as well as across the day as children use writing to think, reflect, and respond to learning. Written responses provide teachers with

continuum
something that is absolutely continuous

assessment data on children's knowledge of subject matter as well as their ability to express what they've learned. Thinking of development along a continuum is more helpful. The stage levels presented and described in earlier chapters provide a guide for understanding each writer's achievement. Children's place on the continuum at the beginning of first grade depends on the literacy experiences they've had beforehand. It would be wonderful if all children started first grade with the skills demonstrated by the pre-K and kindergarten writers described in this text. However, when they don't, effective grade 1 teachers find that an infusion of all the principles for fostering literacy interest, motivation to engage in reading and writing, and concepts described in previous chapters cause these children to quickly catch on and catch up to peers that enter grade 1 with more literacy competence (Rasinski & Padak, 2004).

Early writing also supports formal instruction in reading sub-skills universally included in first grade language arts curriculum. Writers practice phonemic segmentation (separating and ordering sounds in a word) and phonics (spelling sounds in a word with appropriate letters). They reread what they've written and decide if it makes sense; they read the writing of peers, discuss its content, and ask the writer questions. As previously described, similar cognitive processes are involved in writing and reading. Writers are practicing linguistic skills used in reading; they're reading text.

You can read without writing, but you can't compose without reading. Murray (1980, 1982) suggests that writers are continuously integrating several activities—collecting, connecting, writing, and reading—as they work. The writer collects ideas (from within or external sources) for a composition; he attempts to connect (organize) the information for a clear and coherent reporting. Then, he writes a phrase—or more. He reads what's written to evaluate how it flows from what precedes it or advances what will come next. Even the youngest writers can identify such acts of reading.

Bissex (1980) reported that her son Paul commented that, when he could write a word, he could read it; that was an empowering realization of competence. When young children recognize that their writing communicates, they *read* it. First grade curriculum that reflects a balanced approach includes instruction and practice in all language processes. Fitting everything into a tight schedule requires out-of-the-box thinking. The example that follows demonstrates such thinking. The teacher solved a dilemma in a creative way that resulted in increased literacy achievement, rich assessment data on children's writing, and opportunities for community building.

Teatime in Print

Colleagues did not envy this teacher's schedule for special classes (e.g. physical education, art, and music); it wasn't optimal. She and the children had a half hour in the morning to get outside gear (coats, boots), backpacks, and lunch pails put away and conduct opening business. Naturally, children wanted to talk as the teacher welcomed them into the room; they tried to share anecdotes about their life outside of school since leaving the day before. The teacher was definitely rushing these community-building interactions in order to get on with necessary tasks. The daily announcements required attention, the office needed attendance information, the cafeteria wanted a lunch count, and the special class teacher expected the class to arrive promptly. Serendipitously, one day the class read an article in their *Weekly Reader* about the practice of daily teatime. The teacher explained that this activity involved getting together with friends and family in late afternoon for tea, light snacks, and, most importantly, conversation. An idea inspired by the article struck her that evening. The next day the teacher shared her vision for how the class could solve their start of the day dilemma; they could connect with conversations in print. The teacher gave each child a small notebook labeled "Teatime Book". She suggested that whatever they wanted to tell her that morning could be recorded in their book. If they wanted the teacher to read it, they left it open on their desk during special class. The teacher read what they wrote and responded briefly while the children were away. The children loved the idea; their enthusiasm never faded.

Immediately, they dove into their teatime books each morning; they used the teacher's responses as models for structure and spellings. Children talked to their peers and shared what they'd written, allowing the teacher to efficiently complete opening tasks. This teatime paid huge dividends. When the children returned to the classroom, you couldn't hear a pin drop as they poured over every word in the teacher's response and discussed what she had said with a tablemate. This dialog in print built strong bonds, created authentic literacy practice, became a rich source of assessment data for instruction, and allowed targeted modeling. As the teacher reflected on a child's message, she learned about the child's interests, concerns, and experiences. She also identified what the child needed to learn about writing. Many other teachers use dialog journals with similar results.

A first grade teacher (not in a classroom described in this chapter), recently shared examples from dialog journals she keeps with her class (Figures 8.1 and 8.2). Children write in the "You" column and she responds in the "Me" column. Mickey and John reported on how pleased they were with classroom activities. Mickey says, "I like you for doing centers." John asked, "Remember when we talked about animals? That was fun." Getting such feedback is really important; it doesn't matter how engaging and appropriate we believe an activity to be. What matters is how children perceive its relevance.

Children's perspectives can inform us, revealing what's working for them—and what isn't. Writing classrooms create safe outlets for sharing opinions, knowledge, and personal information.

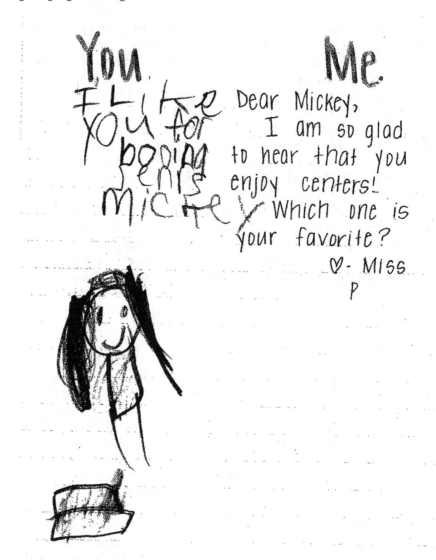

FIGURE 8.1
Mickey's Journal

Common Threads in Exemplary Writing Classrooms

Writing samples from the two first grade classrooms visited similarly demonstrate how children use writing and their growth in skills. These children write in their journal at the beginning of every day. They write personal narratives or report on events and new learning; they share this journal writing with peers. They also use writing across the day to think, reflect, and organize ideas, making lists of what they've learned, responding to prompts for longer essays, writing letters, composing responses to literature, and recording observations. They use writing for the same reasons it's used in the wider world—to communicate, describe events, or demonstrate knowledge. Numerous writing samples from these classrooms are available on the companion website.

One classroom is in a small city in a northeastern state; the other is in a K-12 charter school in a large New England city. Both teachers are

You   Me

Rember   John,
When   Yes I remember
we Takt   talking about animals.
about   That was fun! I
and meb   love baby animals.
that   Maybe we will see
fun-John   some when we
             visit the farm!

♥- Miss
     P

FIGURE 8.2
John's Journal

experienced early childhood educators. A comparison of writing samples from the beginning and end of the school year reveals how each child's writing improved in features associated with message and conventions. For example, early in the school year, Elizabeth had trouble separating spoken words in her message; she wrote macaroni and cheese as one word. Examples from her journal reflect her development as a writer (Figures 8.3–8.5).

Window to a Northeast Small City Grade 1 Classroom

In Mrs. Smith's first grade, children write every day to think, report, describe, communicate, socialize, learn, and all the other possible purposes that drive literate people to construct print. These children haven't necessarily had extensive opportunities to write and read at home or in school before coming to Mrs. Smith's classroom. The day starts with journal writing; children write for the first 30–40 minutes.

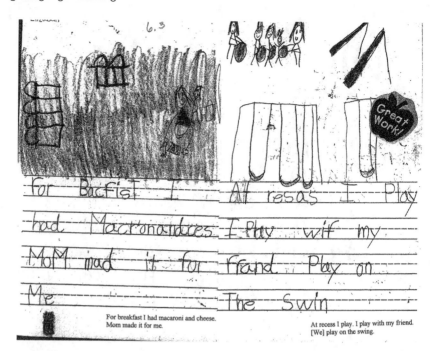

FIGURE 8.3
Sample from
Elizabeth's September
Journal

For breakfast I had macaroni and cheese.
Mom made it for me.

At recess I play. I play with my friend.
[We] play on the swing.

While they write, the teacher takes attendance and the daily lunch count. Using journals as an activity to initiate the day communicates that writing, talking, questioning, sharing, helping each other, and completing a task is honored in this community (Calkins, 1994; Graves, 1983; Hansen, 1987; Kempton, 2007; Short, Harste, & Burke, 1996). Then, Mrs. Smith circulates around the room to support and conference with writers; she publicly comments on effective writing style or word choice she's noticed. When a writer poses a question, she often turns it over to the class. These spontaneous FYIs (Chapter 7) supplement planned mini lessons, creating a teachable moment for the asker as well as anyone who's ready to absorb the information.

Children's writing is always ripe with data to inform focused instructional planning (Clay, 2001b). Figures 8.15 and 8.16 (later in this chapter) provide descriptions and analyses of numerous writing samples collected in this classroom. Each sample analyzed is on the companion website, inviting further collaborative review by individuals or teams of teachers. Mrs. Smith often makes on-the-spot suggestions to individuals or the class based on initial reactions as children read their daily journal entry to her.

Early in the year Mrs. Smith introduces the "five Ws plus H" as a strategy for writing personal narratives. Each word—who, what, when, where, why, and how—is written on a large paper hand that's posted on the wall. The visual reminds writers to ask themselves, "What else can I tell?" Children seldom address all questions in a single entry, but the prompts stimulate more writing every time. Children share their finished entry with Mrs. Smith and three friends—one at a time; pairs select a place in the room (at the rug, in the book nook, or at a table) to read to each other.

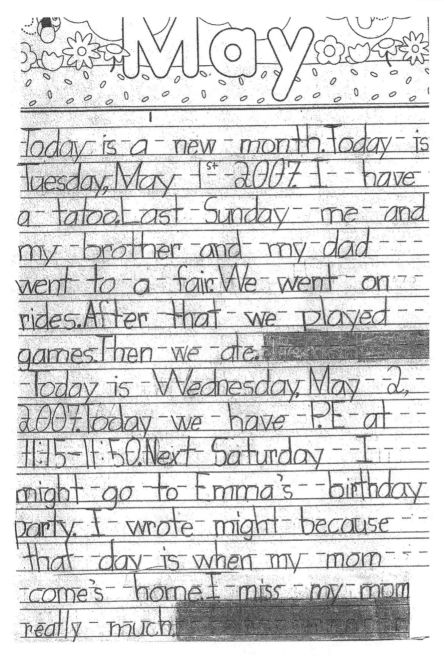

Today is a new month. Today is
Tuesday, May 1st 2007. I have
a tatoo. Last Sunday me and
my brother and my dad
went to a fair. We went on
rides. After that we played
games. Then we ate.
Today is Wednesday, May 2,
2007. Today we have P.E. at
11:15-11:50. Next Saturday I
might go to Emma's birthday
party. I wrote might because
that day is when my mom
come's home. I miss my mom
really much.

FIGURE 8.4
Sample from
Elizabeth's May
Journal

In this classroom, daily writing (encoding) and reading back (decoding) provides practice in both sides of the literacy coin; each reinforces the other. When encoding, children start with ideation (thinking of what they wanted to tell) and move to the word level (sound examination and letter-to-sound matching). Conversely, the flow shifts from reading the words (visual, thinking, and associational aspects) to saying the words (speech) when decoding their own writing. The workout is balanced; multiple linguistic muscles are exercised, but it doesn't stop there. They also write and read to learn across the day.

ideation
the ability of the mind to formulate ideas

FIGURE 8.5
Reflections on
Elizabeth's Writing
Progress in Grade 1

In September, Elizabeth extended her expression to two related sentences. Sound spelling indicates that she can segment sounds and match many of them with letters or letter patterns. She began with a lower case letter, but used capital letters to start the sentences that followed. However, capital letters are used inappropriately within sentences and words. The second September entry has a detailed drawing with a personal statement explaining what she does at recess with her friend. The May entry covers two days. Each is focused on a topic. Elizabeth explained her reason for writing "might go," assuming readers would wonder. This adds a bit of voice. She accurately used the possessive form, but applied it inappropriately later. The writing is neat and clearly readable.

FIGURE 8.6
Children Read
Journals

These first graders also gather each day for modeled writing (writing to children), collaborative writing (writing with children), interactive read-aloud (reading to children), shared reading (reading to and with children), and guided reading (reading with and by children) with follow-up paired rereading (reading by children) and individual responding. A commercial basal reading series (textbook readers) is used, but it's augmented with Mrs. Smith's extensive collection of literature.

basal reading series
textbook reader that includes several reading selections with scripts for teacher-based instruction

The content of language activities supports cross-curricular thematic studies. There's also time for daily D.E.A.R. (drop everything and read). Children gather a basket filled with books at their independent reading level and enjoy time to reread old favorites on a variety of topics. There are more than a few great books to pique everyone's interest. This classroom has more books than some school libraries; Mrs. Smith has built an extraordinary book collection and the children soon know which bins hold their favorites.

FIGURE 8.7
Classroom Library

Children borrow books; every day they take a book (or two) home in their special book travel bag. These are read to an adult. The added practice is like shocking the roots of a newly planted tree. Literacy skills grow quickly and take hold in Mrs. Smith's classroom as well as in the first grade classroom described next in this chapter. The latter is an Urban Charter school classroom, located in a New England state. Quality literature and genuine writing are also central to the curriculum at this site.

Literacy Learning in a Grade 1 Urban Charter School Classroom

Charter schools are guided by a performance contract that details the school's mission, program, goals, number of students, and grade levels served, methods of assessment, and ways to measure success. The contract term varies, but typically ranges from three to five years and may be renewed at that point. Charter schools operate with more autonomy than public schools, but they are accountable to their sponsor, the public, and parents for children's academic performance as well as the fiscal integrity of their operation. Woven skillfully into the tenets of the school's charter, literacy activities in this classroom engage children and have positive academic results.

This urban classroom in a New England state follows a structured curriculum that's intended to be dynamic, comprehensive, and relevant. Ongoing review of curricular designs ensures that these characteristics are maintained. Teachers use internally created materials designed specifically to support the school's objectives and goals.

To support her English Language Arts (ELA) curriculum, Mrs. Wall uses a structured phonics program and a basal series, but children also apply skills learned for authentic purposes.

When children are free to use writing for personal expression, they seldom copy; they invent their own solutions for word constructions needed to produce a meaningful message (Clay, 1987b). They listen for and order sounds and match each with letter(s) associated with it. They find words they need in the room. Sometimes, they construct a new word using parts of a known word; they use /ook/ in *look* to figure out a spelling for *book*. Writing allows authentic practice for phonemic awareness (PA) and phonics; writing makes the content of PA and phonics lessons relevant to these children. The results aren't always conventional, but they show the child's thinking.

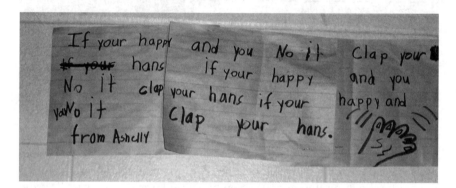

FIGURE 8.8
Wall Chart for Song

Children free to express in written form know how they will use instruction in phonemics and phonetics for their own purposes; the information is immediately relevant to them. Again, interest in function precedes motivation to learn form. Children learn about writing by constructing their own messages with freedom of choice and support from others (Dyson, 2003). But, knowledge of forms (conventions) grows as well in the process—along with motivation to persist in refining one's message. Achievement is evidenced when analyzing children's writing across the academic year.

Figures 8.9–8.11 are samples of Conor's writing at different points in the year. Conor didn't come to first grade with the same writing experience evidenced in Elizabeth's September journal entry (Figure 8.3). He verbally expressed an intended message, but produced only two letters for five words. He read *I*; he read *played* when pointing to the /l/. Then, Conor verbalized the remaining words not represented. Conor's encoding skills grew in an environment that offered daily to, with, and by writing and reading activities.

Children in this classroom write to report their learning in thematic studies, to record observations, and to acknowledge the message presented by a guest speaker (school nurse). Writing samples reflecting these purposes are found on the companion website.

To extend learning and enrich children's responses, Mrs. Wall includes related literature in ELA lessons and content area studies. Ancillary resources motivate deeper exploration of topics; these are more like materials children use outside of school when engaged in literate activities.

ancillary materials
sources (i.e. literature, magazines, media) that support curricular topics and textbooks

"I played basketball this weekend."

CONOr 9/6/06

In September, Conor clearly illustrated his message, but only represented two of the words he read. He wrote I and represented one sound (/l/) in played.

FIGURE 8.9
Conor's Increasing Achievement—September

Conor

2007 January 2, 2007

"Went" "New York" "City"
I Wet to Nyyoc side

Conor's journal entry in January is more readable. Although spelling is unconventional, Conor used the process of segmenting sounds and attaching letters to what he heard. He read, "I went to New York City".

FIGURE 8.10
Conor's Increasing Achievement—January

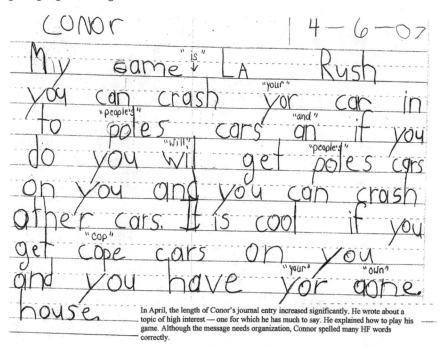

Conor | 4-6-07

My game "is" LA Rush you can crash "your" yor car in to "people's" poles cars "and" an if you do you wil "will" get "people's" poles cars on you and you can crash other cars. It is cool if you get "cop" cope cars on you and you have "your" yor "own" aone. house

FIGURE 8.11
Conor's Increasing
Achievement—April

In April, the length of Conor's journal entry increased significantly. He wrote about a topic of high interest — one for which he has much to say. He explained how to play his game. Although the message needs organization, Connor spelled many HF words correctly.

5/2/07

Dear Mrs Lessard,

I will never get a

"cavity"
cavitie because I'm

eating healthy foods

From,
Noah

FIGURE 8.12
Response to Class
Speaker

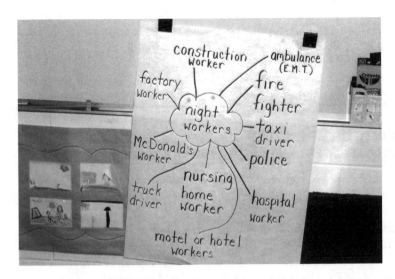

FIGURE 8.13
Content Area Literacy

Books are attractively displayed, allowing easy browsing for D.E.A.R. time. As each lesson begins, objectives are shared with children; this makes the purpose and procedures clear. This classroom is inviting; theme-related displays as well as resources and charts that support reading, writing, and mathematics make wall space functional.

FIGURE 8.14
Book Display

Like the small city classroom, this one is a unique community defined by its members. Both classrooms are *child-centered* in their approach to teaching and children's learning. In child-centered classrooms, teachers teach children, not programs. They make available resources work for learners rather than make learners conform to programmatic structures.

Research-based, Child-centered Literacy Instruction for Reading-writing Classrooms

The theoretical basis for recognizing writing and reading as parallel processes has been previously described and reiterated in this text. Young writers read what they've written (Bissex, 1980; Graves; 1983; Hansen, 1987; Murray, 1980, 1982) in the classrooms described in this book— even before they have formal instruction in reading or begin to read texts constructed by other authors. "Thirty-plus years of research show that immersing children in writing is the most developmentally appropriate first step toward the goal of reading" (Kempton, 2007, p. 81). Engaging children in traditional reading programs before or without approximated writing doesn't make sense; developmental learning takes the learner from the known to the new (Morrow, 1989; Schulze, 2006).

Samples on the website from both classrooms reflect daily writing for a range of real purposes. Routman (2000) concludes, "the most effective kindergarten and first grade teachers demonstrate and promote daily writing" (p. 101). Demonstrations by an experienced writer (writing to and with children, previously described) are a highly effective way to teach writing strategies (Routman, 2000). Children write for social reasons, for play, to tell imaginative stories, to relate personal narratives, to report their knowing, to make lists, and to explore information on a topic—as examples from these classrooms reflect.

The goal is to encourage children to self-initiate topics for writing or responses to a prompt. When they've been immersed in demonstrations, they don't want or need to fill in prepared structures. Effective teachers model writing as they write to and with children. These teachers also draw children's attention to the writing style, structure, and word choice in literature selections shared. Writing causes children to attend to aspects of print that they might otherwise overlook as emergent readers (Clay, 2001a); authors of all ages read like writers, mining ideas and presentation style from the text. Young writers need to think about what they want to say, how print is mapped onto a page (directionality), and how words are constructed (phonemics/phonetics).

Demonstrations from competent writers and time for practice help children understand complexities in the composing process (Mayer, 2007). Children are encouraged to be resourceful and strategic when constructing messages; they are supported over hurdles and inspired to accept challenges. They're allowed to experiment and grow. Mayer states that, "Like reading, writing abilities emerge as children observe and interact with more advanced writers, materials, and print in multiple environments" (Mayer, 2007, p. 34).

Children enter the first grade classrooms described with different literacy experiences and skills; their individual needs are addressed in conferences and mini lessons. Children's growth in organizing an extended message that engages readers is evident in the samples; their writing also demonstrates an expanding repertoire of automatic writing words as well as skills in applying phonetic and visual strategies for spelling words. Figure 8.15 is an excerpt of descriptions of the samples; transcriptions are available on the website. Figure 8.16 evaluates the spelling levels in an excerpt of the sample using the Gentry and Gillett (1993) stages (discussed in Chapter 7).

Small Northeastern City School

Joseph

In September Joseph recorded his message using random letters. His reading of the entry was scribed at the bottom. Throughout the sample journal entries, there are instances where someone (teacher or assistant) scribed a word or two for Joseph. This was accompanied with on-the-spot mental modeling for encoding at the word level—modeling that explained what was heard and how each sound was matched to a letter or letter pattern. In demonstrations, high frequency words, especially non-phonetic ones, were characterized as words that needed to be written (and read) automatically. Such individualized F.Y.I. interactions scaffolded Joseph through roadblocks and encouraged persistence with his writing; without them, his early frustration would have derailed engagement and weakened self-confidence. Many samples don't entirely reflect what Joseph could do independently, but they do indicate what he needed to learn. His progress can be attributed to the teacher's unwavering belief in his potential and the enormous amount of support she provided.

The October benchmark continued to have random letters interspersed with some high frequency words; the message is not known. The drawing of people on the benchmark sample lacks maturity in form. A journal entry from October began conventionally, "We got a ...", but continued with random letters. Joseph's reading of this entry was recorded below it. On a December benchmark, Joseph communicated that he helped his dog, Max, who was under rocks. In February, Joseph started off his entry with voice, but fell into the comfortable listing of people he loves in order to fill space. He had assistance with words in this entry (yesterday, played, Albert, borrowed, called, Spy). The March journal entry began with the list of people loved, but continued with a brief personal narrative. Joseph had one sentence scribed for him. Most of the words are spelled correctly; words he attempted were spelled phonetically. Joseph progressed considerably in sound segmenting and letter/letter pattern matching; he wrote the z backwards in prize. Joseph appears to have written all of the June entry. In places, he wrote only the beginning letter for high frequency words (will, with, the); he ran sentences together and didn't begin the last sentence with a capital letter. Proper nouns were not capitalized (Bob, August, Three in Spiderman Three).

continued overleaf

FIGURE 8.15
Grade 1 Writing
Samples Descriptions

Kyley

Kyley had support to get started on her riddle. The first sentence was scribed. She continued with several informational clues, but didn't end with a question. She punctuated her beginning clues with a period. She correctly spelled a few high frequency words and approximated other words. Kyley's October benchmark sample responded to the prompt with a gist statement. Her second sentence wraps up with a connection to the prompt. Most words are spelled correctly. She spelled "like" correctly, but reversed the letters later. The November journal entry lists a series of unrelated events and thoughts. Most sentences lack punctuation, but she used a question mark after asking, "OK." Sentences without "I" as the first word begin with a lower case letter. Kyley's sound spelling indicates that she segmented sounds and matched letters or letter patterns to sounds heard. In December, Kyley described a Christmas gift. Sentences are punctuated with a period, although the last is a fragment. Most words are spelled correctly; sound spelling is phonetic. The second December journal entry focused on a Christmas gift for a relative. All sentences are related to the topic; many begin with a lower case letter. There's no punctuation in this entry; it's written as a continuous stream of thoughts. Many words are spelled correctly; sound spelling is semi-phonetic and phonetic. Kyley expressed her understanding of the report card grading system before doing a movie review in her February journal entry. High frequency words are spelled correctly; Kyley made close approximations on unknown words. There is voice in Kyley's description of the baseball injury. She asked the question her readers would be thinking. The entry continues with two other unrelated topics. A few sentences are punctuated; some begin with a capital letter. Proper nouns (July, Florida) are not capitalized. Most words are spelled correctly. Kyley's June journal entry has several sentences focused on a single topic. Most words are spelled correctly; misspellings are close approximations.

Large City Charter School

Ashelly

Ashelly made a single sentence entry in September telling what she likes to do. Her illustration is detailed. Ashelly used capital letters inappropriately within the sentence. The use of capital B in this case may be an indication of a b/d confusion; young writers sometimes use the capital letter to solve that problem. There's no punctuation at the end of this sentence. Ashelly wrote a clear sentence to describe her illustration in a literature response completed at home. She didn't use a capital letter at the beginning of the sentence, but ended it with a period. She may have thought it didn't need a capital since the response started in the middle of the line following a prompt. Ashelly wrote to the class to report her observations at the fish tank. It's one long sentence that ends with a period. Capital letters continued to be used within her sentence. In March, Ashelly reported what she learned about polar bears with three run-together sentences that end with a period. She started with a capital letter and followed with all lower case letters in the sentence. Ashelly wrote about the loss of a pet in April. She expanded with several sentences of information for the reader, but continued to run the sentences together without punctuation until the end. She added an illustration of the lost pet.

FIGURE 8.15
Continued

Ashelly demonstrated that she could write creatively, taking on a different role. She wrote a letter as a dog speaking to her owner and punctuated the two sentences appropriately.

Noah

In September, Noah created an elaborate illustration and wrote a sentence to label it. His use of the word been may reflect a speech pattern. A b/d confusion is also noted with this word. Noah's entry a few days later is similar with a detailed illustration and a simple sentence. Neither of the sentences in the first two samples is punctuated. Noah expanded his sentence in an October journal entry; he reported his observations at the fish tank. The writing seems to lack word spacing at the beginning, but Noah may have squeezed in the word "see" after rereading what he wrote. He ended the sentence with a period. In January, Noah wrote a brief personal narrative about how he spent Christmas day. He described two events and closed with a wrap-up sentence. However, the thoughts are run together as one sentence that's punctuated with a period. Noah told one way he'd take care of the Earth after responding to the initial prompts on the page. That statement ends with a period. A wrap-up sentence is used to finish his paragraph. Noah's thank-you letter followed the format for this genre. He made a statement and gave support for his opinion, but didn't punctuate the sentence. Three fact statements reflect what Noah has learned about guppies. Each ends with a period. The first two begin with a capital letter.

FIGURE 8.15
Continued

Small Northeastern City School

Writer's Name	Sample's Title	Grade	Pre-communicative	Semi-phonetic	Phonetic	Trans-itional	Conventional
Joseph	Sad	1	X				
	Benchmark 10/23/06	1	X				we, I, with, play
	Halloween	1	X				we, got, a
	Benchmark 12/06	1		X (nes for needs)	X (roxs, undur)		HF words— helped, he, Dad, dog, my, is
	February Journal	1					X—with assistance from adult
	March Journal	1			X (luve, cuzin, bounsy, frends)		X—with some assistance from adult
	June	1		X (w for will, w for with, t for the, soger for ?, konot for cannot, spudrman for spiderman, me for my, hove, for have)	X (woch, stor, git)		X—many HF words spelled correctly *continued overleaf*

FIGURE 8.16 Overall Stage of Spelling Development Represented in the Grade 1 Samples

Writer's Name	Sample's Title	Grade	Pre-communicative	Semi-phonetic	Phonetic	Trans-itional	Conventional
Kyley	Riddle	1		X (babis for babies, carli for curly, madd for mud)	X (tal, rol)		HF words—am, pink, have, like, to, in, the
	October Benchmark	1		X (esin for ocean, wat for what)	X (liek)		X—most words spelled correctly
	November Journal	1		X (my sehelf for myself, nona for noon, fert for first, tomarow for tomorrow)	X (teric or teret, wock, aftr, werkct, picsher)		X—many words spelled correctly
	December Journal	1			X (diferint, whith, slushies)		X—most words spelled correctly
	December Journal	1		X (be cas for because, casin's for cousin's, thut for thought, their for their, theng for thing)	X (muny, cusins, thats, chrismis, woodin, botum, nothing)		X—many words spelled correctly
	February Journal	1		X (menaes for means, Cindrelar for Cinderella,	X (are for our, supere, nite)		X—many words spelled correctly
	April Journal	1		X (floorda for Florida)	X (thros)		X—most words spelled correctly
	June Journal	1		X (people for people, cosin for cousin)	X (wear for where, difrent, show's)		X—most words spelled correctly

Large City Charter School

Writer's Name	Sample's Title	Grade	Pre-communicative	Semi-phonetic	Phonetic	Trans-itional	Conventional
Ashelly	Beach	1					X
	Best Part	1			X (wotr)		X
	Journal Writing	1			X (snals, rocs, floting)		X
	Polar Bear	1					X
	Scotty	1			X (no for though, sill for still		X
	Owner	1					X
Noah	Home	1			X (den for been reversed b, al)		
	Balloons	1			X (balons)		

FIGURE 8.16 *Continued*

Writer's Name	Sample's Title	Grade	Pre-communicative	Semi-phonetic	Phonetic	Trans-itional	Conventional
	Snails	1		X (snels for snails, rooks for rocks)			
	Christmas	1		X (Cinismes for Christmas, piresits for presents)	X (diner for dinner)		X—several correctly spelled words
	Care of Earth	1			X (that for that's)		X
	Letter	1			X (cavitie)		X
	Guppy	1			X (reversed letters— ocean)		X

FIGURE 8.16 *Continued*

Increased writing vocabularies and sound spelling practice propels children's reading. If they can encode it, they can decode it; if they write it, they will read it. Writing and reading will grow simultaneously and interrelatedly; one reinforces the other (Mayer, 2007; Sampson, 1986). In fact, "children naturally incorporate context, visual, and phonetic clues to decipher their own writing, then transfer these strategies to the reading of books by professional authors" (Avery, 1993, p. 381). In other words, writing directs the way children examine print when they read (Clay, 1987a). Having constructed text, these children know what to look for at the word and message level when decoding.

Building an Automatic Writing Vocabulary

A child's automatic writing vocabulary consists of words he can write all by himself. He knows every detail of these words and writes them without effort. The more varied the child's repertoire of known words for writing, the larger the source he has to draw from when problem-solving the construction of a new or unusual word. Such words may be in his speaking vocabulary or even his reading vocabulary, but they're ones that are new in his writing. Knowing phonics, rimes (i.e. phonograms or word families), and how to sound spell is helpful, but it's not all that's used in spelling English words. We make analogies with known words and filter out patterns that match to spell the new word. "The child who knows a lot of words which are different from one another can generate more words than the child who knows a few spelling patterns well" (Clay, 2001a, pp. 24–25).

phonogram
the rime part of a word. In took, the /t/ is an onset (beginning) and ook is the rime. Phonograms are often called word families (i.e. ake and ick)

The examples from the classrooms described, as well as other examples shared in this text, demonstrate how children build a repertoire of high frequency (HF) words. Daily writing to children (for example, the Morning Message) and with children (the News, LEA) is a context for reinforcing spelling and reading HF words. In shared reading (reading to and with children), guided reading (reading with and by children), and independent reading (reading by children) children practice reading HF words in meaningful contexts. Many teachers post HF words on the wall, and they also display charts listing theme-related words. With repeated use, these words are internalized and children write and read them automatically.

When a word is automatic for writing, it's also a sight word for reading. To increase children's bank of sight words and automatic writing words, effective teachers let them read, read, read; they let them write, write, write! Encoding the word over and over in meaningful messages solidifies it visually and phonetically within varied contexts. Frequent writing increases writing fluency. Knowing how to easily write most of the words you need allows a writer to get ideas down on paper before they're lost. Writers problem-solve unknown words using a combination of word construction strategies. They segment sounds (phonemic awareness) and match them with letters or letter patterns (phonics). Again, the application of skills across language processes has a strengthening effect. Children use phonemic awareness and phonics to encode words; this work strengthens skills in both areas. But, sound spelling isn't enough—not in English. Some words require visual memory of the whole word (for example, "of") or a pattern (such as the pattern for /shun/ in "station").

Respect for Sound Spelling

There is often an aversion to the use of what's been called *invented spelling*. Some teachers, administrators, and/or parents are worried that children will have the incorrect spelling imprinted on their brain if allowed to use it. Even an alternate term—*temporary spelling*—doesn't seem to ease their fears. They have a hard time accepting the premise that writing with invented spelling is a "stepping stone" to early reading (Schulze, 2006, p. 18). Two-year-old Tommy might say, "I want pasketty"—pa (/a/ as in "about")-sketty—when asked for his choice from the menu. The adult will respond, "Oh, you'd like spaghetti. That sounds good." There's a modeling rather than an explicit correction. The parent is not afraid that Tommy will go to graduate school saying pasketty; she's confident that it will get straightened out with experience. If Tommy is still saying pasketty in a few more years, concern leads to screening for speech problems. It's the same with written language.

Children try out the strategies for word construction they've observed, incorporating acquired PA (phonemic awareness) and phonics skills to spell what they hear—*sound spelling* (Scanlon et al., 2010). This label honors what they're actually doing—spelling the sounds heard with letters or letter patterns. Children's sound spelling errors are windows to their creative thinking, confusions, and gaps in learning.

Interesting examples of semi-phonetic and phonetic spelling can be found in writing samples from the grade 1 classrooms described in this chapter. Jacob wrote *nes* for *needs*; Joshua wrote *oshin* for *ocean*. Many more are discussed in the descriptions of individual writers' work. Analysis of sound spellings allows us to home in on what to teach, making instruction efficient; it's targeted on what's needed right now. Spelling and writing assessment are further explored in the next chapter. To ensure the production of worthwhile writing artifacts—ones that show "a significant milestone in the learner's development" (Shea, Murray, & Harlin, 2005, p. 42)—classrooms must CAST for success.

Choice, Audience, Sensitivity, and Time: CASTing for Success

The ingredients for growing successful writers are not secret. Whether emerging or advanced, writers thrive in environments that meet basic human needs (Sagor, 1993).

- They need to feel *competent*—that they can do it.
- They need to feel that they *belong* to this community—the community of writers.
- They need to feel *useful*—that they have something to contribute to the group.
- They need to feel *potent*—that the locus of control (for success) is within them.
- They need to be *optimistic*—believe they will reach proficiency.

Effective teachers recognize that CASTing for writing success addresses these needs.

As repeatedly stated, children write best when the topic is something they know about and care about. Passion for the purpose drives writers to persist and refine expressions, creating ones that captivate readers and infect them with interest. Given *choices* (C) over what and how to write, authors take ownership of the process and responsibility for their products (Calkins, 1994; Graves, 1983; Hansen, 1987; Kempton, 2007; Murray, 1980; Short et al., 1996). "Choice is a powerful motivator; it affects students' desire to read and write" (Schulze, 2006, p. 25).

Good writing takes great effort; sharing snippets as well as completed pieces makes the grind worthwhile. After all, most writing is done to communicate. Young writers need an *audience* (A). Sharing their writing, children give example to others and receive recognition and inspiration in return (Figure 8.6).

Listeners offer compliments, but they also share comments on the writing. Comments seasoned with *sensitivity* (S) are most effective; they nudge writers forward toward improving message content or quality. To ensure the first three ingredients of CAST are delivered, classrooms must carve out room for the fourth. This can be daunting, but it's doable when priorities are set.

Writers need *time* (T) to do their work; it can't be rushed. When daily writing is recognized as authentic practice for phonemic awareness, phonics, building sight vocabulary, thinking, and expressing what you know, then making time isn't difficult. It supplants wasted time given to filling in worksheets. Regularly scheduled writers' workshop provides a time children can count on for writing that they want to do. The classrooms described in this chapter regularly conducted writers' workshop. So too do many other first grade classrooms. They each build a writing community with the workshop protocol.

Writing Workshop in First Grade

recursive
the process of moving forward and doubling back to re-plan, re-draft, or revise as necessary when working on a piece of writing

Writing that's *processed* goes back and forth through layers of refinement until it's published; that's the *recursive* nature of it. In a workshop, first drafts of ideas are revised for content; writers add, delete, or rearrange text after they rethink and refine ideas. They edit the piece for errors before it's published or shared with an audience in some form. Processing their writing is something new for most first graders; it's the next big step in taking on the responsibility of authorship. Writers work hard to make their messages clear, interesting, persuasive, and illuminating for an audience of readers.

Up to this point children's notes and journal writing had been *unprocessed*—left in their original forms. Effective teachers want children to understand why writing is processed and when it's left unprocessed. Writing used to think, reflect, or organize ideas—writing that will not go public (such as notes or lists) is usually left unprocessed. Parents and teachers look at children's unprocessed writing for information about their development; it's an artifact for assessment. Writing for a wider audience is processed (i.e. revised and edited) before it's shared. Effective grade 1 teachers introduced procedures and expectations for writers' workshop gradually; during workshop time, children process pieces of writing. The sections that follow describe a framework for initiating writers' workshop in the classroom. They include anecdotes about young writers that relate to different steps in the process. These are memorable vignettes, shared by teachers in various writing classrooms—including the classrooms described in this chapter. The stories make it clear that the writing process can be transformational on a personal and community level.

Organizing the Room

Establish clear expectations for behavior; a simple posted list helps children remember these. It's also a reference that can be quickly pointed to when halos slip (Figure 8.17). The teacher asks, "Are you following Number 4?" The children write at tables where they have the support of tablemates. They know they can talk; there is the constant hum of a hive when a workshop is productive. There is some social talk, but a small measure of that is also important for building community. Resources are plentiful; these include pictionaries and dictionaries for first graders. Children also have personal dictionaries.

pictionary
book that displays multiple words associated with an illustration

When they ask for the spelling of a complex word, it's written in their dictionary. As the teacher writes it, she verbalizes thinking about the spelling. HF words are added to the classroom word wall as they're

1. They listen to the lesson of the day. They thoughtfully listen to authors who are sharing.
2. They get their materials and check what they planned to do this day.
3. They follow the steps for process writing. Sometimes, they go back to a step. They are busy writers who always work hard.
4. They talk, they write, and they listen.
5. They quietly help other authors.
6. At the end of each workshop, they think about what's finished and what they'll do next time.
7. They record what they plan to start with next time on the chart and put materials away.

FIGURE 8.17
What Writers Do In the Writers' Workshop

introduced. The Daily News, books, and class charts—additional sources for words needed—are always visible.

A teacher recently shared a cue folder she constructed to support young readers and writers. A familiar decoding strategy cue card, HF words, the alphabet with pictures for sound clues, and other letter-sound reminders are pasted onto manila folders and laminated. Children set the folder up on their desk when reading or writing; they don't have to look far to find cues for literacy success. (An example of a folder of sound cues and HF words can be found on the companion website.)

Organizing Materials

There's a place for everything and everything is returned to its place. That's the mantra for order and sanity in an efficient classroom. Teachers want to be able to get what they need when they need it. They also want children to realize that we are more productive in an organized environment; a well-maintained classroom ensures that lessons are learned. The efficient writing classroom looks like the last scene in *Mission Organization* (HGTV show that demonstrates how to efficiently organize spaces). Paper is in one spot—organized by type, color, and size. Markers, pencils, staplers, scissors, hole punch, rulers, and paste are in designated locations. Writing folders are organized in baskets. Dictionaries and pictionaries are on a shelf; books are in the library. In order for everyone to have ready access to tools, children need to be stewards of classroom resources and materials.

Topics for Writing

The teacher begins with homework. She asks children to think about five things they know a lot about. Kempton (2007) states, "Children can write only when they get in touch with what they think and feel" (p. 81). If a child can't come up with five topics, the teacher tells her to ask someone at home for suggestions. The next day, the teacher shares a list she's created for herself. The teacher's sharing continues as she strategically models each step of the process with personal writing. This allows children to observe a writer in action—using the craft. Then, volunteers follow, presenting their expert list.

As children report, the teacher records each topic on a sheet of paper in their writing folder; it's titled "Things I Want to Write About". The teacher explains, "When you know about something, you have a lot to tell. You can use this list for writing topics. If you think of more, we can add them. We can also cross off any if you change your mind." Children often decide they'd like to write about a topic on someone else's list; that's fine. Writers get ideas from each other, but they spin them in different directions. The teacher tries to identify additional topics whenever they come up.

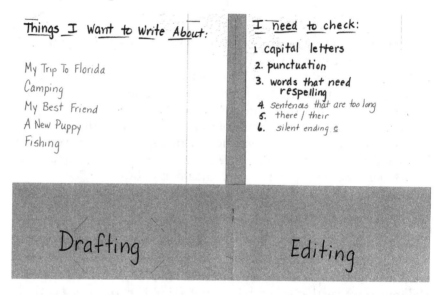

FIGURE 8.18
Topics for Writing

Children don't always realize that authors find stories in the fabric of their lives. One morning as children were coming into the classroom, a teacher overheard them talking about ghosts on Angling Road. It was around Halloween. She couldn't help but comment, "Real ghosts?" They turned to her since she hadn't been part of the conversation from the start and adamantly stated, "Yes, they ARE real! Everybody knows it and we even heard them last night." "Oh, really," the teacher said apologetically. "That would be a great topic to write about because I don't live in this town and I've never heard about them. I bet other readers would want to know. We've read stories that had two authors. Maybe, you two could work together on a book—*The Ghosts on Angling Road*. When you get settled, add that to your topic list."

Going Through the Steps: Together at First

After everyone has a list, the teacher has children select one topic for writing. She asks someone to be her partner; they talk about their selected topics. The partner's job is to listen, ask questions, and let the writer know what additional information a reader would want or like to know.

Brainstorm:
    THINK of story ideas.
    What do you want to write about?
    What do you want to tell your audience of readers? Talk to someone
        about your topic.
    Make notes, a web, or sketches to organize the way your writing
        will go.

Draft:
    Give it a go! Write your story.
    Get your ideas on paper.
    If you're not sure about spelling, spell words they way they sound—
        use sound spelling. Words can be fixed later.

Rehearse:
    Try out your writing with a partner, the teacher, or a small group.
    Read it out loud.
    How does it sound? Does it need changes?
    What does your audience wonder? Use a suggestion from the
        audience to improve your writing.

Revise:
    Make changes in your writing.
    Add new information, take out a part, or rearrange the order.

Share:
    Read your revised writing to a partner, the teacher, or a small group.
    Does it sound right now? Does the audience understand your
        message?

Edit:
    Check your writing for errors.
    Did you start sentences with a capital letter?
    Did you end each sentence with a punctuation mark?
    Did you use capital letters at the beginning of important words?
    Try to fix words you know or can find in the room.
    Underline words you need help fixing.

Conference:
    Meet with the teacher to talk about your writing.

Publish:
    Copy the edited draft in your best handwriting.
    Put your writing on display for others to enjoy.

Celebrate:
    Feel proud! You're a published author.

FIGURE 8.19
Our Steps for Process
Writing

When the demonstration is finished, children work with a peer; they talk about what they'll tell. Articulated ideas then need to be organized.

The group reconvenes; the teacher models how to bundle and sequence ideas, explaining that writers decide on a way that works for them. The teacher tells children that she makes a list (notes) and/or sketches what she's planning to tell. Then, children try it; they think about ideas they've verbalized and the input from their partner. They list or sketch. This is the *brainstorming* and planning step. It involves initial decision-making and organizing. The key is flexibility; changes can always be made in plans.

Brainstorming Steps

- Think about your topic and what you want to tell. Talk to someone about it.
- Get ideas from your listener. What did your listener want to know?
- Make notes or sketches. Plan what you will tell and how you will organize ideas.

With their road map (notes or sketches), writers are ready to *draft*. The teacher shows them how she uses her notes to guide sentence construction. She gets her ideas down so they don't fly away from memory. The teacher demonstrates how she represents sounds in a word when unsure how it's spelled; she shows how resources in the room help her spell other words. The teacher reads back what she's written and checks her notes as she goes along. Children review the behaviors they've observed. The teacher helps them articulate a series of drafting steps before they begin to write. This procedure continues as subsequent steps are modeled, creating concise guidelines for writers to follow.

Drafting Steps

- Use your notes or sketches to write ideas in sentences.
- Find words you need in the room—on the wall, on charts, or in books.
- You can ask a friend at your table for help.
- Use sound spelling when necessary. We will edit later.
- Read over your writing.

The teacher circulates to assist as children draft their ideas as clearly as they can, using available resources for spelling. She encourages children to use sound spelling for harder words; they'll fix them later. The teacher suggests rereading as children write—checking to see if they've forgotten anything important. Since everyone is staying together this first time through the steps, first completers silently read while others work on their draft.

The teacher suggests reading more on a topic before trying to write about it. Todd wanted to write about real bears. When the class was at the library, the teacher helped him find informational books on bears. He read these while others finished their draft. Todd learned how to prepare for writing an informational text; he read up on the topic. Then, he worked on his draft. When drafts are ready, children read them aloud to hear how the composition sounds as a whole.

Oral readings of the draft—before and after revision—are included as separate steps. The first is called *rehearsal* (before revision). *Sharing* comes after revision. The teacher models rehearsal; she reads her draft aloud. The audience considers, "Does this writing make sense? Does it sound right?" Listeners respond with compliments—"I like how … " and comments—suggestions for revision of content.

The teacher plans an additional model; she has a colleague demonstrate the rehearsal step with her. The colleague begins by complimenting something in the teacher's writing before commenting on what's needed for clarity or how ideas could be rearranged. Following this additional demonstration, children rehearse with their writing. They read their draft to a partner or a small group. The audience responds to the writer with compliments and comments. There's a lot of assisting going on at this time—teacher-to-child and peer-to-peer. Rehearsal helps children appreciate that they're writing for an audience as well as themselves. They need to know what readers perceive as unclear. Appreciating the reader's perspective is a big step; it's an understanding that takes time and feedback to develop.

Rehearsal Steps

- Read your writing out loud to a friend, the teacher, or a small group.
- Think about how it sounds. Does it need changes?
- Your listener will give you a compliment—praise for something in your writing.
- Your listener will give you a comment—a suggestion to improve your writing.

Billy wrote a story about the school nurse. After his rehearsal, Ella suggested that he needed to add the name of the school nurse. Billy didn't think that was necessary. "Everyone knows Mrs. Martin is the nurse, he said." Ella persisted, "What if people who don't go to this school read your book? They won't know who it is." Billy hadn't thought about that wider audience. Rehearsing helped him understand that writing can go beyond the neighborhood. When he revised, Billy added her name so everyone would know that Mrs. Martin was the central figure in his book.

Revision follows rehearsal. The teacher emphasizes that revision is hard work, but writers know it's very important. It's done to improve one's message—to make it clear and more interesting to a reader. Revision requires the writer to add, delete, or rearrange text. Revision is about improving content; it's different from editing. Young authors in the writers' workshop are required to make at least one revision based on a comment offered in rehearsal. They can seek help from the person who offered it. After revising, children are ready to learn about the *share* step—the second oral read-aloud to an audience.

Revision Steps

- Use your own ideas and one suggestion from a listener to improve your writing.
- Add new information, take out a part, or rearrange ideas.
- The listener who offered the comment can help you.

The teacher reads her revised draft aloud to model the *share* step. The audience responds with their reactions. Does it sound right after revising? Do listeners understand the message now? The children decide whether the teacher is ready to go on. She wants them to understand that authors often step backwards to revise, draft, or plan more before going ahead. That's the recursive nature of processed writing. The steps are not rigidly linear; writers move back and forth through them. After the teacher demonstrates, each writer shares his writing with an audience in the same way.

Sharing Steps

- Try out your revised writing.
- Read it out loud to a friend, the teacher, or a small group.
- Does it sound better? Is it complete?
- Is it the way you want to tell your ideas?

Now, the teacher's writing needs to be edited. She draws children's attention to the editing checklist in their writing folder (Figure 8.18). Initially, only the first three items are listed. The teacher checks her writing against each point using the guiding questions. Then, children edit their writing using the same checklist.

One teacher continually demonstrates the editing process throughout the year using the Morning Message. Frequently, she explains that her Morning Message needs to be edited; she asks the children to help her as they read it together. Figure 8.20 shows a message Mrs. Wilson left for the class when she had to attend a school meeting one morning. The resource room teacher worked with the children to edit it. The activity evoked a review of the purpose and format for friendly letters as well as conventions related to sentence fragments, capitalization, and punctuation. Children use these models to initiate editing on their own writing, but they also receive adult help for this step.

Before Editing:	After Editing:
June 17, 2008	June 17, 2008
dear class	Dear Class:
i havea meeting this morning mrs black will work with YoU Back soon i miss YoU.	I have a meeting this morning. Mrs. Black will work with you. I'll be back soon. I miss you.
Love, ms wilson	Love, Ms. Wilson

FIGURE 8.20
Morning Message on Chart Paper for Reading and Editing

Although teachers frequently confer with writers throughout the process, they call the next step in this model the *conference*. Specifically, it's an editing conference.

Editing and Conferencing Steps

- Edit your writing. Check for errors.
- Did you start sentences with capital letters?
- Did you end each sentence with a punctuation mark?
- Did you use capital letters at the beginning of important words?
- Check for misspelled words you can fix.
- Underline words you need help spelling.
- Did you do everything on your editing checklist?
- Sign up for an editing conference.
- The teacher will help you do a final edit. Sound spellings will be revised.

The teacher marks an asterisk next to the name of any writer she confers with during the workshop, whether it's a brief conversation or a longer editing session (Figure 8.21). The protocol for the management chart is explained in the next section. This system keeps everyone on track and chugging along!

Name	11/6	11/7	11/8	11/9	11/10
Becky A.	D*	D	Reh/D	Rev/S*	E
Brian A.	C*	P	P	P*	B/D*
Melissa B.	P	P*	B/D*	D	Reh/D*
Jeremy C.	B/D*	D*	D	Reh/D*	Rev/S
Amanda D.	Rev/S	E*	C*	P	P
Tommy H.	D	D*	Reh/D	Rev/S*	E
Sam N.	C*	P	P	B/D*	D*
Claire P.	Rev/S	E*	C*	P	P
Lynn S.	P	P	B/D*	D	D*

FIGURE 8.21
Management Chart for Daily Activity in the Writers' Workshop

With a glance at the chart, the teacher knows with whom she's interacted as well as the step the writer was working on when they talked. Each writer has a final editing conference with the senior editor—the teacher. The teacher uses the Conference Checklist to guide the conversation and make anecdotal notes (Figure 8.22). Any personal goals and instructional focus related to editing are added to the writer's editing checklist (Figure 8.18), making it individualized after the first three items. Numbers 4, 5, and 6 for editing on Figure 8.18 reflect specific editing goals for the writer—each followed instruction during a conference. Children frequently compare editing goals with peers; they can be heard sensitively pointing out a need for similar corrections in the writing of others. This was an unexpected extension of writers' workshop style teaching.

Author _____Title of Piece_____

Content:
Description of the Composition

Does the writing convey meaning to the reader? _____
Can the author read it? _____
Is the author's intent to convey a message? _____
Is there evidence of revision? _____
Comments:

Mechanics:
• Punctuation used   (.) _____ (?) _____ (,) _____ (!) _____ (" ") _____
Comments:

• Capital letters: inappropriately used _____ missing where needed _____
Comments:

• Spelling: Random letters _____ Semi-phonetic _____ Phonetic _____
                Lots of conventional spelling _____
Examples of sound spelling:

Strengths of this piece:

Instructional focus in this conference:

Goal for the next piece of writing:

FIGURE 8.22
Editing Conference
Checklist

Edited work is ready for *publication*. This involves dressing up the writing piece for everyone to see. The teacher shares her published work, showing how she used her best handwriting to rewrite every corrected word and sentence. Then, she illustrated her work (Figure 8.23).

Snow Day

A lot of snow covered the trees.
It was higher than my knees.
We made snow angels all around.
They stayed so still without a sound.

FIGURE 8.23
Teacher's Story

Publishing Steps

- Copy the final draft in your best handwriting.
- Illustrate your work.
- Put your writing on display for others to enjoy.

The children work on publication. Sometimes, parents type up final drafts following identified page breaks; the children cut and paste typed text into blank books before illustrating pages. As pieces are published, the class enjoys listening to readings by the authors—just like in a bookstore. It's a class celebration of the author's accomplishment. Every so often, teachers have an authors' tea and invite family and other classes to the readings.

Celebrating Steps

- Feel proud! You're a published author.
- Sit in the Author's Chair. Read your work to an audience.

Beyond the First Publication

After the first publication, things change a bit; this time can be hectic without a plan for order. A posted schedule for the workshop sets the agenda (Figure 8.24); the wall charts remind students what to do at each step. Writers move forward onto other pieces of writing at their own rate. Some spend more time on a step than others; some write more text than others, but all are involved in the process.

Mini Lesson (10 minutes)
Status of the Class (5 minutes)

General Writing Time (35 minutes)
    Follow Steps of the Writing Process
    Independent Reading

Whole Class Share (5 minutes)
Status of the Class (5 minutes)

FIGURE 8.24
Writers' Workshop

Hillary wanted to write about her cat, Tomasino. The resultant draft was forty-two pages long—a birth-to-old age memoir. The teacher suggested doing several books, creating a series. But, Hillary was determined that all of Tomasino's adventures would be told in one book. This was a labor of love; each step took weeks. Hillary worked with passion and persistence because this was important to her. She learned a lot about writing through this single long publication. However, shorter pieces of processed writing can be powerful too.

Bobby lost his mother in an automobile accident. Several months after it happened, he wrote a five-page—one sentence per page—book titled, *Shopping With Mom*. The children were sensitive, but curious. They asked many questions in the rehearsal and share. Bobby answered every one directly and openly. It was amazing! The teacher had a huge lump in her throat. It stayed there throughout the editing conference. Bobby sat proudly in the Author's Chair to read; he cherished that book. The personal impact of the process overshadowed what he learned about writing that time. Writing helped him make memories permanent with words and pictures; it nurtured empathy in the community. Other writers took time to find their voice. But, when they did, the blossoming was something to behold!

James was a repeater. In September, his self-confidence was low. But, that all changed in Mrs. Cleary's first grade. James flourished; he became a prolific writer. He was invited to read his story, *A Fish's Journey*, as an introduction for Bill Martin Jr., a well-known children's author, at a local Reading Council's conference. The audience and Mr. Martin were held spellbound by James's choice of words and use of literary techniques— ones he'd noticed other authors use.

James wrote, "One day a family of perch was swimming in a stream. One of the baby perch was curious. He swam out of the cave. He went out of the stream and into a pond. Now's when the journey begins ... A quick current creek was ahead." James knew this work was a masterpiece; he and Bill Martin Jr. were fellow authors. Balancing a room of writers like Hillary, Bobby, and James—at various steps, with different purposes and abilities—can be daunting. Having consistent procedures makes it possible.

Managing the Flow

Writers' workshop activities require an established sequence, although the number of minutes can vary on different days (Figure 8.24). The children need to understand what happens at each point. The teacher starts with a mini lesson. The topic of the mini lesson emerges from ongoing assessment of writers' needs as well as their readiness for a gentle nudge forward. Read-alouds frequently start off the mini lesson; these provide exemplars of writers' craft on multiple levels. There's always so much to talk about—so many golden examples to mine from a well-written book.

Then, it's time to check the status of the class—what everyone will be working on that day. The teacher looks to the class management chart (Figure 8.21); it reminds children what they've planned to do in the next writing time.

When writers pack up their folders each day, they think about where they are and what they need to do next. Then, those who plan to brainstorm in the next workshop put their folder away in the brainstorming box. On the chart, the teacher marks B after each child's name. She does the same for the other steps, recording the next day's plan for each child on the chart. When each workshop session begins, the teacher simply refers to this chart for a status of the class. She calls children up to get their folders by the step they planned to work on; this makes accessing materials orderly and efficient. And, everyone knows what to do. They also know that independent reading is the fallback option when waiting for an editing conference; they can also help a classmate by being in a rehearsal or share group if they're in the editing conference queue during the general writing time.

Children work in a self-directed mode during the general writing time; the teacher assists as needed, holding on-the-spot conferences with writers or sitting in on rehearsal or share meetings. She also meets with children for individual editing conferences and completes the conference form (Figure 8.22) as they edit together. These interactions typically uncover rich examples of writing that beg to be shared. The teacher asks children to do just that at the closing meeting. As the time for general writing comes to an end, the teacher announces the two-minute period for children to tie up what they're working on and plan what they'll do in the next session. Folders are collected (as described) before coming together. During this closing meeting, children selected that day to share present mini demonstrations or the teacher shares observations. The teacher's comments flow from information she's recorded on particular editing conference forms as well as anecdotal notes taken while interacting with writers and small groups.

Assessment During Writers' Workshop

Writers' workshop provides an extensive amount of data—anecdotal notes, editing conference forms, and children's writing samples. A regular review of data informs the design of upcoming mini lessons as well as individual conferences. When meeting with parents, the specific data collected speaks volumes. Parents never ceased to be amazed at the concrete evidence of literacy growth right before their eyes! They become the best advocates for endorsing a *write into reading* approach in the primary classroom. Children are reading the words and messages they've created. In a community of authors, children support fellow writers, reading one another's work and suggesting revisions.

Beyond its value for applying specific literacy-related skills, writing is used to assess learning and assess *for* learning across content areas. It can and should guide overall literacy instruction. But, it can only inform instruction in meaningful ways when the writing children do is open and free rather than formulaic or copied correctness.

Interventions for struggling writers within the workshop approach are built on careful assessment, differentiated instruction, patience, and sensitive support. In a writers' workshop classroom several children will likely move beyond the emergent stage; they're ready to consider more sophisticated components (traits) of text. They need intervention too. Chapter 9 explores recognizing when to differentiate for writers beyond emergent. The traits of quality writing—ones these writers are prepared to consider and apply in their own work—are discussed in Chapter 9.

Extending the Discussion

- Examine the grade 1 writing samples available at the companion website with colleagues or course members. Partner up to examine all samples from a particular child. Be prepared to discuss this child's development with the group.
- Collect writing samples from a local grade 1 or your own classroom. Discuss each with others. Determine where these writers fall on the continuum. What would you recommend for scaffolding these learners—nudging them forward?
- Visit a grade 1 classroom that has writers' workshop time or consider writing workshop in your own grade 1 classroom. What protocols are followed? How does the teacher scaffold writers? Describe children's level of enthusiasm, confidence, and purpose when writing.
- Discuss how to initiate writers' workshop in a school in a developmentally appropriate way—in a way that complements the reading program. Invite an administrator to the discussion or interview an administrator for input.

nine
Differentiating for Fluent Young Writers

Advanced First Grade Writers

The descriptions of writing samples found in Chapters 6, 7, and 8, as well as the stage designations, are typical for many children in pre-K, kindergarten, and first grade. As you, individually or collectively, review these with writing pieces on the website, you'll notice additional points of achievement and areas for growth. That always happens when looking through different lenses; a singular analysis is never exhaustive. Teachers are meant to recognize similarities with writing done in their classroom; pre-service teachers will make connections with student writing in classrooms where they've participated. The website resources are intended to generate rich discussions. But, sometimes the stage levels described don't go far enough.

The performance of a few young writers in kindergarten may exceed the stage levels. First grade writers also demonstrate accelerated progress in day-to-day journal entries found on the companion website. They've stretched creative wings; Veronica's story in Figure 9.1 indicates a readiness for scaffolding in more sophisticated writing elements. The direction for that scaffolding is discussed in this chapter.

The rich man and woman

Once upon a time in a far far away land thare was a poor widow he lived in Santiago. Thay were so poor the only thing thay coud eat was hard bred. One day a rich man came to town. The old man and woman beged for mony. Little did thay no the man was a robber. Becs allmost Everybuty was just about poor. And then the man and the lady reckandised his Face and then thay rememberd he was the man that stold thare mony. thay saw a gardin. thay started throwing tomatows at the man the mad got mad. He got out of his careig [carriage] and got on his hours [horse] and went home. The nexed day the man came and left in a hery [hurry]! When the man went home and went to sleep. Then the man and lady brocke into his house. Thay Got all of his Gold. Just then the man wocke up. Luckly thay din't Get cawt. And thay touk the Gold Back to toune. Thay went to every house and Gave them some Gold and the toune was rich. And the man that stold the mony went to Jall.

FIGURE 9.1
Veronica's Story

Recognizing talented writers is important. They need differentiated instruction—instruction that's responsive to their competence level; it ensures that enthusiasm for writing grows. Identifying individual needs requires knowledgeable observations of the writing children produce. Some young writers in first grade are ready to learn more about *traits* (characteristics) that define quality writing (Calkins, 1994; Culham, 2003; Graves, 1983; Murray, 1980).

writing traits
qualities or characteristics
of good writing

The traits discussed in this chapter are ones introduced to all writers when they move beyond emergent levels of performance; that may be in grade 2 for many and grade 3 for others (Morrow, 2009; Tompkins, 2010). However, the traits should be introduced to advanced first grade writers like Veronica as an appropriate intervention for them.

Gathering Evidence Anthropologically

Effective teachers are astute *kid watchers* (Goodman, 1985). They observe students in a manner similar to that of an anthropologist or animal researcher; teachers as kid watchers make note of children's behaviors, patterns, interests, motivations, and changes (Shea et al., 2005). "Like the anthropologist, the effective teacher watches from afar and takes copious notes on what she observes" as children engage in daily classroom activities that involve writing (Shea et al., 2005, p. 22). Then, she moves in close to respond to individual needs and nurture individual writers in their journey forward from wherever they are on the continuum of development. As comfort and trust grow, teachers can interact openly with writers, asking questions about intent, content, and style. Together, observations and interactions form the basis for decisions about instructional interventions. Young writers are part of the assessment process; they reflect and evaluate their work before contributing to goal setting. Without astute observations and discourse, interventions can become futile interference (Nutbrown, 1999).

Learning Snapshots

Teachers could keep mental notes as they watch and talk with writers; some try, but the process becomes cumbersome. They run out of brain space because there are just too many problems to note or milestones to mark. Anecdotal records relieve memory of that burden; they create lasting snapshots of learning milestones, capturing events that might otherwise be forgotten.

Good records consist of brief notes taken across multiple writing activities for a variety of purposes. The key is to have a *system* for compiling the information—one that's easy to access and consistent. No one method is best; it all depends on what works for you. If it's not convenient, like the example that follows, you'll surely abandon it—like an overly complicated kitchen gadget.

As the teacher walks around the writers' workshop or assists children with free writing during the day, she uses a system for making positive notes. She tells each writer what she's writing. "Brett, I'm writing that you have an interesting journal entry today. I like what you said and the words you used. I know your friends will want to hear this." Many teachers use a page of mailing labels for their notes; they write the date and child's name with a comment. At the end of the day, they remove each and stick it on a sheet in the child's writing folder. That way, every writer has a sequentially dated collection of comments. The teacher often reviews these when conferencing; she uses them to set goals. Figure 9.2 shows how these notes are accumulated for reflection and planning.

At the end of the day, dated address labels with anecdotal notes are added to a list in the child's portfolio. Reflections are recorded and plans are made.		
Student: Nate	Year: 2007–2008	
Dated observation	What does this show?	How do I respond?
3/10 *Nate's drawing of the beach had lots of detail accompanied by a single label.*	*Nate tells visually, but he has begun to add print.*	*Scaffold him as he extends the label to a sentence.*
3/24 *Nate wrote* jri *for* dry.	*He's confusing /j/ and /d/, but heard /r/ and /i/ sequentially*	*Continue to distinguish words with* dr *and* j *beginning sounds. Compare ending of* my, by, cry, sky, dry *where /i/ is spelled with* y

FIGURE 9.2
Anecdotal Notes

Assessing What Advancing Writers Know and Need to Know

Teaching *in the moment* and *for the moment* yields efficient forward growth. Walker (2008) suggests that teachers need to teach diagnostically and "assess changes in students' reading and writing *as* they teach" (p. 18). Veronica's story included basic story elements of characters, setting, problem, events leading to a solution, and resolution in her story written in March of first grade, but they ran together; the writing also lacked transitions. Helping her decide where to break for a new paragraph (or new page) would facilitate further discussion of specific components (*traits*) of quality writing (e.g. ideas, organization, transition sentences, word, choice, conventions) (see Figure 9.3). *Teaching diagnostically* is cyclical. Teachers carefully observe the learner's performance on a task, evaluate what it means, make decisions about the next instructional step or series of steps, and implement teaching toward each objective. Then, they observe the learner's response to the intervention just delivered and continue the cycle (Walker, 2004). The diagnostic teaching cycle applies to any instructional interaction.

diagnostic teaching
a teaching strategy that combines assessment with instruction. The teacher matches teaching interventions with identified learning needs to scaffold the learner toward the target performance

---

The rich man and woman

Once upon a time in a far far away land thare was a poor widow he lived in Santiago. Thay were so poor the only thing thay coud eat was hard bred.

One day a rich man came to town. The old man and woman beged for mony. Little did thay no the man was a robber. Becs allmost Everybuty was just about poor. And then the man and the lady reckandised his Face and then thay rememberd he was the man that stold thare mony.

thay saw a gardin. thay started throwing tomatows at the man the mad got mad. He got out of his careig [carriage] and got on his hours [horse] and went home.

The nexed day the man came and left in a hery [hurry]! When the man went home and went to sleep.

Then the man and lady brocke into his house. Thay Got all of his Gold. Just then the man wocke up. Luckly thay din't Get cawt.

And thay touk the Gold Back to toune. Thay went to every house and Gave them some Gold and the toune was rich.

And the man that stold the mony went to Jall.

FIGURE 9.3
Veronica's Story Revised

To ensure consistency when reviewing data from multiple informal samples, a common understanding of universal traits of good writing—those continually refined throughout a writer's life—is useful. Some relate to function; others relate to form. Primary writers gradually acquire the characteristics when nurtured with time, choice, and ownership (Calkins, 1994; Graves, 1983; Hansen, 1987; Short et al., 1996; Turnbill, 1983). Respect for the thinking behind and meaning expressed in children's writing is essential. Instruction flows from that. Part of the conversation with Veronica went like this.

> T: What do you know about Santiago? Why did you choose that for the setting of your story?
> V: My friend's mother lived there when she was a little girl. She told me about Santiago so I wanted the man and lady to live there.

T: You wrote, "… there was a poor widow"? Do you know what "widow" means? Why did you use that description?

V: My mom said our neighbor is a widow because her husband died. She's poor too because she didn't have a job when her husband died.

T: Yes, she's a widow; a man whose wife is dead is called a widower. If the character who lives in Santiago is a man, he's a widower.

T: How did you decide to write about catching a robber and getting back what was stolen?

V: I heard kids talking on the bus about robbers and getting stuff back—and that robbers go to jail.

T: You really put together a lot of ideas from different places. Writers do that all the time when creating new stories.

V: I like to do that. I like to make stories. I tell them too. Sometimes I write them down.

T: Let's read your story together. We can make it more understandable for readers if we make breaks where you start to tell a new part. Good writing keeps sentences that tell the same part together. As we reread your story, we'll think about when it seems to change to a new part. For example, when are you finished telling about the characters and setting? Where does the next part begin?

Armstrong (1990) observed, "meaning must be held central to children's writing … one of the most important tasks in interpreting children's work is to describe its patterns of intentions" (p. 15). The teacher worked with the content of this child's writing, respecting her intended message (function), while introducing information about improving an element of form.

Efficient instruction requires an on-the-run examination of students' writing and teaching that meets their immediate needs. As children work during the scheduled time for writing, the teacher, as workshop leader, scaffolds young apprentices. She circulates the room to:

- intervene when a writer has *writer's block*. The teacher initiates a conversation that gets the writer talking; this helps him realize what he wants to say and how it might be said;

  writer's block
  the writer is stuck; he can't think of a topic or what to write next

- note how fluidly authors are generating a first draft (Chapter 8)—one that reflects ideas expressed in their plan for writing;
- join a rehearsal or share group to contribute to the discussion, offering compliments and comments to authors. The depth and quality of comments offered by audience members also provides information on responders' understanding about writing craft;
- have an editing conference with a writer (Chapter 8). The teacher reviews the entire piece of writing with the author to edit, discuss how the work will be published, and set goals for further writing. The conference checklist (Figure 8.22) guides the teacher's note-taking. The list of traits is used with authors who have moved beyond

emergent writing (Figure 9.4). Both forms document data that informs instructional decision-making.

Assessment is focused on the writing piece as a product that reveals current level of performance. It's also centered on the child's discussion as an indication of an ability to explain and self-reflect on his work. Collaboratively, the teacher and writer decide on goals for the child's next piece of writing. Sometimes, children are reluctant to accept a new challenge; they've become comfortable in their attained level. At other times, a writer shows vague signs of readiness (for example, by using but confusing quotation marks), but the teacher is unsure whether he's ready to grasp the intricacies of a new skill. This frequently happens with young advanced writers who are trying to incorporate conventions or styles they've noted in literature they've experienced.

If a writer (or group of writers) appears interested in a more sophisticated step, effective teachers introduce and discuss it; they respond to needs and interests revealed in the child's work and talk. What form or structure is he trying to use? It can be introduced immediately—during the conference. Or, it might be taught the next day as a mini lesson to a small group or to the individual who wants to know.

Acquiring new skills doesn't always come easily. But, that doesn't mean they can't be understood in the moment. Competent teachers appreciate that reality; they consider alternate presentations and additional scaffolded practice before abandoning instruction when the writer doesn't grasp something on a first try. They "look for another way to adjust instruction for literacy development" (Walker, 2008, p. 18). The goal is to help the writer move forward—write better. The writing conference offers an opportunity to discover and teach the small next step a writer needs to take.

Talking With Writers

Several researchers and authors have described a predictable pattern for effective teacher-writer conferences (Calkins, 1994; Graves, 1983; Hansen, 1987; Phenix, 1990; Robb, 1998; Short et al., 1996; Turnbill, 1983). The tone and content of an effective conference are always positive, where the teacher offers compliments about what's working in the writing before sensitively offering a comment to improve it. The writer contributes his perspectives during the conference, making the review collaborative.

Ray (2004) outlines a conference pattern that involves *active* decision-making—a pattern that integrates the research. The teacher:

- watches to notice specifics in the writer's work;
- is patient and respectful of the writer's involvement with his work. She uses *wait time*—allowing the child to finish the thought he's engaged with or sentence he's writing before initiating a conversation;

- asks the child to talk about his piece of writing. Leading questions help to focus this conversation. The teacher asks, "What part of this writing do you like the best? Which parts don't sound right to you? What parts were hard to write? What parts do you especially like?"
- responds to the content of the writing. The teacher might say, "I like the way you describe the characters. I can picture them. Your words remind me of ... I laughed (or felt sad) when you wrote ... I feel suspense with the words ... I wonder what will happen next";
- considers all she knows about the writer while observing and listening. The teacher knows the writer's history of growth in writing;
- asks the writer how she can help; she decides on one (or two if they're related) teaching point that addresses the immediate need. The teacher sensitively challenges the child to set achievable writing goals while demonstrating confidence that he can meet them.

With young writers, the teaching point might be how to tell more, listen for and sequence sounds, or match sounds to appropriate letters. The teaching point for Veronica was to establish appropriate breaks in her storytelling. The teacher had planned a mini lesson as an individual conference with Veronica. She shared a familiar book with chapters and guided Veronica to notice the structure and how sentences in each paragraph are related. This occurred before the dialog shared earlier in the chapter. Together, they decided how to group the sentences in Veronica's story. Veronica cut sentences apart and pasted them together as paragraphs (Figure 9.3). Now, she can add more content to each paragraph or work on transition sentences.

Small nuances of difference in written performance are important; it takes time to perfect a skill. The teacher, as evaluator, pieces together collected evidence of growth; accumulated data lead to the emergence of patterns. Evaluation of learning involves placing a value on data, revealing the direction and nature of change in children's writing development. Reading data and understanding their significance are time consuming; it requires thoughtfulness and persistence. But, the payoff is huge. Effective assessment leads to informed instruction—instruction that's efficient in its focus and precisely on target. Writers get what they need when they need it. "Assessment is meant to be diagnostic. It's about discovering where you're strong, so-so, confused, and just don't get it" (Shea et al., 2005, p. 1). The process is the same for all learners at any level of learning. To make these fine distinctions, there's a stream of assessment *for* learning (Stiggins, 2002).

Effective teachers continually assess all children's writing to make decisions *for* their learning. They think, "How should I guide this writer? What can he do? What specifically does he need *right now*—teaching, re-teaching, reinforcing, clarifying, or nudging? Where do I start?" Anecdotal notes and data-gathering forms (such as editing conference forms—Figures 8.22, 9.4, and 9.5) provide the grist for timely individual FYI lessons as well as small group or class mini lessons.

Teaching the Traits: Balancing Function, Style, and Form

It's important to maintain a developmentally appropriate balance between function and form with young writers. "Writers only become writers when they have something to say" (Nutbrown, 1999, p. 74). Numerous actual and vicarious experiences—ones that build background knowledge on a range of topics and stimulate further curiosity—provide grist for expanded writing (function). But, writers beyond the emergent stage want to construct messages others can read; they become increasingly interested in refining conventions (forms) in their writing. Competent teachers know that responding to the *teachable moment*—when students are ready for and need the information—is critically important. Continued struggles with the forms of writing lead to frustration and abbreviated expressions. Elements of function and form must be nurtured in ways harmonious with children's natural development. Common characteristics—*traits*—of quality writing have been well-documented (Calkins, 1994; Culham, 2003; Graves, 1983; Hansen, 1987; Murray, 1980; Phenix, 1990; Short et al., 1996). A frame for considering them in a balanced approach ensures appropriate attention to all.

composition
process of constructing a written message

Nutbrown (1999) describes three categories for organizing the traits (characteristics) of quality writing. These include *composition* or the process of constructing meaning with print as the sign (meaning) system. Writing begins with thinking about the ideas that will be replicated in print. The next category is *communication*. The writer attempts to communicate in a way that grabs and holds his reader's attention. This includes a skillful use of structures (genres) matched to intended messages as well as the personal voice of the teller. Specific writing structures guide the reader's comprehension while voice adds life to the ink and paper; voice is a window onto the author's personality. The third category is *secretary*; it relates to the mechanics (forms, including spelling, grammar, and punctuation) and appearance (neatness) of writing. However, caution is suggested with this category. When secretarial elements are given prime importance in early writing, development is usually stifled (Larson, 2002). The elements should be part of editing a final draft for presentation.

communication
expressing a message in a way that enables others to receive it (e.g. by listening or reading)

secretary
relates to the mechanics or correct conventions for printed language

Using the checklist (Figures 9.4 and 9.5), teachers document a writer's growth in the traits from beginning to early fluent levels as it occurs across early elementary grades. Each trait has notable markers. The checklist in Figure 9.5 identifies common needs that can be met with small group instruction.

Composition

Assessing the quality of young children's writing can be accomplished by looking at productions through particular lenses associated with each trait (Culham, 2003; Nutbrown, 1999). There's no hierarchy of

Name _____   Date_____

Record the date when significant evidence has been gathered to support the determination of skill level as **Beginning**, **Developing**, or **Early Fluent**

Skill	Beginning	Developing	Early Fluent
Composition			
Ideas			
• writing is focused on a theme			
• strong, relevant ideas are used to address the theme			
• ideas are supported with relevant, interesting, important, or informative details			
• message is clear to author and reader			
Organization			
• effective opening			
• ideas flow logically, building on each other			
• transitions between ideas and sentences are smooth; sentences blend together			
• effective closing			
Sentences			
• uses simple sentences			
• expands sentence with details and descriptors			
• constructs appropriate compound sentences with conjunctions (e.g. and, but, or)			
• creates appropriate sentences of varied length, type, and style			
Vocabulary			
• colorful language is used appropriately			
• precise language is appropriately used			
• interesting words are used appropriately			
• effectively incorporates new words from literature and conversations			
Communication			
Purpose			
• intention directs the writing			
• writer can explain his intention			
• uses writing for multiple purposes			
• appropriately matches purpose to genre for writing			
• effectively writes in different genres			
• has a sense of audience; considers needs and interests of readers			*Continued overleaf*

FIGURE 9.4 Writing Checklist

Skill	Beginning	Developing	Early Fluent
Voice			
• a personal tone comes through—a sense that the writer is speaking to a reader			
Secretary			
Mechanics			
• tracks print while reading message back; notices missing words			
• Spelling (Beginning = semi to early phonetic Developing = phonetic; Early Fluent = transitional to conventional)			
• appropriate punctuation			
• appropriate capitalization			
• standard grammar			
Appearance			
• print progresses from L to R, line under line (unless purposefully placed for aesthetic reasons)			
• correct letter formation			
• appropriate spacing between letters, words, sentences			
• clear handwriting			
• generally neat			

Comments:

Date/Comment

FIGURE 9.4 *Continued*

development, but each dimension adds to the whole. As children write and listen to or read the writing of others (authors and peers), they internalize an understanding of composition as an expression of ideas in print.

Ideas

Young children's ideas for writing typically reflect life experiences, conversations, and literature read to them. At first, their thinking through print seems like a stream of consciousness—a bouncing stream or one that flows from a single topic. It's important to assess the development of the child's focus. Does the writing have a topic? Does the writer construct strong ideas related to the topic? Are interesting, important, or informative details presented to support the theme? The strength of ideas and the details that support them persuade a reader to engage with the author—to learn or be convinced, inspired, or entertained.

Name _____   Date _____

B = beginning   D = Developing   F = Fluent

List writers →																											
Skill	B	D	F	B	D	F	B	D	F	B	D	F	B	D	F	B	D	F	B	D	F	B	D	F	B	D	F
Composition																												
Ideas																												
• writing is focused on a theme																												
• strong, relevant ideas are used to address the theme																												
• ideas are supported with relevant, interesting, important, or informative details																												
• message is clear to author and reader																												
Organization																												
• effective opening																												
• ideas flow logically, building on each other																												
• transitions between ideas and sentences are smooth; sentences blend together																												
• effective closing																												
Sentences																												
• uses simple sentences																												
• expands sentence with details and descriptors																												
• constructs appropriate compound sentences with. conjunctions (e.g. and, but, or)																												
• creates appropriate sentences of varied length, type, and style																												
Vocabulary																												
• colorful language is used appropriately																												
• precise language is appropriately used																												
• interesting words are used appropriately																												
• effectively incorporates new words from literature and conversations																												

Continued overleaf

FIGURE 9.5 Writing Checklist for Group Analysis

List writers ⟶	B	D	F	B	D	F	B	D	F	B	D	F	B	D	F	B	D	F	B	D	F	B	D	F	B	D	F
Skill	B	D	F	B	D	F	B	D	F	B	D	F	B	D	F	B	D	F	B	D	F	B	D	F	B	D	F
Communication																											
Purpose																											
• intention directs the writing																											
• writer can explain his intention																											
• uses writing for multiple purposes																											
• appropriately matches purpose to genre for writing																											
• effectively writes in different genres																											
• has a sense of audience; considers needs and interests of readers																											
Voice																											
• a personal tone comes through—a sense that the writer is speaking to a reader																											
Secretary																											
Mechanics																											
• tracks print while reading message back; notices missing words																											
• Spelling (Beginning = semi to early phonetic; Developing = phonetic; Early Fluent = transitional to conventional)																											
• appropriate punctuation																											
• appropriate capitalization																											
• standard grammar																											
Appearance																											
• print progresses from L to R, line under line (unless purposefully placed for aesthetic reasons)																											
• correct letter formation																											
• appropriate spacing between letters, words, sentences																											
• clear handwriting																											
• generally neat																											

Comments:

Date/Comment

FIGURE 9.5 *Continued*

Organization

Organization of expression is a difficult concept. Abundant experience in verbalizing ideas develops awareness of the features that make it easier for an audience to comprehend the message. Like any verbalized story, effective writing piques the reader's interest with its opening sentence or paragraph. Attention is maintained when there's a logical flow of well-sequenced ideas. Transition words and sentences are the glue that connects ideas; they eliminate jolts and pauses in the reader's message processing. Organized writing weaves pieces together in a closing that evokes a sense of completion.

In June of first grade, Brett and Jason worked together to write a report on dolphins. Their earlier report writing was a string of ideas on the topic—a stream of facts that were most interesting to them. Like Veronica, they hadn't considered how to structure their information, although both had been reading books organized by subtopics and paragraphs. The teacher planned several mini lessons throughout the class research project. These included planning subtopics to be researched (i.e. characteristics of the animal, where it's found, typical behaviors), researching information for each subtopic, drafting a paragraph that sticks to the topic, and putting pieces of the report together. The boys used what they learned in the lessons to organize ideas with a paragraph for each subtopic (Figure 9.6). It's a first step toward report writing with more refined features (i.e. distinct introduction and conclusion, identified subtopics, and transitional sentences).

Dolphins are gray. They have a fin that sticks out of the water. Dolphins have a blowhole for breathing. It's on their head. They can live for 30 or 40 years.

Dolphins live in the ocean. Dolphins live in aquariums too. You can see dolphins at Marine Land. You can see dolphins if you are on a big ship in the ocean.

Dolphins eat fish. They swim and flip. They can be trained to do many tricks. Dolphins make high-pitched sounds too. It's like talking to other dolphins.

There are different kinds of dolphins. Dolphins are mammals. The mother dolphin makes milk in her body. She feeds the milk to the baby dolphin.

Dolphin babies are called calves. They are born under the water. Calves stay close to their mother for one year.

Scientists study dolphins. They write books about them. We read some books and learned about them. We like dolphins.

FIGURE 9.6
Dolphins

Sentences

Children who have been exposed to good conversational models, invited to participate in extended conversations, and immersed in quality literature followed by book talks are primed for writing. They have the experience necessary to construct sentences that are increasingly complex, rich in detail, and varied in length, style, and type. They construct with the materials they have; input highly affects output. Where early language input is limited, effective teachers infuse their teaching with healthy doses of effective language models to ameliorate differences. All children are marinated in quality literature and experiences followed by discussion of the content and connections made with each.

Vocabulary

Words are important; they have power. Precise words clarify meaning; they lessen the potential for misunderstanding. The right words in the right places make the writing interesting, poetic, and memorable. Children acquire such words in the same way they acquire the material for constructing good sentences.

Communication

The desire to communicate seems inherent—something we're driven to do. People talk to those around them. But we have archaeological evidence that humans sought to spread their messages beyond the neighborhood—to later generations. Before writing, people made their stories permanent with ideographic markings. Cave drawings report the trials, tragedies, and triumphs of their creators. As alphabets were established, written messages were constructed for similar purposes. Children verbalize ideas, wants, and needs at a very young age. As they interact with others they learn how to revise and refine their expression, increasing understanding and response from the listener. The introduction of marking tools leads to ideographic representations of ideas (drawing)—illustrations for verbal text.

Drawings—by children or cave people—can be interpreted as they stand, but the interpretation may differ from the intention. Alphabetic systems allow people to construct messages that more fully explain their ideas—their stories. But, written productions are also open to interpretation. When authors in any sign system (print, music, art, dance) go public, they no longer own the meaning. They maintain intended meaning, but audiences are entitled to different interpretations. Understanding how this works, grants literal readers the freedom to infer. When teachers think out loud, explaining how they make an inference, they let readers know that it's more than all right to add personal information between the lines; it's expected.

For example, a teacher demonstrated what she had concluded about a story setting and character traits. She explained,

> The author said the old house has a broken porch; it needs paint. And, a broken window has boards nailed to it. The yard is messy with junk, weeds, and tall grass. I think no one lives there. Or, the person who lives there can't fix those things. It says Billy's wondering about the noises he's heard coming

from the house. He's going to ask a friend to go with him to investigate. I think Billy's curious—and cautious. He wants to know, but he's wise enough to have someone come with him in case there's danger. Readers do this all the time. They combine what they know with the information in the story and make inferences like I just did. Writers put in enough information—particular clues—so readers will *infer*. Readers infer—add—details that connect their experience and what they know to the story. You should do it too. It helps you understand a story.

Purpose

Writers write to communicate vital personal stories, whether small or grand. "Children's writing often reflects events which are important to them, real and imagined happenings, [and] the plots of favorite or influential stories they have read or heard told to them" (Nutbrown, 1999, p. 73). Young children also write to report what they've learned from research, experimentation, or experience. Passion is the driving force that spurs writers on when the work is difficult. In school, purpose is often set by a teacher-directed prompt or petition (Cole, 2009). But, the best prompts and petitions are open-ended; choice and ownership ignite the responder's intrinsic motivation to engage. Purpose guides decisions related to structure, style, and formality, whether the writing is self-initiated or requested.

Voice

Finding your voice in writing comes with maturity, the cumulative effect of exposure to good models, and lots of writing practice. Some people become adequate writers without ever finding their voice. Voice is hard to describe, but you know it's there when you "hear" it. You hear voice in such elements as a writer's tone, word selection, or injection of humor. Celebrate the budding of voice in young children's writing. Nurture its growth by sharing literature filled with voice and guiding children's efforts to find their own.

Secretary

The very act of marking—the process and production—is initially what stimulates the child. He's observed those around him using writing so he mimics that action. The child's production looks like writing; the act feels like writing. Response from others leads the child to associate a message with his marking. But, only he can decipher it. For his message to be readable by others, the child must begin to use print that others can read. In minute steps, the writer becomes his own secretary. With help, he manages compositions, checking messages for interest, clarity, and accuracy.

Mechanics

The term "mechanics" refers to the expected forms for standard usage in written language. It includes correct spelling, grammar, and punctuation. Teachers evaluate children's stage of spelling development before grouping them for instruction (Figures 9.7). Mechanics also includes the format appropriate for a genre (e.g. business or friendly letter, poetry). The use of conventions grows developmentally with effective instruction, time for practice, targeted feedback, and, most importantly, respect for the writer's effort and his intended message.

Semi-phonetic	Phonetic	Transitional
Word awareness	Short vowels	Double letters (grass)
Syllable awareness	Long vowels	Regular verbs (e.g. w/ed)
Awareness of onset and rime	Initial blends	Irregular verbs
Alphabet (recognition, matching)	Consonant digraphs	Making plurals
Phonemic awareness	Final blends	Irregular plurals
Initial consonants	Vowel digraphs	Compound words
Final consonants	"R" controlled vowels	Prefixes/suffixes
Medial consonants	Diphthongs	Abbreviations
		Homonyms
		Contractions
		Possessives
		Silent letters

FIGURE 9.7
Class List on Spelling Continuum

Appearance

We're told not to judge a book by its cover; a great story can reside under a wretched binding. But, in the case of writing, people tend to ignore this maxim. When writing's messy, readers get discouraged. They easily assume the message doesn't warrant getting mired in the muck. As children learn the principles of letter formation and develop fine motor skills, their ability to control appearance improves. Drawing attention to exemplars—writing that's legible, neat, and free of erasure or written-over letters helps. However, it's unwise to allow young writers to become compulsive about neatness. Try to encourage a reasonable approach.

This spectrum of traits represents long-term goals; young writers are never expected to have mastered them. Authors continue to refine their craft over a lifetime. But, it is important to keep an eye on the destination while living in the moment. When you don't know where you're going, you won't know whether you've arrived. In conferences, we discuss the work with a writer, suggest revisions, support the process of polishing the piece, and help him set new goals.

Documenting a Continuum of Learning

Periodically, teachers review data accumulated over time (e.g. across a given reporting period) and form conclusions about a writer's growth. They place a *tentative value* on the myriad of data gathered through assessment. In other words, they make an evaluation *of* learning—of the writer's growth on a continuum (such as a spelling continuum class list or primary writing checklist) or against a benchmark of expected growth at a specific point. Figure 9.8 shows a comparison of assessment for learning and assessment of learning (Nutbrown, 1999; Stiggins, 2002).

Assessment *for* Learning	Assessment *of* Learning
• purpose is to inform next instructional step	• purpose related to accountability
• is ongoing, in-the-lesson; it's formative	• occurs after a block or unit of study; it's summative
• focused on the individual's knowledge acquisition	• compares achievement to benchmark
• requires understanding of child and concept development	• requires ability to follow directions for test administration
• effectiveness highly connected to the teacher–learner relationship	• teacher–learner relationship is not a critical factor; another adult can administer the measure
• children's work and behavior becomes the focus of analysis	• specific prompts are followed to elicit responses
• looks for patterns across triangulated data	• items related to particular skill limited in number and context

Adapted from Nutbrown, 1999; Stiggins, 2002.

FIGURE 9.8
Assessment *for* Learning and Assessment *of* Learning

When significant evidence of a writing trait has been accumulated from anecdotal notes and writing samples, the teacher notes it on the checklist (Figure 9.4). She checks and dates her conclusion in the Beginning column. After additional accumulation of evidence reflects that the skill is maintained and expanding, a check and date is placed in the Developing column. A third body of evidence designates that the learner has reached the Early Fluent level with the skill; this is noted with a check and date. The checklist records the glass filling; the focus is on what has been accomplished and setting the next goal (Shea et al., 2005). It mirrors a learning continuum—a journey that's not completed in a single academic year. And, basic writing skills—including those attained —need to be continuously monitored and practiced during and beyond the primary grades. Evidence of growth in the writing traits is revealed in tasks accomplished across the curriculum—across the grades.

Multiple Assessments for a Complete Picture

Many schools adopt formal tests and programs aimed at preparing students for state assessments. Most states now include a writing component in their ELA (English Language Arts) test as well as content area tests. When used effectively, local tests and programs prepare children for the format of state tests. But, the skills taught and measured with these only scratch the surface. There's so much more to writing if one is to understand and use it fully in life. Developing individual talent in creative writing is very important; such writing is personally fulfilling. It also adds enormously to a culture—to the human spirit. But, much writing in school and out of school involves the ability to respond to a *prompt* (question) or *petition* (request to explain, describe, define) in a coherent, cohesive manner. Children need to develop a broad range of writing skills (Cole, 2006, 2009). Observations of others using writing in multiple aspects of daily life (making notes, lists, letters, e-mails) help children realize that writing proficiency allows them to emulate those behaviors.

prompt
a question or premise presented to a writer to initiate a written response

petition
a request for a written explanation, description, or definition

When deciding what to collect, the teacher as anthropologist considers the *purpose* of collecting—What am I looking for? To answer that question fully, a deep understanding of literacy concepts and child development is necessary. After teaching Veronica about making transitions within her story, the teacher reinforced the concept in modeled writing and, using books, read aloud to show how other authors do it—in narrative, exposition, or poetry. She watched for independent attempts to use transitions in future writing.

Teachers gather data related to target skills as children work on tasks that incorporate them. The teacher considers, Is this behavior an appropriate example of the concept? Does it require the writer to apply the concept? Did the task stimulate an *authentic representation* (use of the concept as it's used outside of school—writing a letter, notes, or e-mail) of the concept? Pedagogical (teaching) knowledge directs the teacher's gathering of valid evidence in response to both questions. The knowledgeable teacher is at the center of assessment that has instructional utility.

Day by day, positive engagement with writing—writing used for learning and living in a community—builds persistence with refining skills. It always comes down to a personal appreciation of purpose. The learner asks, "Why does this matter to me?" Any child wants to develop and improve a behavior that serves him well. Authentic uses for writing (such as writing notes, lists, stories, essays, poems, plays, or reports) in the classroom and recognition of useful writing done outside of school generate self-motivating purpose while expanding specific and broad skills. Each production of writing provides a microcosm of evidence. As pieces of a puzzle, the collected efforts form a picture of growth when connected. The picture is clearer with selected writing samples as informal data because these weren't created under stress, with time limits, or in response to a prompt loosely connected or not at all connected to the curriculum. Writers that are invested in their work acquire the persistence needed to refine skills. They have a passion for sharing a fully refined message; they enjoy the construction process even though it requires great effort.

Enjoying the Journey

Sometimes, we're so close to the forest we miss the trees; at times, young writers appear to be at a standstill. However, a careful review of assessments verifies growth—even when changes are miniscule and take time.

Marking the checklist (Figure 9.4)—by item and level (beginning, developing, early fluent)—as previously described, allows immediate identification of accomplishments and areas not yet mastered. Collaboratively, the teacher and learner determine where they'll go next.

Teachers acknowledge milestones with writers; each child's journey needs to be littered with recognized triumphs. Celebrations make the rough patches endurable.

With overall goals in mind, assess writers on a daily basis—observe how they work independently, use the print around them (e.g. wall charts, word walls, alphabet cards, books) or seek help from and offer help to peers (Kempton, 2007). Notice the uniqueness of children's development as well as their needs. Appreciate errors as windows into their thinking and a true compass for teaching plans. "They [errors] often signal that the child is reaching out to some new facet of written expression, and that he needs help toward some new learning" (Clay, 1987a, p. 58). It's particularly important to analyze the writing of bilingual children to assess what they understand about the relationship of the two languages and their point of development in each (Rubin & Carlan, 2005) since bilingual and multilingual children often use symbols and strategies across languages that have different forms and conventions (Hirst, 1998).

We can and must ensure that all children become capable, as well as enthusiastic, writers right from the start. Early success and positive dispositions about literacy activities sustain and extend motivation to pursue the knowledge and skills that lead to language proficiency.

Extending the Discussion

- Using the checklist, analyze writing samples from an advanced first grade writer or children in your classroom. Plan small group instruction based on identified common needs.
- Discuss how you will introduce these writing traits to children who are ready to work at this level.
- Find literature selections that demonstrate particular writing traits. Outline a plan for sharing the books and examining each author's demonstration of the trait.
- Create a letter to parents that explains your plan for working with their child as an advanced writer. Suggest how they can reinforce your instruction.

ten
Conclusion

Young children need teachers who are well-grounded in child and literacy development as well as sound pedagogical practice. They need teachers who continue to build on that knowledge through professional development, collegial interactions, and deep reflection. And, they need teachers who are allowed to use their expertise to teach diagnostically, differentially, and in developmentally appropriate ways. These teachers work as professionals; they're not scripted technicians, mandated to follow every step and word of a program whether or not it fits the needs of children—whether or not it's even theoretically sound. The writing shared in this text came from classrooms with such teachers—ones who crafted writing and literacy activities aligned with foundational perspectives on early literacy (Rowe, 2008). The children came from homes where parents responded to their learning explorations with sensitivity and soft teaching. The children in these environments were immersed in literate activities; their writing reflects it.

Complementing Developmental Learning

Some programs for literacy instruction—ones with rigid scope and sequences—appear incompatible with Sylvia Ashton-Warner's (1963) concept of *organic learning*, making the practices they outline a futile endeavor. The child's motivation to participate slowly atrophies as others take control over his behaviors; however well-intended, scripted teaching subverts the child's role in directing learning.

The child's writing must be "his own affair ... The more it means to him the more value it is to him" (Ashton-Warner, 1963, p. 54). Learning grows organically with sensitive nurturing and simple basic ingredients.

Experimenting Through Play

Children learn through their play. They're motivated to engage because they're in charge of how it goes; it isn't play without that element.

Bringing literacy into the play domain is easy. Props (such as restaurant menus in the kitchen, garage work orders in the truck area, or post office cubbies) direct children's attention to using print in imaginative ways—in the same way they play with spoken language (Newman, 1984). Inattention is never a question during play. A child would experiment with water toys in the bathtub until he turned into a prune.

Children like to *muck around a bit* with writing materials. They're content using what they know about print and how it works; they elaborate creatively. But, when the pressure for correctness is high, children shut down. Their "up tight gotta be right" state produces tentativeness and real fear about making any uncertain marks. They would rather appear unwilling than unable. Writers aren't born; they're made. The construction zone for that making is lengthy, messy, and bumpy—filled with the debris of starts and stops as well as frustrations and triumphs. Through it all, accomplished writers acknowledge having the support of others and great mentors along the way. However, being a writing mentor is a challenge in today's educational climate.

Schools are highly stressed about achievement; they forget that natural learning doesn't follow from one neat step to the next (Papert, 1980). In school, children learn to avoid experimentation for fear of being wrong. But, "errors benefit us because they lead us to study what happened, to understand what went wrong, and, through understanding, to fix it" (Papert, 1980, p. 114). The path back to balance between discovery and instruction will be blazed by teachers who kindle the flame of effective pedagogical practice.

Self-directed Learning

Children's own purposes inspire them to write. "The whole exercise of creative writing, the reaching back into the mind for something to say nurtures the organic idea and exercises the inner eye" (Ashton-Warner, 1963, p. 55). Intention may be the most important factor leading to persistence at the task (Clay, 1987a).

Teachers need to honor young children's priority for function (Feldgus & Cardonick, 1999). The child is the decider; he chooses why to write, when to do it, what to tell, and how to say it (Morrow, 2009). Young children find lots of reasons to write—ones that are personally important and connected to their lives. When self-determination and experimentation are suppressed, writers lose interest. They can't write about things they don't know about or care about—in ways they don't understand. That principle is basic and critical for all authorship. Like the thread from a spider that anchors it to the web, it's been reiterated throughout this text that theories and practices must be connected to writers' schemata and passions. The principle must be at the heart of a school's writing curriculum.

Avoidance leads to *aliteracy*; sadly, this condition is noticed in many struggling older writers. Aliteracy is defined as the tendency of capable readers and writers to choose not to engage in literate activities (Harris &

Hodges, 1981). They write only when they have to—without voice or passion. The cure is supported engagement for personally meaningful purposes. Ensure time for writing in a safe environment, choice of topics, and ownership of the work. These ingredients are topped with strategically offered models that demonstrate reasons, content, and styles for writing.

Social Aspects of Learning

Children need to observe others reading and writing in natural ways. "What an individual can learn, and how he learns, depends on what models he has available" (Papert, 1980, p. vii). Soft teaching begins with adult models in the child's home environment; it continues with educators who apply developmentally appropriate practice while "grabbing teachable moments, grabbing the teachable kid running by" (Kingston, 1963, p. 9). Modeling produces a visual image of how something is created or accomplished. Models offer possibilities rather than exemplars to be replicated; they broaden the child's schemata for his own thinking and creating.

In effective writing classrooms, children also respond to authentic requests for writing. They've observed adults writing in response to a prompt or petition from others; they know this is part of the business of living. Both are authentically connected to one's work or living in a family and broader community. Navigating this writing is a functional and critical life skill.

Classrooms—ones that are microcosms of real world learning—make similar calls for writing. Typically these are connected to units of study, collective inquiry, or personal reflection. Prompts and petitions that generate the most creative thinking are open-ended, offering a range of options for content and style, allowing voice to emerge in the creation. Responding to calls for writing can be done in tandem; more heads and hands make the job easier. Relationships are built in shared toil. Children learn from each other while practicing the skills needed to work in harmony with others.

Learning in Harmony

Children need to collaborate with other writers. "To create is to construct, and to construct collaboratively is to lay the foundations of a peaceful community" (Ashton-Warner, 1963, p. 11). I've worked in many classrooms as a literacy specialist. As a college instructor, I visit literacy specialist interns in local classrooms. And, as a researcher, I've visited classrooms across the United States and in other countries. I feel the ethos—the tone—of a classroom the second I enter it. It's intangible, but very real. Tone is "a condition that is or is not implicit in every group of people working together" (Ashton-Warner, 1963, p. 84). It can be a condition of peace that envelops you warmly, making you instantly feel like a member of the community. Or, it can firmly reinforce the fact that you are an outsider. Tone reverberates in the room's physical arrangements, the degree of child-centeredness in routines and curriculum, the teacher's demeanor, and personal interactions. Children, like anyone else, are deeply affected by tone.

Writers thrive in caring communities—where their work is appreciated. One might say a tree falling in a distant forest doesn't make a sound unless someone hears it. Likewise, writing doesn't communicate unless someone reads it and grasps the message. Most writing is produced for reading. Sometimes, the reader is also the creator—when it's personal writing to think, reflect, or organize ideas. Writers also reach out to communicate through their productions. There's vulnerability in that social contact. Writers hope that an audience will consider their message, appreciate their right to self-expression, and treat them and their work respectfully. Caring is a cornerstone of a writing classroom; it permeates all interactions, providing a safe haven for social, emotional, and cognitive growth. "The primary aim of every educational institution and of every educational effort must be the maintenance and enhancement of caring" (Noddings, 1984, p. 172). The effective writing teacher knows intuitively that she must "support his [the child's] efforts . . . He [the child] must be aware always that . . . he is more important, more valuable, than the subject" (Noddings, 1984, p. 174).

Why Write Right Now?

We should allow children to write right from the start, because that's what children want to do. Allowing it demonstrates that we value what's inherent in their nature. Children don't order their learning as adults sequence instruction. They accept that living in the world requires an integrated application of a myriad of skills to accomplish complete tasks. They seek to develop competence in a range of seemingly disparate skills at once. However, many current school practices work against this logic.

Young children who explore the writing system start with approximated productions of the whole; they've noticed print's functions and seek to participate. This attention leads them to question and examine closely the parts that make up that whole—the forms and conventions that facilitate communication. Young writers work on the parts in order to apply them back to the whole; they've intuited that the ultimate purpose for these pieces *is* the message. *Whole-part-whole* is the natural learning pattern for any new skill (Temple et al., 2008). Conversely, learning literacy in many schools today seems to start and focus on parts.

The drive—fueled by mandates for federal funding—to break literacy into pieces to be taught and tested separately has produced learners who bark at print on demand, but haven't learned to attend to meaning or love a good book. They say sounds and words—with increasing speed—but fail to process these into a coherent whole. Reports show that reading comprehension scores for grades 1 to 3 are down (IRA, 2008). Meaningful early writing has also been neglected—even eliminated in places.

Could we have expected a different result, when the emphasis in schools was on isolated skills?

Teachers given the "flexibility, resources, and evidence as to what is effective" (IRA, 2008, p. 4) apply their pedagogical skills in designing effective literacy programs that meet the needs of all children. When we deeply understand language learning—when that knowledge guides our teaching—children write into reading and read as writers. The processes develop in parallel, each supporting the other.

Bibliography

Allen, R. (1976). *Language experience in communication.* Boston, MA: Houghton Mifflin.

Allington, R., & Cunningham, P. (1996). *Schools that work: Where all children read and write.* New York, NY: HarperCollins.

Anderson, R., & Freebody, P. (1981). Vocabulary knowledge. In J. Guthrie (Ed.), *Comprehension and teaching: Research views* (pp. 77–117). Newark, DE: International Reading Association.

Anderson, R., Hiebert, E., Scott, J., & Wilkinson, I. (1984). *Becoming a nation of readers: The report of the commission on reading.* Washington, DC: The National Institute of Education.

Applebee, A. (1980). Children's narratives: New directions. *The Reading Teacher, 34*(2), 137–142.

Armstrong, M. (1990). Another way of looking. *Forum, 33*(1), 12–16.

Ashton-Warner, S. (1963). *Teacher.* New York, NY: Simon & Schuster.

Avery, C. (1993). *... And with a light touch: Learning about reading, writing, and teaching first graders.* Portsmouth, NH: Heinemann.

Bagley, D. (1937). A critical study of objective estimates in the teaching of English. *British Journal of Educational Psychology, 7,* 57–71.

Bandura, A. (1998). *Self-efficacy: The exercise of control.* New York: Freeman.

Bear, D., Invernizzi, M., Templeton, S., & Johnston, F. (2000). *Words their way: Word study for phonics, vocabulary, and spelling instruction.* Upper Saddle River, NJ: Prentice Hall.

Beaty, J. (2009). *50 Early childhood literacy strategies.* Upper Saddle River, NJ: Pearson.

Beaty, J., & Pratt, L. (2011). *Early literacy in preschool and kindergarten: A multi-cultural perspective.* New York, NY: Pearson.

Beck, I., McKeown, M., & Kucan, L. (2002). *Bring words to life: Robust vocabulary instruction.* New York, NY: Guilford.

Behymer, A. (2003). Kindergarten writing workshop. *The Reading Teacher, 57*(1), 85–88.

Bissex, G. (1980). *GNYS at work: A child learns to read and write.* Cambridge, MA: Harvard University Press.

Bissex, G. (1984). The child as teacher. In H. Goelman, A. Oberg, & F. Smith (Eds.), *Awakening to literacy* (pp. 87–101). Portsmouth, NH: Heinemann.

Bloomfield, L. (1933). *Language.* New York, NY: Henry Holt.

Bodrova, E., & Leong, D. (1996). *Tools of the mind: The Vygotskian approach to early childhood education.* Englewood Cliffs, NJ: Merrill/Prentice Hall.

Bodrova, E., & Leong, D. (1998). Scaffolding emergent writing in the zone of proximal development. *Literacy Teaching and Learning*, 3(2), 1–18.

Bodrova, E., & Leong, D. J. (2007). *Tools of the mind: The Vygotskian approach to early childhood education* (2nd ed.). Upper Saddle River, NJ: Pearson/Merrill Prentice Hall.

Bond, G. L., & Dykstra, R. (1967). The cooperative research program in first-grade reading instruction. *Reading Research Quarterly*, 2(4), 4–142.

Branscombe, N. A., Castle, K., Dorsey, A., Surbeck, E., & Taylor, J. (2003). *Early childhood curriculum: A constructivist perspective*. New York, NY: Houghton Mifflin.

Bredekamp, S. (Ed.). (1987). *Developmentally appropriate practice in early childhood programs serving children from birth through age 8*. Washington, DC: National Association for the Education of Young Children.

Bredekamp, S., & Copple, C. (1997). *Developmentally appropriate practice in early childhood programs*. Washington, DC: National Association for the Education of Young Children.

Bredekamp, S., & Rosegrant, T. (Eds.). (1992). *Reaching potentials: Appropriate curriculum and assessment for young children. Vol. I*. Washington, DC: NAEYC.

Brodsky-Chenfield, M. (2007). Handcuffed in the garden of thorns. *Reading Today*, 25(1), 20.

Bruner, J. (1986). *Actual minds, possible worlds*. Cambridge, MA: Harvard University Press.

Burns, M., Snow, C., & Griffin, P. (Eds.). (1999). *Starting out right: A guide to promoting children's reading success*. Washington, DC: National Academy Press.

Caine, R. N., & Caine, G. (1997). *Education on the edge of possibility*. Alexandria, VA: Association for Supervision and Curriculum Development.

Calkins, L. (1994). *The art of teaching writing*. Portsmouth, NH: Heinemann.

Cambourne, B. (1984). Language, learning and literacy: Another way of looking at language learning. In A. Butler, & J. Turbill (Eds.), *Towards a reading-writing classroom* (pp. 5–10). Portsmouth, NH: Heinemann.

Cambourne, B. (1988). *The whole story: Natural learning and the acquisition of literacy in the classroom*. New York, NY: Scholastic.

Cambourne, B. (1995). Towards an educationally relevant theory of literacy learning: Twenty years of inquiry. *The Reading Teacher*, 49(3), 182–192.

Cambourne, B. (1999). Conditions for literacy learning: Turning learning theory into classroom instruction: A mini case study. *Reading Teacher*, 54(4), 414–429.

Campbell, R. (2004). *Phonics naturally*. Portsmouth, NH: Heinemann.

Cecil, N. (2007). *Striking a balance: Positive practices for early literacy*. Scottsdale, AZ: Holcomb Hathaway.

Chall, J. (1967). *Learning to read: The great debate*. New York, NY: McGraw-Hill.

Clark, L. (1987). Invented versus traditional spelling in first graders' writings. *Research in the teaching of English*, 22, 281–309.

Clay, M. (1980). Early writing and reading: Reciprocal gains. In M. M. Clark, & T. Glynn (Eds.), *Reading and writing for the child with difficulties* (pp. 27–43). Educational Review Occasional Publications No. 8, Birmingham, England.

Clay, M. (1987a). *What did I write?: Beginning writing behavior*. Portsmouth, NH: Heinemann.

Clay, M. (1987b). *Writing begins at home: Preparing children for writing before they go to school*. Portsmouth, NH: Heinemann.

Clay, M. (1991). *On becoming literate: The construction of inner control*. Portsmouth, NH: Heinemann.

Clay, M. (1993). *An observational survey*. Portsmouth, NH: Heinemann.

Clay, M. (2001a). *Change over time in children's literacy development*. Portsmouth, NH: Heinemann.

Clay, M. (2001b). Exploring with a pencil. *Theory Into Practice*, 16(5), 334–341.

Cole, A. (2003a). It's the teacher, not the program. *Education Week*, 22(26), 33.

Cole, A. (2003b). *Knee to knee, eye to eye: Circling in on comprehension*. Portsmouth, NH: Heinemann.

Cole, A. (2004). *When reading begins*. Portsmouth, NH: Heinemann.

Cole, A. (2006). *Right-answer writing*. Portsmouth, NH: Heinemann.

Cole, A. (2009). *Better answers: Written performance that looks good and sounds smart* (2nd ed.). Portland, ME: Stenhouse.

Coles, R., & Goodman, Y. (1980). Do we really need those oversized pencils? *Theory Into Practice, 19*(3), 194–196.

Collins, K. (2004). *Growing readers: Units of study in the primary classroom*. Portland, ME: Stenhouse.

Culham, R. (2003). *Six + 1 traits of writing*. New York, NY: Scholastic.

Cummins, J. (1979). Linguistic interdependence and the educational development of bilingual children. *Review of Educational Research, 49*, 222–251.

Cunningham, J. (2002). The National Reading Panel Report. In R. Allington (Ed.), *Big brother and the national reading curriculum* (pp. 49–74). Portsmouth, NH: Heinemann.

Cunningham, P., & Allington, R. (1994). *Classrooms that work: They all can read and write*. New York, NY: HarperCollins.

Dahl, K., & Farnam, K. (1990). *Children's writing: Perspectives from research*. Newark, DE: International Reading Association.

Denzin, N., & Lincoln, Y. (1994). *Handbook of Qualitative Research*. Thousand Oaks, CA: Sage.

Dickenson, D. K., & Tabors, P. O. (2001). *Beginning literacy with language: Young children learning at school and at home*. Baltimore, MD: Brookes.

Dodge, J. (2005). *Differentiation in action*. New York, NY: Scholastic.

Doyle, B., & Bramwell, W. (2006). Promoting emergent literacy and social/emotional learning through dialogic reading. *The Reading Teacher, 59*, 554–564.

Durkin, D. (1966). *Children who read early: Two longitudinal studies*. New York, NY: Teachers College Press.

Dyson, A. (1982). Reading, writing, and language: Young children solving the language puzzle. *Language Arts, 59*, 829–839.

Dyson, A. (1985). Individual differences in emerging writing. In M. Farr (Ed.), *Advances in writing research. Vol 1: Children's early writing development* (pp. 5–125). Norwood, NJ: Ablex.

Dyson, A. (2003). *The brothers and sisters learn to write: Popular literacies in childhood and school cultures*. New York, NY: Teachers College Press, Columbia University.

Ehri, L. (1975). Word consciousness in readers and prereaders. *Journal of Educational Psychology, 67*, 204–212.

Elkonin, D. (1963). The psychology of mastering the elements of reading. In B. Simon, & J. Simon (Eds.), *Educational psychology in the USSR*. Stanford, CA: Stanford University Press.

Elley, W. (1989). Vocabulary acquisition from listening to stories. *Reading Research Quarterly, 24*(2), 175–187.

Evans, R. (1979). The relationship between the reading and writing of syntactic structures. *Research in the Teaching of English, 13*(2), 129–135.

Farnan, N., Lapp, D., & Flood, J. (1992). Changing perspectives in writing instruction. *Journal of Reading, 35*(7), 550–556.

Feldgus, E., & Cardonick, I. (1999). *Kid writing: A systematic approach to phonics, journals, and writing workshop* (2nd ed.). Chicago, IL: Wright Group/McGraw-Hill.

Ferreiro, E., & Teberosky, A. (1989). *Literacy before schooling*. Portsmouth, NH: Heinemann.

Fields, M., Groth, L., & Spangler, K. (2008). *Let's begin reading right* (6th ed.). Upper Saddle River, NJ: Pearson Education.

Fisher, D., Flood, J., Lapp, D., & Frey, N. (2004). Interactive read-alouds: Is there a common set of implementation practices? *The Reading Teacher, 58*(1), 8–17.

Fisher, J. (1991). *Joyful learning: A whole language kindergarten*. Portsmouth, NH: Heinemann.

Freeman, M. (2003). *Teaching the youngest writers*. Gainesville, FL: Maupin House.

Galperin, P. Y. (1992). Organization of mental activity and the effectiveness of learning. *Journal of Russian and East European Psychology, 30*(4), 65–82.

Garan, E. (2004). *In defense of our children*. Portsmouth, NH: Heinemann.

Gentry, J. R. (2005). Instructional techniques for emerging writers and special needs students in kindergarten and grade 1. *Reading & Writing Quarterly, 21*(2), 113–134.

Gentry, J. R., & Gillet, J. W. (1993). *Teaching kids to spell*. Portsmouth, NH: Heinemann.

Goodman, K. (1982). Acquiring literacy is natural: Who killed cock robin? In F. Gollasch (Ed.), *Language & literacy: The selected writings of Kenneth Goodman, Vol. II* (pp. 243–269). Boston, MA: Routledge & Kegan Paul.

Goodman, K. (1996). *On reading*. Portsmouth, NH: Heinemann.

Goodman, K., Smith, E., Meredith, R., & Goodman, Y. (1987). *Language and thinking in school* (3rd ed.). New York, NY: Richard Owen.

Goodman, Y. (1984). The development of initial literacy. In H. Goelman, A. Oberg, & F. Smith (Eds.), *Awakening to literacy*. Portsmouth, NH: Heinemann.

Goodman, Y. (1985). Kidwatching: Observing children in the classroom. In A. Jaggar, & M. T. Smith-Burke (Eds.). *Observing the language learner*. Newark, DE: International Reading Association.

Goodman, Y. (1989). Children coming to know literacy. In W. Teale, & E. Sulzby (Eds.), *Emergent literacy: Writing and reading* (pp. 1–14). Norwood, NJ: Ablex.

Graves, D. (1981). *A case study observing the development of primary children's composing, spelling, and motor behaviors during the writing process* (Final Report No. NIE-G-78-0174. ED 218-653). Durham, NH: University of New Hampshire.

Graves, D. (1983). *Writing: Teachers and children at work*. Portsmouth, NH: Heinemann.

Graves, D. (1994). *A fresh look at writing*. Portsmouth, NH: Heinemann.

Graves, M. (2006). *The vocabulary book: Learning and instruction*. New York, NY: Teachers College Press and Urbana, IL: National Council of Teachers of English.

Graves, M., Juel, C., & Graves, B. (2007). *Teaching reading in the 21st century* (4th ed.). New York, NY: Allyn & Bacon.

Hall, M. A. (1976). *Teaching reading as a language experience*. Columbus, OH: Merrill.

Halliday, M. (1975). *Learning how to mean: Explorations in the development of language*. London: Edward Arnold.

Halliday, M. (1994). *An introduction to functional grammar* (2nd ed.). London: Edward Arnold.

Hansen, J. (1987). *When writers read*. Portsmouth, NH: Heinemann.

Harris, T., & Hodges, R. (Eds.). (1981). *A dictionary of reading and related terms*. Newark, DE: International Reading Association.

Harste, J., Burke, C., & Woodward, V. (1983). *The young child as writer-reader, and informant* (Final Report No. NIE-G-89-0121). Bloomington, IN: Language Education Department.

Harste, J., Woodward, V., & Burke, C. (1984). *Language stories and literacy lessons*. Portsmouth, NH: Heinemann.

Hart, B., & Risley, T. (1999). *The social world of children learning to talk*. Baltimore, MD: Brookes.

Hart, B., & Risely, T. (2003). The early catastrophe: The 30 million word gap by age 3. *American Educator*, Spring, 6–9.

Heath, S. (1983). *Ways with words: Language, life, and work in communities and classrooms*. New York, NY: Cambridge University Press.

Heath, S. (1989). Separating "things of the imagination" from life: Learning to read and write. In W. Teale, & E. Sulzby (Eds.), *Emergent literacy: Writing and reading* (pp. 156–172). Norwood, NJ: Ablex.

Hedrick, W., & Pearish, A. (2003). Good reading instruction is more important than who provides the instruction or where it takes place. In P. Mason, & J. Schumm (Eds.), *Promising practices for urban reading instruction* (pp. 6–24). Newark, NJ: International Reading Association.

Hill, E. (1980). *Where's Spot?* New York, NY: G. P. Putnam's Sons.

Hirst, K. (1998). Preschool literacy experiences of children in Punjabi, Urdu and Gujerati speaking families in England. *British Educational Research Journal, 24*(4), 415–429.

Holabird, K. (2002a). *Angelina ballerina's colors.* Middleton, WI: Pleasant Company Publishers.

Holabird, K. (2002b). *Angelina and Henry.* Middleton, WI: Pleasant Company Publishers.

Holdaway, D. (1979). *The foundations of literacy.* New York, NY: Ashton Scholastic.

Horn, M., & Giacobbe, M. E. (2007). *Talking, drawing, writing: Lessons for our youngest writers.* Portland, ME: Stenhouse.

Huberman, A. M., & Miles, M. (1994). Data management and analysis methods. In Denzin, N., & Lincoln, Y. (Eds.) *Handbook of qualitative research* (pp. 428–444). Thousand Oaks, CA: Sage.

International Reading Association (IRA). (1998). The studies that mattered. *Reading Today, 15*(6), 28.

International Reading Association (IRA). (2008). IRA issues statement on Reading First report. *Reading Today, 25*(6), 1 and 4.

International Reading Association and National Council of Teachers of English (IRA & NCTE). (1996). *Standards for the English language arts.* Newark, DE and Urbana, IL: IRA and NCTE.

Iredell, H. (1898). Eleanor learns to read. *Educator,* 233–238.

Jago, M. (1999). Bilingual children in a monolingual society. In David, T. (Ed.), *Young children learning* (pp. 156–167). London: Paul Chapman.

Jensen, E. (1998). *Teaching with the brain in mind.* Alexandria, VA: Association for Supervision and Curriculum Development.

Jensen, E. (2001). Fragile brains. *Educational Leadership, 59*(3), 32–36.

Johnson, B. (1999). *Never too early to write.* Gainesville, FL: Maupin House.

Johnston, P. (2004). *Choice words: How our language affects children's learning.* Portland, ME: Stenhouse.

Kane, T. (2001). *The fairy houses series.* Lee, NH: Light-Beams.

Karpova, S. (1966). The preschooler's realization of the lexical structure of speech. In F. Smith, & G. Miller (Eds.), *The genesis of language* (pp. 43–55). Cambridge, MA: The Massachusetts Institute of Technology Press.

Kempton, S. (2007). *The literate kindergarten: Where wonder and discovery thrive.* Portsmouth, NH: Heinemann.

Kibby, M. (1989). Teaching sight vocabulary with and without context before silent reading: A field test of the focus of attention hypothesis. *Journal of Reading Behavior, 21*(3), 261–278.

Kingston, M. (1963). Foreword. In S. Ashton-Warner, *Teacher* (pp. 7–9). New York, NY: Simon & Schuster.

Kirkland, L., & Patterson, J. 2005. Developing oral language in primary classrooms. *Early Childhood Education Journal, 32*(6), 391–395.

Klenk, L. (2001). Playing with literacy in preschool classrooms. *Childhood Education, 77*(3), 150–157.

Kostelnik, M., Soderman, A., & Whiren, A. (2007). *Developmentally appropriate curriculum: Best practices in early childhood education* (4th ed.). Upper Saddle River, NJ: Prentice Hall.

Kucer, S. (1985). The making of meaning: Reading and writing as parallel processes. *Written Communication, 2,* 317–336.

Kuskin, K. (1971). Tiptoe. In C. Huck, W. Jenkins, & W. Pyle (Eds.), *When something happy happens* (p. 33). Glenview, IL: Scott Foresman.

Laliberty, E., & Berzins, M. (2000). Creating opportunities for emerging biliteracy. *Primary Voices K-6, 8*(4), 11–17.

Laminack, L. (1990). Possibilities Daddy, I think it says possibilities: A father's journal of the emergence of literacy. *The Reading Teacher,* 43(8), 536–540.

Laminack, L. (1991). *Learning with Zachary.* New York, NY: Scholastic.

Larson, J. (2002). Packaging process: Sequences of commodified pedagogy on students' participation in literacy events. *Journal of Early Childhood Literacy,* 2(1), 65–94.

Lincoln, Y., & Guba, E. (1985). *Naturalistic inquiry.* Newbury Park, CA: Sage.

Makin, L., Diaz, C. J., & McLachlan, C. (2007). *Literacies in childhood: Changing views, challenging practice.* New York, NY: MacLennan & Petty.

Manzo, K. (2007). Reading curricula don't make cut for federal review. *Education Week,* 27. Retrieved from http://www.edweek.org/ew/articles/2007/08/15/01 whatworks_web.h27.html accessed 10/17/10.

Martens, P. (1998) Growing as a reader and writer: Sarah's inquiry into literacy. In R. Campbell (Ed.), *Facilitating preschool literacy* (pp. 51–68). Newark, DE: International Reading Association.

Martin, T., Lovat, C., & Purnell, G. (2007). *The really useful literacy book.* New York, NY: Routledge, Taylor & Francis.

Matthews, M., & Kesner, J. (2003). Children learning with peers: The confluence of peer status and literacy competence within small-group literacy events. *Reading Research Quarterly,* 38(2), 208–234.

Mayer, K. (2007). Emerging knowledge about emergent writing. *Young Children,* 62 (1), 34–40.

McGee, L., & Richgels, D. (1996). *Literacy's beginnings* (2nd ed.). Needham Heights, MA: Allyn & Bacon.

McGill-Franzen, A. (2006). *Kindergarten literacy: Matching assessment and instruction in kindergarten.* New York, NY: Scholastic.

McLaughlin, M. (2003). *Guiding comprehension in primary grades.* Newark, DE: International Reading Association.

McNaughton, S., Parr, J., & Smith, L. T. (1996). *Processes of teaching and learning in literacy—writing.* Final Report to Ministry of Education. Research project No. ER 35/5335, Ministry of Education, Wellington.

Meek, M. (1991). *On being literate.* London: Bodley Head.

Miller, D. (2002). *Reading with meaning.* Portland, ME: Stenhouse.

Montessori, M. (1966). *The secret of childhood* (7th ed.). M. J. Costelloe, Trans. New York, NY: Ballantine Books. (Original work published in 1960.)

Mooney, M. (1990). *Reading to, with, and by children.* Katonah, NY: Richard Owens.

Moore, P., & Lyon, A. (2005). *New essentials for teaching reading in PreK-2.* New York, NY: Scholastic.

Morrow, L. M. (1983). Home and school correlates of early interest in literature. *Journal of Educational Research,* 76, 221–230.

Morrow, L. M. (1989). *Literacy learning in the early years: Helping children read and write.* Englewood Cliffs, NJ: Prentice Hall.

Morrow, L. M. (2004). *Literacy development in the early years* (5th ed.). Boston, MA: Allyn & Bacon.

Morrow, L. M. (2009). *Literacy learning in the early years: Helping children read and write* (6th ed.). Englewood Cliffs, NJ: Prentice Hall.

Moss, B., Leone, S., & Dipillo, M. (1997). Exploring the literature of fact: Linking reading and writing through information trade books. *Language Arts,* 74(6), 418–429.

Moustafa, M. (1997). *Beyond traditional phonics.* Portsmouth, NH: Heinemann.

Moustafa, M. (2000). Phonics instruction. In D. S. Strickland, & L. M. Morrow (Eds.), *Beginning reading and writing* (pp. 121–133). New York, NY: Teachers College Press.

Murray, D. (1980). Writing as process: How writing finds its own meaning. In T. Donovan, & E. McClelland (Eds.), *Eight approaches to composition teaching* (pp. 7–12). Urbana, IL: National Council of Teachers of English.

Murray, D. (1982). Teaching the other self: The writer's first reader. In D. Murray (Ed.), *Learning by teaching* (pp. 164–172). Montclair, NJ: Boyton Cook.

Myhill, D., & Jones, S. (2009). How talk becomes text: Investigating the concept of oral rehearsal in early years' classrooms. *British Journal of Educational Studies*, 57(3), 265–284.

Nagy, W., Anderson, R., & Herman, P. (1987). Learning word meaning from context during normal reading. *American Educational Research Journal*, 24(2), 237–270.

Nagy, W., & Herman, P. (1985). Incidental vs instructional approaches to increasing reading vocabulary. *Educational Perspectives*, 23, 16–21.

Nagy, W., Herman, P., & Anderson, R. (1985). Learning words from context. *Reading Research Quarterly*, 20(2), 233–253.

National Institute of Child Health and Human Development (NICHHD). (2000). December. Report of the National Reading Panel. *Teaching children to read: An evidence-based assessment of the scientific research literature on reading and its implications for reading instruction* (NIH Publication No. 00-4754). Washington, DC: NICHHD.

Neuman, S. B., & Celano, D. (2001). Access to print in low-income and middle-income communities: An ecological study of four neighborhoods. *Reading Research Quarterly*, 36(1), 8–26.

Newkirk, T. (1989). *More than stories: The range of children's writing*. Portsmouth, NH: Heinemann.

Newman, J. (1984). *The craft of children's writing*. Portsmouth, NH: Heinemann.

Newman, S. (1997). Guiding your children's participation in early literacy development: A family program for adolescent mothers. *Early Childhood Development and Care*, 119–129.

Newman, S. (2004). Introducing children to the world of writing. *Early Childhood Today*, 18(4), 34–39.

Noddings, N. (1984). *Caring: A feminine approach to ethics & moral education*. Los Angeles, CA: University of California Press.

Norris, E., Mokhtari, K., & Reichard, C. (1998). Children's use of drawing as a pre-writing strategy. *Journal of Research in Reading*, 21(1), 69–74.

Nutbrown, C. (1999). *Threads of thinking: Young children learning and the role of early education* (2nd ed.). Thousand Oaks, CA: Sage.

Ohanian, S. (1999). *One size fits few: The folly of educational standards*. Portsmouth, NH: Heinemann.

Ong, W. (1982). *Orality and literacy: The technologizing of the word*. London: Methuen.

Owocki, G. (1999). *Literacy through play*. Portsmouth, NH: Heinemann.

Owocki, G. (2003). *Comprehension strategy instruction for K-3 students*. Portsmouth, NH: Heinemann.

Owocki, G. (2007). *Literate days: Reading and writing with preschool and primary children*. Portsmouth, NH: Heinemann.

Papert, S. (1980). *Mindstorms*. New York, NY: Basic Books.

Pappas, C., Keifer, B., & Levstik, L. 1999. *An integrated language perspective in the elementary school*. White Plains, NY: Longman.

Paratore, J. (2003). Building on family literacies: Examining the past and planning the future. In A. DeBruin-Parecki, & B. Krol-Sinclair (Eds.), *Family literacy: From theory to practice* (pp. 8–27). Newark, DE: International Reading Association.

Parsons, S. (2005). *First grade writers*. Portsmouth, NH: Heinemann.

Perlmutter, J., Folger, T., & Holt, K. (2009). Pre-kindergarteners learn to write: A play on words. *Childhood Education*, 86(1), 14–19.

Phenix, J. (1990). *Teaching writing: The nuts and bolts of running a day-to-day writing program*. Markham, Ontario: Pembroke.

Pinnell, G. S., & Fountas, I. (1998). *Word matters*. Portsmouth, NH: Heinemann.

Platt, P. (1977). Grapho-linguistics: Children's drawings in relation to reading and writing skills. *The Reading Teacher*, 31(3), 262–268.

Portalupi, J., & Fletcher, R. (2005). *In the beginning: Young writers develop independence* (DVD). Portland, ME: Stenhouse.

Rasinski, T., & Padak, N. (2004). *Effective reading strategies: Teaching children who find learning to read difficult.* Upper Saddle River, NJ: Pearson.

Rasinski, T., & Padak, N. (2009). Write soon! *The Reading Teacher, 62*(7), 618–620.

Ray, K. (2004). *About the authors.* Portsmouth, NH: Heinemann.

Ray, K., & Glover, M. (2008). *Already ready: Nurturing writers in preschool and kindergarten.* Portsmouth, NH: Heinemann.

Richgels, D. (1995). Invented spelling ability and printed word learning in kindergarten. *Reading Research Quarterly, 30,* 96–109.

Richgels, D. (2001). Invented spelling, phonemic awareness, and reading and writing instruction. In S. Neuman, & D. Dickinson (Eds.), *Handbook of early literacy research* (pp. 142–155). New York, NY: Guilford.

Robb, L. (1998). *Easy-to-manage reading & writing conferences.* New York, NY: Scholastic.

Roe, B., Smith, S., & Burns, P. (2005). *Teaching reading in today's elementary schools* (9th ed.). New York, NY: Houghton Mifflin.

Routman, R. (2000). *Conversations: Strategies for teaching, learning, and evaluating.* Portsmouth, NH: Heinemann.

Rowe, D. (2008). Social contracts for writing: Negotiating shared understandings about text in the preschool years. *Reading Research Quarterly, 43*(1), 66–95.

Rubin, R., & Carlan, V. (2005). Using writing to understand bilingual children's literacy development. *The Reading Teacher, 58*(8), 728–739.

Ruddell, R. (1969). Psycholinguistic implications for a system of communication model. In K. S. Goodman, & J. T. Flemming (Eds.), *Psycholinguistics and the teaching of reading* (pp. 61–78). Newark, DE: IRA.

Rushton, S. (2001). Applying brain research to create developmentally appropriate learning environments. *Young Children, 56*(5), 76–82.

Rushton, S., & Larkin, E. (2001). Connecting developmentally appropriate practices to brain research. *Early Childhood Education Journal, 29*(1), 25–33.

Rushton, S., Eitelgeorge, J., & Zickafoose, R. (2003). Connecting Brian Cambourne's conditions for learning theory to brain/mind principles: Implications for early childhood educators. *Early Childhood Education Journal, 31*(1), 11–21.

Sagor, R. (1993). *At-risk students: Reaching and teaching them.* Swampscott, MA: Watersun Press.

Sampson, M. (1986). *The pursuit of literacy: Early reading and writing.* Dubuque, IA: Kendall/Hunt.

Scanlon, D., Anderson, K., & Sweeney, J. (2010). *Early intervention for reading difficulties: The interactive strategies approach.* New York, NY: Guilford.

Schickedanz, J. (1990). *Adam's righting revolution.* Portsmouth, NH: Heinemann.

Schulze, A. (2006). *Helping children become readers through writing.* Newark, DE: International Reading Association.

Scott, R. (1993). *Spelling: Sharing the secrets.* Toronto, Ontario: Gage.

Sendak, M. (1963). *Where the wild things are.* New York: Harper & Row.

Shea, M. (1992). *Children's concepts of print prior to formal instruction.* Unpublished doctoral dissertation. SUNY at Buffalo.

Shea, M. (1997). Thoughts on affirming young children's literacy efforts. *The Language and Literacy Spectrum, 7,* 56–57.

Shea, M., & Murray, R. (2000). Spelling in English: A critical thinking, problem-solving process. *Balanced Literacy Instruction, 7*(1), 37–46.

Shea, M., Murray, R., & Harlin, R. (2005). *Drowning in data?: How to collect, organize, and document student performance.* Portsmouth, NH: Heinemann.

Sheehan, T. (2009). *Vocabulary in beginning reading.* University of Oregon: Institute for the Development of Educational Achievement. http://reading.uoregon.edu/voc/voc_sbooks_4.php, retrieved 10/17/10.

Short, K., Harste, J., & Burke, C. (1996). *Creating classrooms for authors and inquirers* (2nd ed.). Portsmouth, NH: Heinemann.

Sidelnick, M., & Svoboda, M. (2000). The bridge between drawing and writing: Hannah's story. *The Reading Teacher, 54*(2),174–184.

Sinclair, H. (1989). Foreword in E. Ferreiro, & A. Teberosky, *Literacy before schooling* (pp. v–vi). Portsmouth, NH: Heinemann.

Smith, F. (1983). *Essays into literacy: Selected papers and some afterthoughts.* Portsmouth, NH: Heinemann.

Smith, F. (1988). *Joining the literacy club.* Portsmouth, NH: Heinemann.

Smith, J., & Elley, W. (1997a). *How children learn to read.* Katonah, NY: Richard C. Owen.

Smith, J., & Elley, W. (1997b). *How children learn to write.* Katonah, NY: Richard C. Owen.

Snow, C., Burns, M., & Griffin, P. (Eds.). (1998). *Preventing reading difficulties in young children.* Washington, DC: National Academy Press.

Soderman, A., & Farrell, P. (2008). *Creating literacy-rich preschools and kindergartens.* New York, NY: Allyn & Bacon.

Squire, J. R. (1983). Composing and comprehending: Two sides of the same basic process. *Language Arts, 60*(5), 581–589.

Stahl, K. (2004). Proof, practice, and promise: Comprehension strategy instruction in the primary grades. *The Reading Teacher, 57*(7), 598–609.

Sticht, T., Beck, L., Hauck, R., Kleinman, G., & James, J. (1974). *Auding and reading: A developmental model.* Alexandria, VA: Human Resources Research Organization.

Stiggins, R. (2002). Assessment crisis: The absence of assessment *for* learning. *Phi Delta Kappan, 83*(10), 758–769.

Stotsky, S. (1975). Sentence combining as a curricular activity: Its effect on written language development and reading comprehension. *Research in the Teaching of English, 9,* 30–71.

Stotsky, S. (1983). Research on reading/writing relationships: A synthesis and suggested directions. *Language Arts, 60,* 627–642.

Strickland, D. S., & Barnett, W. S. (2003). Literacy intervention for preschool children considered at risk: Implications for curriculum, professional development, and parent involvement. In C. M. Fairbanks, J. Worthy, B. Maloch, J. V. Hoffman, & D. L. Schallert (Eds.), *52nd Yearbook of the National Reading Conference* (pp. 104–116). Oak Creek, WI: National reading Conference.

Strickland, D. S., & Schickedanz, J. A. (2004). *Learning about print.* Newark, DE: International Reading Association.

Sulzby, E. (1985). Kindergartners as writers and readers. In M. Farr (Ed.), *Advances in writing research: Vol. 1, Children's early writing* (pp. 127–199). Norwood, NJ: Ablex.

Sulzby, E. (1990). Assessment of emergent writing and children's language while writing. In L. Morrow, & J. Smith (Eds.), *Assessment for instruction in early literacy* (pp. 83–108). Englewood Cliffs, NJ: Prentice Hall.

Sulzby, E. (1996). Roles of oral and written language as children approach conventional literacy. In C. Pontevecorvo, M. Orsolini, B. Burge, & L. B. Resnick (Eds.), *Children's early text construction* (pp. 25–46). Mahwah, NJ: Lawrence Erlbaum.

Taylor, D. (1983). *Family literacy: Young children learning to read and write.* Portsmouth, NH: Heinemann.

Taylor, D. (1993). *From the child's point of view.* Portsmouth, NH: Heinemann.

Taylor, D., & Dorsey-Gaines, C. (1988). *Growing up literate: Learning from inner city families.* Portsmouth, NH: Heinemann.

Teale, W. (1982). Toward a theory of how children learn to read and write naturally. *Language Arts, 59*(6), 555–570.

Teale, W. (1984). Reading to young children: Its significance for literacy development. In H. Goelman, A. Oberg, & F. Smith (Eds.), *Awakening to literacy.* Portsmouth, NH: Heinemann.

Teale, W. (1986). The beginning of reading and writing: Written language development during the preschool and kindergarten years. In M. Sampson (Ed.), *The pursuit of literacy: Early reading and writing* (pp. 1–29). Dubuque, IA: Kendall/Hunt.

Teale, W., & Yokota, J. (2000). Beginning reading and writing: Perspectives on instruction. In D. S. Strickland, & L. M. Morrow (Eds.), *Beginning reading and writing* (pp. 3–21). Language and literacy series. Newark, DE: International Reading Association.

Temple, C., Nathan, R., Temple, F., & Burris, N. (Eds.). (1993). *The beginnings of writing* (3rd ed.). Boston, MA: Allyn & Bacon.

Temple, C., Ogle, D., Crawford, A., & Freppon, P. (2008). *All children read: Teaching for diversity in today's diverse classrooms* (2nd ed.). Boston, MA: Allyn & Bacon.

Tobin, R. (2008). Conundrums in the differentiated classroom. *Reading Improvement, 45* (4), 159–169.

Tomlinson, C. (1999). *The differentiated classroom: Responding to the needs of all learners.* Alexandria, VA: ASCD.

Tomlinson, C. (2001). *How to differentiate instruction in mixed ability classrooms* (2nd ed.). Alexandria, VA: ASCD.

Tompkins, G. (2010). *Literacy for the 21st century: A balanced approach* (5th ed.). New York, NY: Allyn & Bacon.

Torrey, J. (1969). Learning to read without a teacher: A case study. *Elementary English, 46*(5), 550–556.

Trushell, J. (1998). Emergent writer as emergent "reader": Juliet makes her mark. *Reading, 32*(1), 29–32.

Turbill, J. (1983). *Now, we want to write!* Rosebery, NSW, Australia: Primary English Teaching Association.

Turbill, J. (Ed.). (1984). *No better way to teach writing!* Rosebery, NSW, Australia: Primary English Teaching Association.

Vacca, J., Vacca, R., Gove, M., Burkey, L., Lenhart, L., & McKeon, C. (2009). *Reading and learning to read.* New York, NY: Allyn & Bacon.

Veatch, J., Sawicki, F., Elliot, G., Barnett, E., & Blackey, J. (1973). *Key words to reading: The language experience approach begins.* Columbus, OH: Charles E. Merrill.

Vukelich, C., Christie, J., & Enz, B. (2002). *Helping young children learn language and literacy.* Boston, MA: Allyn & Bacon.

Vygotsky, L. S. (1978). *Mind and society: The development of higher mental processes.* Cambridge, MA: Harvard University Press. (Original work published in 1930, 1933, 1935.)

Vygotsky, L. S. (1986). *Thought and language.* Cambridge, MA: MIT Press.

Vygotsky, L. S. (1987). *The collected works of L. S. Vygotsky* (R. W. Rieber, & A. S. Carton, Trans.). New York, NY: Plenum Press. (Original works published in 1934, 1960.)

Walker, B. (2004). *Diagnostic teaching of reading: Techniques for instruction and assessment* (5th ed.). Upper Saddle River, NJ: Pearson.

Walker, B. (2008). Adjusting instruction to meet students' needs. *Reading Today, 25*(6), 18–19.

Walshe, R. D. (1982). *Every child can write.* Rozelle, NSW, Australia: Primary English Teaching Association.

Weaver, C. (1998). *A balanced approach to reading: Becoming successfully and joyfully literate* (video tape and facilitator's guide). Bothell, WA: The Wright Group.

Webster, D. (1996). *Webster's new universal unabridged dictionary.* New York, NY: Barnes and Noble.

Weinberger, J. (1998). Young children's literacy experiences within the fabric of daily life. In R. Campbell (Ed.), *Facilitating preschool literacy* (pp. 30–50). Newark, DE: International Reading Association.

Wells, G. (1986). *The meaning makers: Children learning language and using language to learn.* Portsmouth, NH: Heinemann.

Whitmore, K., & Goodman, Y. (1995). Transforming curriculum in language and literacy. In S. Bredekamp, & T. Rosegrant (Eds.), *Reaching potentials: Transforming early childhood curriculum and assessment* (pp. 146–166). Washington, DC: National Association for the Education of Young Children.

Whitmore, K., Martens, P., Goodman, Y., & Owocki, G. (2005). Remembering critical lessons in early literacy research: A transactional approach. *Language Arts, 82*(5), 296–307.

Wohlwend, K. (2008). From "what did I write?" to "is this right?": Intention, convention, and accountability in early literacy. *The New Educator, 4*, 43–63.

Wood, D., Bruner, J. C., & Ross, G. (1976). The role of tutoring in problem solving. *Journal of Child Psychology and Psychiatry, 17*, 89–100.

Yoos, G. (1979). An identity of roles in writing and reading. *College Composition and Communication, 30*, 245–249.

Zimmermann, S., & Hutchins, C. (2003). *Seven keys to comprehension.* New York, NY: Three Rivers Press.

Index

Note: Page numbers for illustrations appear in **bold**.